BOATBUILDING MANUAL

ROBERT M. STEWARD

International Marine Publishing Company
Camden, Maine

Copyright © 1970 by the
International Marine Publishing Company
Library of Congress Catalog Card No. 77-133677
International Standard Book No. 0-87742-014-9
Printed by Maine Coast Printers
Rockland, Maine, USA
(Copyright 1969 by the Poseidon Publishing Company)
Second Printing, 1971

CONTENTS

FOREWORD

THE LIGHTS often showed bright, late in the evening, at the Mizzen-top in Huntington, New York and continue at Anchordown here in Darien. I have enjoyed a lifetime influenced by the talk of small boats—their design—their building and their use. Most rewarding of all aspects, perhaps, are the letters that come along—letters extolling the grand experience encountered in the building of a boat!

There has always been great satisfaction—a justified feeling of accomplishment—related to making things with our own hands. In this age of specialization I believe there is even more satisfaction—as well as relaxation and a challenge to our individual ability and in-genuity. Few things involve the many skills required as that in building a boat, each essential for its successful completion. Possibly nothing else is as rewarding.

Further, nicely fashioned and well built boats are growing more and more expensive. To build your own may well be a practical solu-tion—as well as rewarding. Surely the joys of being afloat are manifold, and those experienced aboard a boat you have built with your own hands are immeasurable.

Bob Steward, being exceptionally well qualified by his long ex-perience in the "world of small ships," has produced a clearly written text of merit and great worth. After years that began as an apprentice, he worked in several small boat yards before joining the highly respected office of naval architect Philip L. Rhodes where he spent many years engaged in the designing and planning of numerous power and sailing yachts, as well as commercial boats. The period of the second World War found him in an engineering capacity working between various yards and design offices. Far more pleasant work was resumed at the war's end involving yachts—and Bob accepted a position with a West Coast firm as superintendent of yacht repair and construction. Sometime later he returned to the East Coast where a number of yacht designs were produced, ranging from 22 to 73 feet, which required his experienced supervision of lofting and construction. The warmer clime beckoned, with its slower pace and easier living, and Bob continued his work involving the designing and supervision of numerous yachts. Presently he is a Florida builder, where he is concerned with the design and progress of outstanding power yachts.

Bob Steward has given us the benefit of his long experience in the yacht design and building world. Surely this comprehensive and practical material, so well presented, will provide the amateur boatbuilder, *as well as the professional,* with a world of valued and valid information. He has covered all phases of the subject and has brought us up to date on all manner of contemporary building methods and material. The professionally made illustrations provide a clear understanding of accepted methods utilized in building boats today.

Bob has provided us with all of the essential information required to build a boat—no more grand "monument to spare time" can be imagined.

JOHN ATKIN, S.N.A. & M.E.

Anchordown
Darien, Connecticut
1969

PREFACE

DURING a meeting a number of years ago with Boris Lauer-Leonardi and the late Andy Patterson, Editor and Business Manager respectively of the fine old Rudder magazine, it was decided that I should write some articles about boat construction aimed at the amateur and, hopefully, of some value also to the professional. This decision resulted in a series of twenty consecutive monthly pieces that were so well received that they were made into a book. The reception of this, too, was enthusiastic, and soon after it was introduced, the book was published abroad in French. Letters of approval were received from afar. One that lingers in my mind was from a Turkish naval officer who not only bought the book, but also built a boat from my plans. Then again Olin Stephens, famed yacht designer, told me how the French edition was of value to him on an inspection trip in Europe when the book illustrations served to break a language barrier between him and a builder. Things like this are heartfelt because in so small a field the monetary reward must, unfortunately, be secondary.

As time went on the number of requests for the book showed that a revision was in order. So now we have Boatbuilding Manual, again done with the enthusiasm of Boris as a prime mover, although there have been times when the midnight oil was burning low that I was not so happy with his prodding. The new book has been rewritten, but includes a little of the old as well as techniques I have picked up in the interim, and new materials that have been accepted.

Do not think that this or any other book can teach all there is to know about boatbuilding. The best we can hope for is to give some guidance to those with the urge to build a boat, an urge that usually is greatly rewarding, and trust that this book, plus a good set of plans from an understanding and experienced designer, will lead to the realization of a dream for many who otherwise could not enjoy boating and the sea.

Assuming he has ability with woodworking tools, and is armed with plans and the elements of boatbuilding set forth in this book, there is no reason why an amateur cannot turn out a creditable boat, but he is cautioned not to be too pretentious at first. Better to start with something small, like a dinghy, to acquire the feel of boat construction, then go on to a larger craft.

The author wishes to thank Philip L. Rhodes for the use of some photographs; Fred Bates for his experience with strip planking; Joe Schabo of Goldelier magazine for tracking down the remarkable photo of the Gulfstream 42 in frame; William G. Hobbs for the use of the same photo; and, once again, my family for patience on days when I was drawing or writing when we should have been fishing or sailing.

ROBERT M. STEWARD

Jacksonville, Florida

Chapter 1

GENERAL

M ANY CAPABLE persons fear building a boat due to lack of knowledge of certain essentials, including the important problem of how to start. During the past two decades especially, more and more people have learned to skilfully use both hand and electric tools for household chores and improvements, making furniture and the like, and turn out creditable jobs. Although they are aware of the finished shape of a boat from having seen and no doubt admired many in boat yards and afloat, or even in their favorite department store nowadays, they are mystified by a lines plan for a hull and the attendant table of offsets, and the thought of actually bending wood or other material to curves is discouraging to most. Thus they are unnecessarily deprived of the fascinating pastime of small boatbuilding.

Constructing the first boat, seeing her grow from plans and a pile of flat boards to a shapely form, provides hours of fun, and when carefully done is a source of great pride to the builder on launching day. Unlike a piece of furniture, the finished product is not placed in a corner of a room to be eventually forgotten, but is useful for years of pleasure afloat.

The purpose of this book is not to teach the skills of an expert boatbuilder, but to introduce small boat construction by explaining the elementary problems involved during the several steps from the time the hull is begun until water first laps at the keel.

It is impossible to briefly cover all the information needed to build every type of boat. If you are fortunate enough to live in a boat building area much can be learned from observation, and it should be borne in mind that a set of plans drawn by a reliable naval architect is a source of detailed information pertinent to a particular boat. The author cannot help but assume that the reader has acquired the ability to use ordinary carpenter's tools, for these are sufficient to build some boats and, of equal importance, knows how to keep tools sharp. Also, that a good set of plans is to be used for the building project.

It is not likely that one considering the building of a boat will be totally unfamiliar with boats, and most probably either a sailboat or a powerboat is desired. The urge to build a boat stems from somewhere, whether from reading boating magazines, from previous ownership of a boat, or from enjoying trips in the boat of a friend. It may even be that a choice has been made between a flat, round or vee bottom boat.

The ordinary flat bottom rowboat that abounds in harbors and on lakes is really quite simple to construct, needing but a few forms to shape the hull and having a minimum of beveled parts. Little layout work is necessary. However, a flat bottom boat has definite limitations in its usual form, so unless one is content to frequent sheltered waters a more pretentious and seaworthy boat will be required, entailing the construction of one of the vee bottom family of hulls or a round bottom boat. It is a matter of opinion whether a round bottom hull is more work than a vee bottom or vice versa.

A round bottom hull has curved transverse frames, sometimes called ribs, which are shaped by steaming or soaking in boiling water until supple, then they are bent either directly on the hull framework or over forms in the shop and located in the hull after they have cooled and set. Most boats of the size a beginner would build have frames bent right in the hull, and the bevel necessary to have them conform to the hull shape is twisted in during the bending process. Do not let this scare you. When working with relatively light material the bending is not unduly difficult and can be mastered after a few attempts. In fact it can be a great deal of fun. The process will be described in more detail further along during a discussion of framing.

The bending of wood by steaming or boiling is not restricted to round bottom construction alone, as it is entirely possible that certain parts of vee bottom boats, such as the forward ends of bottom planks, will not bend on the boat cold and must be made limber for them to fit the shape of the hull.

The frames for a vee bottom boat are made from a full size drawing of the hull lines, then set up and left in the hull as permanent members of the structure, thus eliminating the work and material needed for the temporary molds necessary to shape the frames of a round bottom boat. But on the other hand, the chine pieces or corners in the sections of a vee bottom hull must be carefully worked to bevels that continually change from bow to stern and this can be a job calling for some nice fitting. The frames, too, are all beveled and each is usually made up of as many as seven carefully fitted and securely fastened parts.

Arc bottom hulls, as exemplified by such boats as the Penguin, Star and Comet classes of sailboats, are but a modification of the vee type bottom and require the same type care in framing, although it is simple to plank the bottom except when it is of plywood. An arc bottom hull has what is called compound curvature. In the case of plywood this means bending the panel in two directions, which the material by nature resists, and the necessary forcing requires the use of clamps to press it against the bottom framing properly. But many amateurs have done this successfully.

The relative merits of the hull types are argued far and wide, but just about everyone will admit that there will never be a vee bottom hull as handsome as a well designed round bottom boat, especially for a sailing craft.

Figures 1-1 and 1-2 show the essential differences between the framing of flat, vee, arc and round bottom hulls. Although the lower ends of the frames in the round bottom boat are shown butted against the keel, it is sometimes possible, depending upon hull shape, to install them in one piece, extending from the deck on one side to the deck on the other side. In contrast, note the number of pieces that make up a frame for a vee bottom boat. On the other

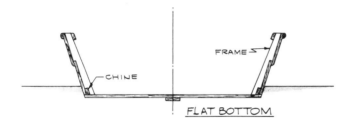

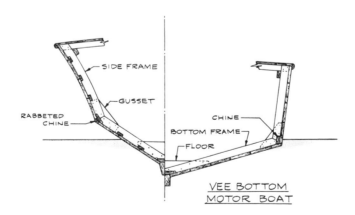

FIGURE 1-1. *Typical construction sections through vee and flat bottom boats*

3

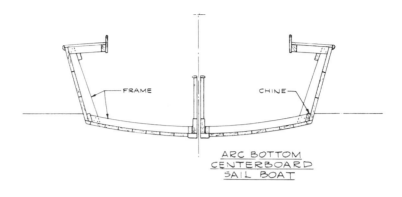

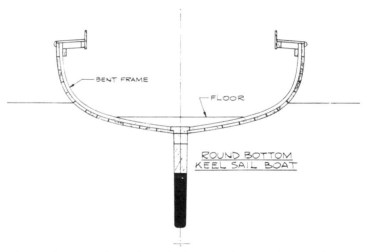

FIGURE 1-2. *Sections through typical arc and round bottom hulls*

hand the frames are spaced farther apart than in a round bottom boat, thus the frames are far fewer in number.

Figure 1-3 is a section through a rather normal sailboat of the cruising or ocean racing type, and is typical of either the so-called deep keel or combination keel and centerboard type boats, the latter being of shallow draft. This sort of boat is not recommended for the very first attempt unless the amateur has helped on a similar job or has watched enough of this kind of construction that he will not become discouraged when on his own. The

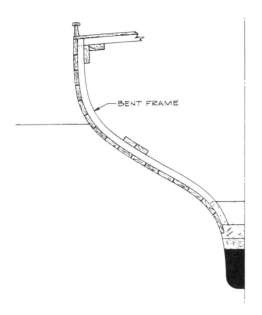

FIGURE 1-3.   *Midship section of ocean racer type sailing yacht showing bent frame with reverse curve*

framing is more difficult due to reverse (S) curves in many of the frames, the planking is a tougher job than a simpler hull, and there is a lot of heavy work getting out the backbone and deadwood.

It is possible to gain an introduction to boatbuilding by purchasing and assembling a "knockdown" or "kit" boat. There are numerous of the latter available, usually vee bottom outboard motorboats with plywood planking. Most are furnished with beveled parts, requiring but care in setting up the frames to turn out a successful boat. There are still one or two producers of "knockdown" boats which are actually set up by the builder, pre-drilled and fastened (with the exception of the planking), then taken apart for shipment. Needless to say, it does not pay to do this for the smaller boats. It is remarkable how much value can be purchased in some brands of kit boats, considering the cost of the materials furnished, and the layout work eliminated for the builder. Making a kit boat, though, does not give the same sense of accomplishment as starting from scratch, but the type does have a place for those who do not have as much spare time as others, or are satisfied with the type of boat that is offered in kit form.

5

Scanning the advertisements in the boating press one might think that this is the age of the plastic boat, and it is true that hundreds of different sail and motorboats are now made of fiber glass reinforced resin. The hulls and other parts are made from expensive molds and must be produced in quantity to be economically feasible, thus quantities of each design must all be the same. Wooden boatbuilding, however, is far from dead. Boats of wood are still made by stock builders and scores of custom built wooden yachts and commercial boats are turned out each year. In fact, the techniques of wooden boatbuilding are used in the plastic boat field for making the molds for fiber glass parts and for finishing boats with fiber glass hulls. In the latter case the wood finish, particularly the cabin interior, provides a warmth never achieved by synthetic materials. Yachts with metal hulls, steel or aluminum, are also finished with wood.

Chapter 2

PLANS

A SET OF plans is needed for a boatbuilding project unless it has been decided to build a kit boat. Seldom does one want to build just any boat—rather there is an urge to own a certain type, either power or sail, and usually there is an idea about size suitable for the intended use. There are several sources for plans, and ample time should be spent on the search for a design to make sure the boat will meet the requirements.

Knowledge of arrangements feasible for various lengths of boats can be obtained by scanning the design sections of the monthly boating magazines. These small drawings are ample for study of what is offered by the design, and the naval architect can be contacted for further information. Some of the boating magazines, also mechanical magazines, have a choice of plans for sale that have been run as "how-to-build" articles over the years and make available plans to a larger, more practical scale than the drawings that appeared in the magazines. One of the plywood manufacturers' associations also has a selection of plans for boats with plywood planking. Naval architects advertise in the boating magazines and often have a catalog of their plans that are for sale to builders. Many of the small sailboat one-design classes are organized in associations to control racing, and for a small fee issue plans to insure that all boats in the class will be as alike as possible.

Regardless of the source for plans, try to determine whether they are sufficiently detailed for you to understand the construction completely. It cannot be emphasized too strongly that good plans are well worth the price charged because the cost is but a small percentage of the total cost of the boat. The cost of plans might be considered as insurance that the finished boat in which you have invested money and time will be a success.

Some designers do not draw the profusion of details that a new builder would like to have, and that is where this book should be of much help.

The reader is cautioned against making changes in the hull lines, heights of superstructure or relocation of major weights. Such procedures can result in unsatisfactory performance at least, or even downright reduction of seaworthiness. Consult the designer before making a major change, and if he advises against it you will be better off using plans that will give you what you want without departure from the drawings.

Chapter 3

TOOLS

THE TOOLS needed for building a boat depend upon the type of project to be undertaken, and it is best to start with a small craft, perhaps a dinghy, to get the feel of the work—the difference between boatbuilding and common carpentry. The construction of a plywood planked boat, either a kit or one started from scratch, calls for only a minimum of tools. The usual assortment

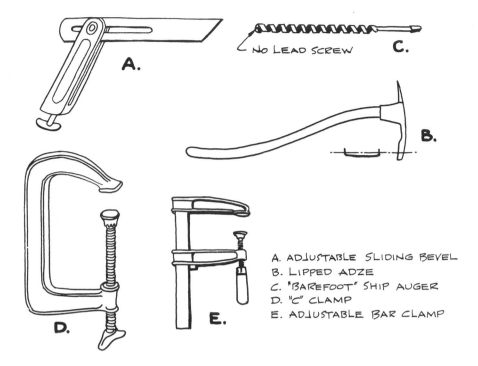

No LEAD SCREW C.

A.

B.

A. ADJUSTABLE SLIDING BEVEL
B. LIPPED ADZE
C. "BAREFOOT" SHIP AUGER
D. "C" CLAMP
E. ADJUSTABLE BAR CLAMP

D.

E.

FIGURE 3-1. *A few boatbuilding tools not always found in the home work-shop*

of home workshop tools such as a hammer, hand saws, planes, chisels, screw-drivers, brace and bitts, hand drill, etc., are sufficient to build many boats. One other item the amateur may not have when starting a boat is a number of clamps, either the "C" or bar type. It seems as though one never has enough of these and they really are indispensable. The one power tool that is well worth the money in labor saving, even for the simplest of boats, is a quarter inch electric drill.

Other hand tools such as a drawknife, spokeshave, bullnose plane, rabbet plane and round bottom plane are out of the ordinary but very handy in the building of some boats. If not on hand these can be added as the need develops.

Essential tools for layout work, and useful from start to finish, are a twenty-four inch carpenter's framing square, level, dividers and a carpenter's pencil compass. Also a rule or tape for measuring, of course, but not a cloth tape that stretches. For making your own long bolts from rod stock a few thread cutting dies and a die holder will be needed. Another handy tool, one that a boatbuilder cannot do without, is an adjustable sliding bevel such as Stanley Tools No. 25 or No. 18. This is used for transferring bevels from drawings to the lumber and picking up bevels in many ways as you will learn. Needless to say, both carpenter's and machinist's vises will be used.

A relatively new hand tool on the market is the Stanley Surform, which features a unique disposable blade made in Sheffield, England, and which can be bought in most good hardware stores. The most common holder for the blade is shaped like a large file with a built-in handle, and there is also a holder that is curved and has a handle like a plane. It cuts wood, plastic and soft metal easily and can be used for many jobs during boatbuilding.

It takes a lot of fastenings to make a boat sound, so for the electric drill you will needs twist drills. These come in two kinds, carbon steel and high speed. Be sure to get the latter kind even though more expensive because drilling a series of holes in hardwood or metal heats the drills and the carbon steel bits will burn and become useless.

In all but the smaller boats there will be some holes required for long bolts. These can be bored with ship augers available with and without center lead screws. The latter, called "barefoot" by boatbuilders, are preferred because it is easier to keep a hole on a straight course. If auger holes are made with power, a heavy duty slow-turning electric drill is a must. Some builders, and you must develop your own technique, like to use a twist drill rather than an auger. If the standard drills are not long enough you must have them extended by welding a rod onto the drill shank and trued up, the extension to be smaller than the drill diameter if necessary to fit in the drill motor chuck.

You will learn that a great many wood screws are used in modern boat construction. All of the screws must have drilled holes either to drive them in hardwoods or to prevent soft woods from splitting. To reduce the number of separate drilling operations there are patented countersinks and counterbores on the market. Both of these tools first drill a hole for the body of the screw, then the countersink follows up by shaping the hole to take the head of the screw, while the counterbore drills a straight sided hole for a wood plug. Both of these gadgets have an adjustment for depth of hole and they are both valuable time savers because they eliminate many back and forth changes of drills and working twice on every hole. These are shown in the chapter on fastenings. Unfortunately the range of sizes is not as extensive as may be desired.

There are also some recently developed similar drilling tools of more inexpensive construction that more or less do the same job. These drills look as though they are stamped out of a steel sheet to the profile of a screw and have two diameters, one for clearance of the screw shank, and one about equal to the diameter of the screw at the root of the threads, and some makes have a stop on the shank of the drill to control depth of the hole. One name for these drills is wood screw pilot bits, and they are sold in sizes for various diameters and lengths of screws. They can be burned drilling hardwoods but they are cheap and thus expendable. These bits are also shown in the chapter on fastenings.

Old hand boatbuilders often grind twist drills to a tapered point similar to a gimlet, especially when a hole is to be made completely through the wood for a rivet or clout nail fastening. The tapered point does not tear the wood as the drill goes through.

One of the traditional tools of the boatbuilder is the adze. This tool is shaped like a hoe and is still in use in yards that build vessels with heavy timbers. Boatbuilders usually use the lipped adze which is a smooth cutting type with curled edges at the ends of the blade. The adze is used diagonally across the grain, and when in the hands of a skilled workman is a wonderful tool for working heavy pieces of wood. The adze can also be dangerous to the limbs when in the hands of the inexperienced, so it is best to learn how to use one under the guidance of someone who has plenty of adze time under his belt.

As we progress it will be apparent that some hand tools have been omitted from the foregoing, but mention has been made of most you will ever need and the chances are good that your home workshop is already equipped with many of them. If not, go ahead and start your boat anyway because none of the hand tools is really expensive and can be bought as you go along.

Power tools in the home workshop are more common now than ever before. By far one of the most useful for boatbuilding is the band saw and it should be twelve or fourteen inch size. For straight cuts, very handy especially for much of the interior joinerwork in a cabin, an eight inch circular table saw with tilting arbor and a four inch jointer are suitable. A portable circular saw is a poor substitute for a table saw but does have some use, particularly for cutting up plywood panels. It can also be used for cutting curved planking out of lumber if the planking is not too thick and the saw set to cut out little more depth than the plank thickness. A saber saw is invaluable for cutouts such as for portlights in the hull and hatch openings in plywood decks. As in the case of the quarter inch electric drill, do not buy the cheapest saber saw you can find. Stick to a good grade in a good brand because even reputable makers have competitive lines and better lines, the difference being in bearings and power, thus in life. Somewhat of a luxury for small boats is an electric screwdriver, but a tremendous labor saver when quantities of anything but small screws are to be driven.

One of the most labor saving power tools is the sander, and it helps prevent boredom, too. The disc sander is good for such jobs as cutting down the seams of planking and for sanding fiber glass. For finishing, the orbital sander is about the best, whether for wood or fiber glass, and the belt sander is much used by the pros for smoothing up joinerwork. Again, quality is important in sanders, so don't skimp.

Another power tool that might be considered a luxury, but an enormous labor saver during the construction of boats upwards of twenty five feet long, is an electric plane. Not one of the heavy monsters that takes a real man to handle, but a lightweight one such as the three inch plane made by Skil. This tool has even been used for smoothing up lead ballast keels.

This is all that will be said about tools because, as mentioned in the introduction, familiarity and a certain ability with woodworking tools has been assumed.

Chapter 4

WOOD

WOOD IS ONE of the easiest materials from which the amateur can build a boat and remains a favorite of many professionals despite the great growth of synthetic materials. Not all woods are suitable for boatbuilding, however, so as we go along there will be comments on those kinds that have proven durable, one of the most desirable qualities sought, and have the strength necessary for a boat.

It is beyond the scope of this book to more than scratch the surface on the subject of wood, even when limited to the trees found in the United States alone, so we will limit our discussions to the small number of commonly accepted boatbuilding woods and how the lumber is manufactured from the logs. A few reasons for the elimination of certain woods from boatbuilding are brittleness, softness, weakness, susceptibility to decay and shortness of growth. On the other hand there are time tested woods available that have the necessary qualities and seldom can these types be found in an ordinary lumber yard. Boat material should be selected with care and might be difficult to find, but fortunately almost every area where boats are built has a yard that fully understands the needs of the boatbuilder, and the amateur is advised to seek the aid of such a supplier to obtain the high grade lumber needed for long hull life. There should be no compromise in the matter of lumber quality, for when the labor of the builder is considered, the extra cost and trouble of good material is of little consequence.

Sawing of Lumber

Grain is formed by the angle of the annual rings with the face of a board and has much to do with the suitability of the lumber for use in boats. The grain in manufactured boards depends upon how the lumber is cut from the logs. After a tree has been felled and trimmed to a log it is easy for the lumberman to run the log through a saw and cut it into boards as shown in A of Figure 4-1. This is called plain sawing and all but one or two of the boards sawn

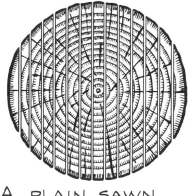
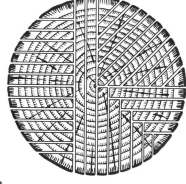

A. PLAIN SAWN   B. QUARTER SAWN

FIGURE 4-1.

from the log in this manner are called slash grain or flat grain. A more expensive and more wasteful method of cutting up the log, B in Figure 4-1, is called quarter sawing and the resulting boards are known as rift, vertical or edge grain boards. It can be seen from Figure 4-2 that a few boards from the middle of a plain sawn log have rift grain same as quarter sawn lumber, but the majority of the plain sawn boards are not desirable for boatbuilding as will be shown.

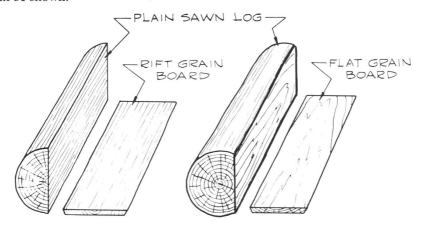

FIGURE 4-2.

Seasoning

Wood for almost any purpose at all must be dried or seasoned to reduce the moisture content present when the tree is cut, at which time the content may be as much as half or more the weight of the log. There are two ways that wood contains moisture, that absorbed by the cell walls and that which is free within the cell cavities. When the wood has taken on as much as the cells will hold the wood is said to be at the fiber saturation point. In this condition the moisture content of the wood averages about twenty-five per cent, and no shrinkage takes place until this percentage is reduced. Seasoning is the process of reducing the moisture content to about fifteen per cent, an acceptable level for boatbuilding material, and during the seasoning the wood shrinks. After it seasons to whatever level is wanted, speaking not only of boatbuilding, wood shrinks further if more moisture is removed and swells if more moisture is taken on. Shrinking or swelling is greatest in a direction parallel to the annual rings, thus slash grain boards cup more than rift sawn and appear as shown in Figure 4-3A after seasoning. Shrinkage of rift sawn lumber tends more toward reducing thickness than width, producing boards with greater dimensional stability than flat grain (Figure 4-3B), and for this reason rift sawn lumber is desirable for planking, decking and other boat parts.

There are two methods used for seasoning wood and the mention of them just might start an argument in the local boat shop. There are those

13

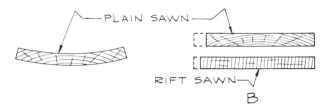

FIGURE 4-3.

who will accept nothing but air dried lumber, a process that can take several years depending upon the thickness of the pieces. Nevertheless, it is generally accepted that air dried wood is the best for boatbuilding, and on numerous occasions the writer has seen this being done right in the boat yard. On the other hand modern production cannot wait too long for material, so the lumber is placed in a kiln to be dried in a number of days. Boat lumber dried by this method must be done with care because the normal product of the kiln will have a moisture content as low as eight per cent, whereas time has shown that regardless of the drying method the moisture content of boat material should be between twelve and sixteen per cent, with many accepting fifteen per cent as ideal. Moisture content, incidentally, is expressed as a percentage of the lumber weight when oven dry.

Drying in a kiln speeds up the evaporation of moisture, causing fast drying on the surface and slow drying of the inside, and is said to affect both the strength and elasticity of the wood. Lumber for boats must not be too green or it will shrink and check excessively during the building period, nor must it be too dry or it will absorb moisture and swell unduly. In the case of some types of planking the latter condition could be very serious.

There are meters made for determining the moisture content of wood and they must be used properly for correct results. The best procedure for the amateur is to leave the selection of the wood to the experts who understand the requirements of boatbuilding. These people also know that boat lumber should not have large knots and checks, decay or nondurable sapwood.

Kinds of Wood

In the northeastern parts of the United States, where we like to think boatbuilding in this country was born, the practice of using certain available native woods was established long ago and time has proven its worth. Through the years lumber from other parts of the country, as well as material

14

from foreign lands, has been added to the list of suitable woods, with substitutions of local products being made in certain areas as a result of satisfactory experience with the wood for the building of boats. As a typical example, frames would be of oak in the majority of localities, but keel, deadwood and other backbone members might be yellow pine in the South, white oak in the Northeast, Alaska cedar or Douglas fir on the West Coast. As long as the wood is proven it makes little difference, but a boat involves too much work to gamble with untried materials that may rot in a short time or be brittle and not hold fastenings.

As a guide we give here a list of good woods, together with principal properties and approximate weight per board foot (one foot square by one inch thick) at twelve per cent moisture content.

White Oak

Weight about 4.2 pounds (heavy). Durable, stiff, strong and holds fastenings exceptionally well. Easily steam bent, thus excellent for frames, but for this purpose the oak should be green, not seasoned. Also used extensively for all backbone members such as keel, stem, deadwood, etc. Good white oak grows in the New England states, and it is axiomatic that the most durable oak, one of the best qualities of this wood, is from trees felled during winter when the sap is not flowing. It should be noted here that there is a much greater supply of red oak than white oak. Red oak is weaker and less durable than white and is to be avoided when it is at all possible to obtain white oak.

Douglas Fir

Weight about 2.9 pounds (medium). Strong and straight grained, useful for stringers, clamps, sometimes for spars as a substitute for Sitka spruce, and for planking when rift sawn. Grows in Oregon, Washington and California. Logs are large, from which veneer is peeled inexpensively for manufacture into plywood panels. Douglas fir is often called Oregon pine. Green fir is often found in lumber yards catering to house builders and this should not be used without further seasoning.

Yellow Pine (longleaf)

Weight about 3.4 pounds (heavy). Strong, very durable and straight grained. Used for stringers, clamps, and for planking if weight is not a factor, also as a substitute for white oak keels, deadwood, etc. May be available in good long lengths in some localities. Has been reported as not durable in fresh water, but we cannot substantiate this. Grows in Southern U.S. in Atlantic and Gulf states.

15

White Pine

Weight about 2.1 pounds (light). Scarce, genuine northern white pine, enormous quantities of which were used in the construction of sailing ships years ago and often for laid decks in yacht building, but this material is seldom seen nowadays. White pine is mentioned here because the wide, clear boards available make it a tempting material for the amateur, but the dubious durability of many varieties make this wood undesirable for boat construction except for interior joinerwork.

White Cedar

Weight about 1.9 pounds (light). Atlantic white cedar, which grows near the Atlantic coast from Maine to northern Florida and westward along the Gulf coast to Louisiana, is also known as juniper, southern white cedar, swamp cedar and boat cedar. It is not strong, but uniformity and resistance to rot make it excellent for planking. Soaks up moisture rapidly but shrinkage is low, both of which qualities are especially good for light lapstrake planked boats that are alternately in and out of the water. Sapwood layer is usually thin. Almost always supplied as "flitches," that is, plain sawn boards with or without bark on the edges. These "boat boards" taper in width same as the tree trunk and can be advantageously used for hull planking.

Port Orford Cedar

Weight about 2.4 pounds (light). Moderately strong, clear and straight grained. Heartwood very resistant to rot. Used for planking and bright finished decks. Grows in southern Oregon and northern California and is a material familiar to the layman as the wood from which vast numbers of venetian blind slats have been made. Has a distinctive spicy odor.

Western Red Cedar

Weight about 1.9 pounds (light). Highly resistant to rot and available in good widths and lengths for planking. This wood, however, is soft and weak, thus not the best material for this purpose.

Cypress

Weight about 2.8 pounds (medium). Moderately strong, heartwood very resistant to rot. Used for planking where weight is not a factor because it soaks up water to a great extent, making for a heavy boat after a short time in the water. Grows in southern low swamplands of the United States.

Sitka Spruce

Weight about 2.4 pounds (light). Moderate shrinkage, high strength for weight and long clear lengths make it ideal for spars. Grows on Pacific Coast in a narrow strip from northern California to Alaska. Not particularly resistant to rot, but this is not detrimental when spars have proper care.

Spruce (northern white)

Weight about 2.4 pounds (light). High strength for weight, not very resistant to rot. Used for deck and hull framing where weight saving is primary consideration. Grows in the New England states.

Philippine "Mahogany"

Weight about 3.0 pounds (medium). This is the market name for woods known as *lauan* and *tangile* in the Philippine Islands and extensively used for planking and trim in this country. It is decay resistant and an excellent material for planking used by the finest of builders for this purpose. When selected for color and grain it is attractive for cabin sides and trim. Somewhat more difficult to finish than true mahoganies, but not unduly so. Hardness and color vary considerably. Holds fastenings well and is relatively inexpensive considering its qualities. According to one large importer the best grade is known as "firsts and seconds" and the better boatbuilders prefer the more expensive, darker red variety.

Other Mahoganies

Weight varies from medium to heavy. Honduras, Mexican and African mahoganies have all been used for planking, exterior finish and interior joinerwork of fine yachts. They are heavier than the so called Philippine mahoganies, are better looking, easier to finish and more expensive. Honduras or Mexican mahogany is a favored first quality planking and finish material. According to Abeking and Rasmussen of Lemwerder, Germany, builders of some of the finest yachts in the world, suitable African mahoganies are Khaya (Ivorensis), Sipo (Utile), Sapeli (Aboudikro) and Niangon (Nyankom), and if this firm uses these kinds they should be acceptable to anyone. In the past this firm stated that there are other kinds of African mahoganies that are not suitable, so here again it is a case of dealing with a reliable supplier of woods.

Teak

Weight about 3.5 pounds (heavy). Not as strong as people think but extremely durable. Has a natural oil that excludes moisture and thus has minimum shrinkage. The acceptable kind is grown in Burma or Thailand, and is so expensive in the United States that the use is reserved for decks and trim. Teak decks are not coated as a rule, and are scrubbed periodically to a whitish finish which, in the opinion of many, has no equal. Varnished teak trim has a rich appearance. Worms are not fond of teak, so this wood is often used to sheath the bottom of a keel as protection in case some of the toxic anti-fouling bottom paint is rubbed off. Teak also contains a gritty substance that dulls tools quickly, adding somewhat to the cost of working.

White Ash

Weight about 3.4 pounds (heavy). Straight grained, strong for its weight and very durable. Used for deck beams as a substitute for oak where reduction in weight is desirable. Suitable for steam bending and used for small boat frames; also a favorite for sailboat tillers and is an old standby for oars.

Hackmatack

Weight about 3.1 pounds (medium), also called larch or tamarack. Tough and durable. Only the roots, from which natural crooks are made are used for boatbuilding. Stems for small boats and knees are cut from these crooks.

Alaska Cedar

Weight about 2.6 pounds (medium). Straight grained, moderately strong, heartwood very resistant to decay. Minimum shrinkage when seasoned. Good for planking and is used for keels in area where grown, southeastern Alaska to southern Oregon. Heartwood is bright yellow, sapwood usually narrow.

Strength vs. Weight

Because a comparison of strengths is of interest, the woods mentioned above are listed below in order of strength, with the weight per board foot again shown.

	pounds		pounds
White ash	3.4	Cypress	2.8
White oak	4.2	Sitka spruce	2.4
Yellow pine	3.4	Northern white spruce	2.4
Douglas fir	2.9	Port Orford cedar	2.4
Teak	3.5	Alaska cedar	2.6
Hackmatack	3.1	White cedar	1.9
Honduras mahogany	2.9	White pine	2.1
Philippine "mahogany"	3.0	Western red cedar	1.9

It is recommended that those who want to learn more about wood acquire the *Wood Handbook* of the Forest Products Laboratory, U.S. Dep't of Agriculture, for sale by the Superintendent of Documents, Government Printing Office, Washington, D.C. 20402.

Plywood

The completely waterproof glues developed comparatively recently have made possible the manufacture of laminated wood veneers into plywood panels that have had a marked influence on the construction of most types of boats. Being made of thin layers of wood securely bonded to each other, they are stiffer than boards of equal thickness and have advantages over regular lumber for many boat parts. Planking, for example, may be made proportionately thinner and because it is stiffer there is less framing required. Both of these factors save weight, of equal importance in either sail or power-boats. Also, in the case of planking, there are fewer seams to leak and due to the construction of the panels there is minimum swelling and shrinking. Other examples are bulkheads and interior partitions, where plywood not only saves weight but also the many hours of labor to make these parts of small pieces put together with painstaking care. A further advantage is that fastenings may be close to the panel edges without fear of splitting.

Although there are exceptions to this, it is not theoretically possible to plank a hull with plywood panels unless the designer has especially shaped the hull for such construction because plywood, like a metal plate, cannot be bent in two directions at once, that is bent to fit on a surface that has compound curvature. Metal plates can be worked in various ways to fit a compound curve but this cannot be done to plywood. However in reference to the exceptions mentioned above it has been found that the bottom planking of certain arc bottom hulls can be made of plywood with the use of strategically located clamps and fastenings. Only experience can help you with this, but nevertheless amateurs have done it the first time they tried.

If you should happen to have a set of plans for the boat you want and get the notion that it should be planked with plywood although the designer has specified otherwise, check with him first to see whether it is feasible. This procedure may save you a major heartbreak.

Even though plywood is not suitable for planking all boats it has a place in the construction of every boat. Besides bulkheads, for which plywood is ideal, it is an excellent material for cabin tops and has all but supplanted solid lumber for decks, either alone or as a sub-deck where planking is desired for appearance.

Plywood is made by laying up thin layers of wood with the grain at right angles to each other, and the number of layers is always odd so that the grain of the face plies is always parallel. The number of plies and their thickness is important. Cheap ⅜ inch thick plywood, for instance, might have two thin faces and a relatively thicker inner ply, a total of three, whereas a better grade will have five plies of wood of about equal thickness each. It can be readily seen that with right angle construction the three ply panel with a thick inner ply will be weak when bent parallel to the grain of the inner ply.

The most common and inexpensive kind of plywood is made of Douglas fir. To obtain the fir veneer for making plywood panels the logs are placed in a lathe and turned against a knife edge that peels the veneer to desired thickness, thus most of the grain is flat grain, called wild grain, and in fir it is indeed difficult to tame sufficiently for a smooth paint finish. Fir also checks badly so the paint finish develops hair line cracks that become greater in number as time goes on. This situation can be helped somewhat by coating the fir with a sealer before painting, using a plywood sealer made by one of the marine paint or plywood manufacturers. The checking of fir plywood faces is much worse where exposed to the weather, but even when used for interior joinerwork a paint finish is a problem when a first class job is wanted. Fir plywood, however, is acceptable for interior work that is to be covered with either one of the modern vinyl wall coverings or with one of the durable laminates such as Formica, also for planking and decking that is to be covered with a synthetic cloth such as fiber glass and resin.

Plywood for any purpose in a boat, whether planking or interior joinerwork, should be the marine grade as a guarantee that the veneers are bonded with waterproof adhesive, that a minimum number of patches are used in the face plies, and that voids in the inner plies are practically nil.

A rather new marine grade of plywood made especially for boat use is available with a facing of phenolic impregnated cellulose fiber on both sides. This type panel is laid up with Philippine mahogany face plies and fir inner plies, so the cellulose fiber over the mahogany results in just about the smoothest surface possible for a paint finish, and the bonding of the fiber covering is such that this material can be used for planking the hull.

Also made in marine grade is plywood with either ribbon grain or rotary grain Philippine mahogany faces. This type panel is also excellent for a paint finish, but the principal use is for natural finished varnished joinerwork. The choice of the grain rests with personal taste.

Plywood Sizes

One large manufacturer of marine grade plywood lists panels generally available as shown below (all dimensions in inches). This is handy information to have when planning your work.

Fir
¼ 3-ply x 48 x 96, 120, 144, 168
⅜ 5-ply x 48 x 96, 120, 144, 168, 192, 216, 240
½ 5-ply x 48 x 96
¾ 7-ply x 48 x 96
1½ 11-ply x 48 x 96

Rotary Grain Philippine Mahogany
⅜ 5-ply 48 x 144
¾ 7-ply x 48 x 96

Ribbon Grain Philippine Mahogany
½ 3-ply 48 x 96

"Duraply" (Cellulose fiber faced)
½ 3-ply 48 x 96
⅜ 5-ply 48 x 96, 120, 144, 168, 192, 216, 240
½ 5-play x 48 x 96
¾ 7-ply x 48 x 96

Exterior Grade Plywood

Many builders, including the writer, have successfully used exterior grade plywood instead of marine grade, but a sufficient number of failures such as delamination have been recorded so that the use of exterior grade is not recommended unless one is absolutely certain that the panels are made with truly waterproof glue, that all voids are plugged by the builder to prevent the entrance of water that can cause rot, and that the weaker construction of the lesser number of plies is suitable for the job. All in all, considering the tremendous amount of trouble that could be caused by failure of the plywood material, the amateur is advised against gambling his labor against the saving in material cost gained by the use of exterior grade.

Cutting Plywood

Due to the thin veneers that make up a panel, plywood tends to splinter on the underside of the cut when sawed, and fir is one of the worst in this respect. A piece of solid lumber clamped on the underside of the panel will eliminate this splintering when it is possible to do so. Cuts should aways be made with the face side up, and a fine toothed crosscut saw must be used. Lightweight portable circular saws are handy when much plywood is to be cut and there are blades with fine teeth made just for this purpose. The edges of plywood panels are best smoothed with a low angle, sharp block plane set for a fine cut and held at an angle to the edge rather than parallel to it.

Laminating Wood

Glued parts of laminated solid wood or plywood can be used in boat construction because of the availability of waterproof adhesives that cure at room temperature. Curved parts can be made with minimum waste of material in some cases and large parts can be made of smaller pieces of wood readily obtained and easily handled. Double diagonal and strip planking as described later are both a form of wood laminating and so is a hollow mast. Aside from boats, small aircraft propellers and tennis rackets are common examples of wood lamination. For boat construction laminated parts are not necessarily cheap due to the time in preparing the form and preparing the material, but the parts are strong, particularly laminated solid wood assemblies of parallel grain construction such as deck beams that would have cross grain in them if sawn from solid stock. Laminations are much less likely to check and split than non-laminated parts, and although laminating does not increase the strength of the wood itself, the strength of the assembly such as the stem for a boat shown in A of Figure 4-4 is greater than if made of solid pieces with joints in the conventional manner.

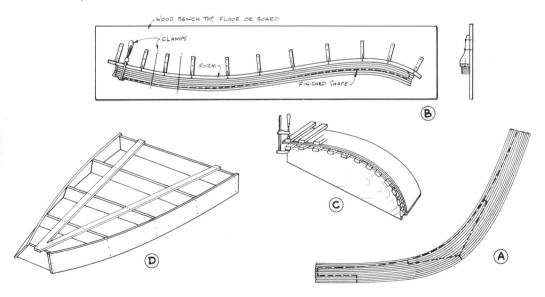

FIGURE 4-4.

22

In B of Figure 4-4 is shown the lamination of a part such as a tiller. A part like this would have cross grain if sawn from one piece of wood. The shape is laid out on a board or the floor and a series of cleats fastened in place to secure the form to which to clamp the lamination.

In almost all laminating it will be found from sad experience that waxed paper must be used to prevent the part from becoming glued to the form.

Another type of form is shown in C. Such a form is used for laminating either plywood or solid stock. In D is sketched a form to glue up right and left hand parts with a twist, such as the bulwarks at the bow of the boat.

Builders with an interest in laminating become quite ingenious at concocting forms for laminated parts that otherwise would be tedious to make or would be inferior to a lamination either strength-wise or from the effects of time.

There is no rule for the thickness of the lamination strips except they must be thin enough to easily take the required shape. If not sufficiently thin you will have a hard time holding them in place prior to clamping.

Prevention of Wood Decay

The first step in the prevention of decay is the selection of woods that experience has proven durable in boats, and it should be remembered that the heartwood of the log is the most resistant to rot. Decay is caused by fungi that feed on the cellulose between the cell walls of wood. For the fungi to grow certain conditions of moisture, temperature and the air must be present and too often, sometimes through carelessness of the builder, these conditions are met. The moisture content must be on the order of 25-30 per cent, the temperature 75-90 degrees F., and the air stagnant. Wood that is always dry does not rot because of the lack of moisture, and wood that is continuously wet does not rot because there is no air present.

There will be more later on the importance of building to avoid leaks in deck and cabin where water can enter and be trapped, just waiting for the right temperature for the fungi to grow.

In addition to the natural decay resistance of some woods and the precautions against leaks that can be taken by the builder, the chemical world has produced chemicals that can be used that are toxic to fungi and marine borers. These preparations are cheap, easy to apply and reduce the chances of decay.

For many years an old standby in boatbuilding are decay preventatives containing copper naphthanate, then pentachloraphenol came along, and more recently TBTO (tributyl tin oxide). All of these are sold under various names by the marine paint manufacturers and are readily available from suppliers. Although we are reluctant to recommend any one as the best, the experience of boatbuilders we have talked with and photos of test panels we have closely examined point up TBTO as the most effective for protection against marine borers and wood destroying fungi.

Any of the preservatives are easy to apply by brushing or dipping, the larger parts being brushed and smaller pieces such as planking butt blocks, short deck beams and the like being dipped in a container of the preparation.

Scantlings

The sizes of the hull parts in boatbuilding, wood or metal, are called scantlings. For instance, the list of scantlings will include the size and spacing of frames, planking thickness, keel depth and width, stem width and sizes of clamps, stringers, deck beams, etc. The actual dimensions may be given as the "siding," generally the smaller dimension, and the "molding," usually the larger and measured vertically. As an example of this, and referring to Figure 12-1A, a deck beam would be sided 1½ inch and molded 2½ inch, while a clamp would be sided 1½ inch and molded 4 inch. The dimensions of frames are an exception to the above because the fore and aft dimension is the siding, and the athwartship dimension the molded size. The terminology is peculiar to boatbuilding and the builder quickly becomes adjusted to the usage.

Chapter 5

FIBER GLASS AND OTHER MATERIALS

Ｗood has been the traditional material for boatbuilding and because of the ease of working by the beginner it remains so, especially for one-of-a-kind construction, but for other reasons, and depending upon the skill and ingenuity of the builder, there are other materials to be considered, sometimes in combination with wood.

Wood and Fiber Glass

When the type of wood hull construction is suitable there is much to recommend covering the wood with resin and fiber glass or other synthetic cloth. The hull planking must be of a stable type such as strip planking, double or triple diagonal planking, or plywood, as compared with normal carvel planking where moisture changes or storage out of water might cause the seams to open and close a considerable amount and crack the covering. When the hull is suitable the covering adds strength, prevents rot, minimizes leaks and weight gain from the absorption of water, and on boats used in sea water particularly the attack and possible destruction by worms and borers is eliminated. The latter by itself is a great advantage by reducing worry due to delays in hauling out of water for bottom cleaning. The weight of the covering does not add much to the overall weight of the boat and when planned in the design the wooden parts can be reduced in size to compensate for the weight of the covering. In anything except very fast boats the added weight does not count for much anyway.

The fabric is usually fiber glass cloth, but polypropylene and Dynel are also used. The resin can be either polyester or epoxy. The latter is more expensive, more time-consuming due to slower cure at room temperatures but has superior adhesion.

Covering is also recommended for plywood decks, cabin tops, and the like, and the covering of joints in cabin sides, etc. to prevent leaks is a genuine boon to the builder when the joined work is to be painted rather than varnished. Taped joints can be sanded to feather edges and made invisible under a paint finish.

Anyone who dabbles with boats will sooner or later want to cover old wood, and there are certain precautions that must be taken for a good job. All old finish must be cleaned off the wood, and the wood must be dry. For instance, in the case of a plywood hull, the boat must be hauled out of the water and put under cover, the old finish stripped, and the wood allowed to dry for several weeks before covering. Epoxy resin is strongly recommended for old wood.

New wood or old, oil base fillers must not be used over the heads of fastenings because it will be softened by the resin. For filling cracks and smoothing gouges use either a polyester automobile body putty, which is very fast drying and can be sanded soon after use, or make a mixture of epoxy resin and a material like Cabosil proportioned to the consistency of putty.

Fiber Glass Hulls

The shiny, commercially produced fiber glass hulls are usually made from a female mold. This requires first making a male "plug" of wood just as though you were building a wooden hull, using strip planking or plywood, whichever is suitable for the hull shape. The plug is then covered with glass cloth and resin and worked to a very smooth finish because every blemish will be reproduced when the female mold is made. When the plug is finished as desired a release is applied so the female will not stick to it, then glass cloth and mat and polyester resin are laid up successively until a mold has been made that is strong and rigid, even to the extent of reinforcing with wood and sometimes steel pipe. To facilitate the future removal of a molded hull from the female mold the latter is often made in two pieces, split on the center line.

When the female mold for the production of a hull has been removed from the plug it is polished and waxed and any blemishes repaired, and then is ready for laying up a hull. Sometimes a partial disc of wood or steel, larger in diameter than the beam of the boat, is added to the mold near each end so the mold can be rolled from side to side while laying up the fiber glass and resin. When the hull is anything larger than dinghy size this minimizes the amount of time the builders must spend actually in the hull while laying up and makes the work mostly downhand. The more you can stay out of the sticky resin the less distasteful the job can be. This presumes that the hull will be made by laying up the laminates by hand and the resin applied with roller and brush. When hulls are produced in large quantity, the resin and even chopped glass fibers can be applied with specialized spray equipment.

How does one make a mold and lay up a fiber glass hull if precise plans and instruction procedures are not available? Observation, experience, and a combination of both. At this writing one of the best books in print is the *Marine Design Manual* listed under Recommended Reading elsewhere in this book. Otherwise, suppliers of resins, cloth and other molding materials usually have knowledgeable representatives who can give valuable information.

It is only natural that enterprising builders should seek ways of building a hull of synthetic materials without the time and expense of making a male plug and the female mold. One way to do this is to set up a framework of molds and ribbands as for a wooden hull and cover it with foam core material such as Plyfoam. This comes in sheets like plywood and can be draped to the hull form when made limber with heat lamps. The outside of the foam is then covered with resin and cloth or cloth and mat, depending upon the requirements, then the hull is removed from the form and the inside surface is covered with a layup, again depending upon what strength is wanted. The resulting hull is of the so-called sandwich construction, can be made strong and lightweight, and has built-in floatation provided by the foam core. Other similar methods are certain to be developed.

The shiny hulls produced from female molds are made inside out in that the glossy gel coat of resin is sprayed in the hull as the first step of the layup. The sandwich type hull mentioned above can be given a finish equal in appearance to the best only by sanding absolutely smooth and then rolling on a gel coat of resin made for this purpose, or painting with one of the several marine finishes made for fiber glass hulls.

Steel

When you stop to think about it, steel is a remarkable material. It is strong, very inexpensive when compared with other metals, and when proper equipment is available it can be worked to almost any shape desired. Relative ease to join pieces by electric welding makes it a material suitable for small craft with a saving in weight over old fashioned riveted construction. One disadvantage of steel is the low resistance to corrosion by sea water. Fortunately the years have brought about improved coatings to protect steel against corrosion, but the coatings must be constantly maintained. An advantage of steel construction is that inner bottom integral fuel and water tanks can be built in, using the hull for one side, enabling larger capacities to be carried than in wooden hulls.

Steel is not a material for the average beginner by any means, but without reflecting for too long the writer can remember two good sized auxiliary sailboats of steel built by people that had not built a boat before. However they did have metal working experience and also had the necessary equipment. The worst fault of these boats were the humps and hollows in the hull plating, and both builders said that they had gained experience so that if they did it again the hulls would not be so rough.

Rough plating of steel hulls is often disguised by skillful application of trowel cement, probably because it is cheaper to do this than to expend the labor needed to smooth the plating by heating and quenching. The roughness of the plating is caused by stresses set up when welding the plating to the frames and the butt welds between the plates. The sequence of welding is of importance in this respect.

Even though steel is an old material, research technicians occasionally invent new alloys of higher strength so that steel hulls can be built lighter today than ever before.

Aluminum Alloys

Certain of the many alloys of aluminum, those that came along in the 1930's containing magnesium and manganese, are satisfactory for boatbuilding. These alloys are relatively high in strength and corrosion resistance and can be satisfactorily welded. At this writing there are vessels in ocean service without any paint above the water line for protection against corrosion, but the bottoms have anti-fouling coatings. Pleasure boats, however, are usually painted for the sake of appearance.

In general terms, alloys of aluminum reduce construction weight over that of steel. This permits the carrying of more deadweight or increasing speed, or of achieving speed with less horsepower, and the fact that commercial operators are using aluminum cannot but speak well for the anticipated longevity.

Several makers of pleasure boats either build only in aluminum or have a line of aluminum boats in addition to those of other materials. Small craft such as dinghies and runabouts of aluminum are made by stretch-forming sheets over male molds to produce a large part or an entire half out of one piece of metal. Otherwise regular transverse or longitudinal framing is used and covered with plating as in steel construction. The cost of aluminum is greater per pound than steel, but there is less of it, and welding is more expensive than steel, so the overall cost is greater than steel.

Many builders of steel boats have converted to aluminum construction with little need to change equipment except for welding but, like steel, it is not a material for the inexperienced beginner. One very important phase of aluminum construction is the prevention of galvanic corrosion between the aluminum hull and dissimilar metals such as seacocks, propellers, shafts, rudders, etc.; also protection from corrosion from stray electrical currents in anchorages. These things can be done and the methods are preferably all spelled out in the plans and specifications for the boat. Lacking this, the marine departments of the aluminum manufacturers can be consulted for help. These companies also provide information about welding, which is quite different from steel. The marine paint makers have systems for painting aluminum and instructions for the very important cleaning of the metal preparatory to coating.

Ferro-Cement

Every now and again there is a wave of enthusiasm about constructing hulls of ferro-cement and it would be a poor bet to say that a beginner will not tackle this system and produce a satisfactory hull. Essentially the system consists of a framework of concrete reinforcing rod interlaced with wire, similar to building and bridge construction, and applying cement so the steelwork is completely imbedded, not exposed to the atmosphere. It is understood that great care must be taken to eliminate voids in the cement, and that the basically heavy weight of the construction makes it impractical for hulls under thirty feet in length.

According to articles in the boating press during 1967-68 there were at least fifty ferro-cement ships and boats under construction and a few naval architects designing in this material.

Chapter 6

FASTENINGS

OMPARED WITH the heavily constructed boats of the old days, almost all modern craft can be considered lightly built. Thus the innumerable fastenings holding the parts together assume extra importance as a primary contribution to a tight seaworthy boat. All fastenings should be sized according to their task, located with thought by the designer and builder, and always driven in carefully drilled holes of proper size so the holding power will be maximum.

Galvanized Iron

The builder will hear that considerable money can be saved by using galvanized iron fastenings. Word has been passed down the line that galvanized fastened boats will last a lifetime, and certainly there are boats here and there that seem to prove this point. On the other hand the writer recently examined a wrecked shrimper on a beach that proved just the opposite.

In the first place the old timers used galvanized iron, whereas what is available today is most likely galvanized mild steel and, secondly, their iron nails and rods were always coated by the hot dipping process. Bared of the coating mild steel is not nearly so resistant to corrosion as iron, and many fastenings today are zinc coated by electroplating that is worthless compared to hot dipping.

Planking has been fastened to frames with either galvanized boat nails or galvanized wood screws. Frames should be at least 1½ inch thick for the nail to be buried in it without going through the frame. With lighter frames the nail goes through the frames and is clinched over on the inside. When poor nails are used the zinc will break off the nail where it is bent, leaving the bare metal without protection right at the start. Many boats have had to be refastened because of corrosion starting at the end of the nail and progressing throughout the length of the fastening. Renailing is an expensive job and the necessity is a good sign that fastenings were inferior or inadequate when the boat was built.

In the case of galvanized wood screws the threads of the smaller sizes are frequently clogged with zinc when they are dipped, and in driving they tear the wood around the hole, reducing the holding power. Despite some good experiences in the past the builder is advised to be sure of his fastenings by using a better metal for parts that are constantly in water. Although more expensive initially, the best fastenings are cheap in the end.

Brass

If a decision is made against galvanized fastenings it might seem that the next best metal would be brass, but the use of this metal for fastening parts exposed to salt water cannot be advised against too strongly. Brass as furnished for the manufacture of screws and bolts is very high in zinc content, perhaps as much as 30%, and in an electrolyte such as sea water the zinc leaves the alloy, so what remains is a spongy copper so reduced in strength that it is practically useless. This is called dezincification and can be expected when a copper alloy is used containing zinc in excess of 16%. There are mechanical disadvantages, too. The high zinc brass alloys are not particularly strong so it is easy to break off screws being driven into hard woods. Brass is all right for the fastening of interior parts such as joinerwork but care should be taken not to use it in the hull.

Silicon Bronze

For every structural fastening in a boat it is hard to beat a copper silicon alloy sometimes called Everdur. It is about 96% copper and is so strong that seldom are fastenings wrung off when being driven and, of major importance, it is highly resistant to corrosion from sea water. The use of this metal removes the risks involved with the brasses and galvanized steel fastenings and is well worth the difference in cost. When it is considered that it takes no more time to drive a bronze screw than other kinds the difference in cost is not as much as the price of the screws alone might indicate, and a point to be remembered is the resale value of a bronze fastened boat.

Monel

This nickel copper alloy ranks above silicon bronze in strength and corrosion resistance but the cost of screws and bolts made from it is much too high for most people to afford. It can be used in conjunction with silicon bronze without fear of much galvanic action between the metals. For instance, Monel is often used for fastening bronze propeller shaft struts and Monel shafts have bronze propellers in direct contact. The strength and stiffness of Monel makes it very satisfactory for Anchorfast boat nails, a popular fastening for some purposes because of the saving in labor over driving screws. See Threaded Nails. Monel as a metal has many uses in boat construction and will be mentioned further.

Copper

Copper has excellent corrosion resistance but because of its softness is suitable mostly for fastenings in the form of flat head nails that are used as rivets or for clout nails sometimes used in hulls with light lapstrake planking.

Stainless Steel

There are many alloys under this common heading. It is recommended that these metals not be considered for hull fastenings unless you are guided by someone that has vast experience and satisfactory proof of corrosion resistance and freedom from galvanic action with other materials being used in the same boat. Without such assurance the use of stainless steel should be limited to applications above water, such as fastening aluminum alloy marine window frames, deck hardware, etc., or such items as stainless steel rub rail moldings. It is believed that Type 316 stainless steel is the most resistant to sea water corrosion, but at this writing such fastenings as Type 316 wood screws are not available except made to order. We know of one builder at least that does have these screws made for his stainless steel trim, but this is out of the question for the small builder in most cases. Other than for fastenings there are several practical uses for stainless steel in boats. Certain stainless steels are being used for propeller shafting and apparently the experience from the standpoint of corrosion resistance and compatibility with bronze propellers has been satisfactory. The strength of these steels is very high. Stainless is also used for wire rope rigging and rigging fittings on spars. As with many materials that might be used in a boat it is best to leave experimentation to others, using it yourself only when you know the application has been proven by time.

Mixture of Metals

The loosely used term "electrolysis" is applied by the average boatman to the corrosion and erosion of metals by electrolysis, cavitation or galvanic action, and usually the destruction of metals is blamed on electrolysis due to lack of knowledge of the other causes. Except for discussing galvanic action between fastenings the subject is beyond the scope of this work.

Sea water is an electrolyte that will cause an electric current to flow between dissimilar metals when in contact or close proximity to each other. When this occurs current will flow from the anode to the cathode, that is, the anodic fitting or fastening will be attacked and gradually destroyed by what is properly termed galvanic corrosion. The intensity of the attack will vary according to the relative positions of the metals in the galvanic series and also upon the relative areas or mass of the metals. The positions in the galvanic series of some metals follow:

> *Anodic* Zinc
> Pure aluminum
> Aluminum alloy
> Steel
> Cast iron
> Stainless steels (active)
> Lead
> Naval brass (Tobin bronze)
> Copper
> Silicon bronze
> Monel
> Stainless steels (passive) *Cathodic*

It is not practical to use only one metal throughout the construction of a hull, so the next best thing is to use metals close to each other in the galvanic series, such as silicon bronze and Monel. These two metals are galvanically compatible and high in strength and corrosion resistance.

Note that stainless steels are shown in the series above in two different positions. As we understand it, the surface of the steel is passivated by chemical treatment to hasten the formation of oxide. This is done to a piece after all machining and working has been finished, and after a thorough cleaning and degreasing. The passivated surface is more resistant to corrosion. Without passivation, or if the surface treatment is destroyed, the corrosion resistance is severely reduced, and the change from one condition to the other is so uncertain that it is best to avoid the use of these metals for underwater fastenings.

We know of a case where a bronze stern bearing casting was fastened with galvanized iron lag screws through sheer ignorance, a perfect example of setting up galvanic corrosion. The dissimilar metals were in contact in sea water, first the zinc disappeared, then the iron was attacked until the bearing finally came loose.

Many boats with bronze hull fastenings have been built with cast iron ballast keels, but in this case the comparitively huge mass of anodic material, the iron keel, would show signs of attack slowly due to its bulk. The bolts securing the keel can be of hot dipped galvanized wrought iron or Monel.

The joint between the keel casting and the wood keel and deadwood should have a liberal dose of bedding compound during assembly and the outside of the iron should have several coats of a vinyl type anti-corrosive paint to act as a barrier to galvanic action.

Screw Bolts

These are ordinary machine bolts with square or hexagon heads and nuts and are made in silicon bronze, Monel and galvanized iron. Longer bolts are homemade by threading a piece of rod on both ends, screwing a nut as a head on one end, peening over the end of the rod to prevent the head nut from turning. Washers of the same material are used under the head and nut. Drilled holes should be the same diameter as the bolt. Screw bolts are used for fastening many backbone parts and have the advantage over drift bolts of being able to be tightened when the wood shrinks.

Well equipped professional builders sometimes head their own long bolts. They have a die, usually for a flat head, and the end of the rod is heated and forged to shape.

Drift Bolts

When bolts must be very long or a through bolt is not practical or necessary, a drift bolt is made from a piece of rod and driven like a large nail. The one end is pointed slightly by hammering, the other has a washer or clinch ring under a driving head formed by riveting the end of the rod. The hole is made about two diameters shorter than the bolt to be driven and should have smooth sides. The size of the hole must be less than the diameter of the bolt for a tight, driving fit. Be careful not to bend the bolt above the timber when driving. When a pair or a series of drift bolts is called for it is best to drive them at an angle (Figure 6-1) to resist strains by locking the parts together. Drift bolts are made of bronze or galvanized iron.

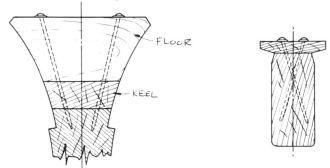

FIGURE 6-1. *Drift bolts are driven at an angle to lock parts*

Carriage Bolts

These are screw bolts with a round button head and a square neck on the shank just under the head which keeps the bolt from turning in the wood. Carriage bolts are used in many parts of the structure such as fastening frames to floors, stringers to clamps, and frames and deck beams to clamps or shelves, and are made in silicon bronze, galvanized iron and stainless steel.

Bolt Threads

The only reason for any fastening is to hold parts together and keep them from moving. Fastenings must be tight in their holes. This is not possible if the bolts have what are called *rolled threads* and bolts of this type are common today because threads formed by rolling instead of cutting are cheaper to manufacture. The unthreaded shank of these bolts is smaller in diameter than the outside of the threads so the shank cannot possibly be tight in the hole. Bolts of this type are all right when the fastening is purely in tension, but this is seldom the case in the hull structure so rolled thread bolts should not be used.

Wood Screws

Flat head screws are used extensively for fastening planking and decking and many other minor parts. They are available from stock made of galvanized iron, brass, silicon bronze and are also produced of Monel and stainless steel.

Tests have shown that screws with sharp, thin threads develop the greatest holding power. Thus galvanized screws have one strike against them from the start because if well coated with zinc the threads are often very rough. Withdrawal resistance of screws used as plank fastenings is theoretically not too critical because the most important function of the fastening is not to keep the plank from springing off, but to prevent it from moving past its neighbor in a fore and aft direction when the hull is being driven through the seas. When such movement occurs the hull is said to "work" and is the cause of leaking seams in a conventionally planked boat. Indeed the primary job of fastenings is to hold the parts together tightly and the area of the wood that bears against the fastenings is very important. In other words, a thick fastening puts more wood to work resisting stresses than a thin one. This fact is a strong argument for screws instead of nails as planking fastenings, especially in the hulls of sailboats with the wringing strains from masts, because for a given length a screw can be used that is thicker than a nail of the same length. The accompanying table, Figure 6-2, shows practice accepted over the years for screw sizes in planking and decking, and if you compare the gauge of any one of the screws with an ordinary boat nail of the same length

FLAT HEAD WOOD SCREWS FOR PLANKING					
PLANK THICKNESS	SCREW LENGTH & GAUGE[1]	SCREW DIAM.	BODY DRILL	LEAD DRILL[2]	PLUG DIAM.
3/8"	3/4" No. 7	.150"	9/64"	No. 44	NONE
1/2"	1" No. 8	.163"	5/32"	No. 40	NONE
5/8"	1 1/4" No. 9	.176"	11/64"	No. 37	3/8"
3/4"	1 1/2" No. 10	.189"	3/16"	No. 33	1/2"
7/8"	1 3/4" No. 12	.216	13/64"	No. 30	1/2"
1"	2" No. 14	.242"	15/64"	No. 25	1/2"
1 1/8"	2 1/4" No. 16	.268"	17/64"	No. 18	5/8"
1 1/4"	2 1/2" No. 18	.294"	9/32"	No. 13	5/8"
1 1/2"	3" No. 20	.320"	5/16"	No. 4	3/4"

[1] MAY BE REDUCED ONE GAUGE FOR DECKING.
[2] FOR HARDWOOD

FIGURE 6-2.

the advantage of screw thickness will be obvious. Unlike common boat nails, Monel Anchorfast nails and Stronghold bronze nails are available in heavy gauges suitable for planking fastenings, but usually must be made to order.

Some will consider the screw sizes in Figure 6-2 to be on the heavy side, but the table is meant for hulls subject to rigorous service such as ocean cruising sailing yachts. The sizes may be reduced by a gauge or so for power and other boats of light construction for sheltered waters. When building from plans, be guided by the fastening sizes specified.

The size of a drilled hole for a screw affects its holding power to an appreciable extent. A general rule to follow for the lead hole drill is 90% of the diameter at the root of the screw threads in hard woods and 70% in soft woods. The lead hole drill sizes in the table are a guide for hard wood such as oak because the threaded part of a screw used for planking is in the frame, but it is best to check the table sizes by driving a few screws in samples of the wood to be used. Most builders use just one drill for screws in mahogany or white cedar planking and oak frames and this is satisfactory if the plank does not split in the way of the unthreaded screw shank. If splitting does occur the table shows a body drill to use through the plank that is slightly under the actual screw diameter. Especially when driving into hardwood it is recommended that either laundry soap or beeswax be rubbed in the threads of screws. This acts as a lubricant and reduces the driving labor.

In the best yacht practice the screw holes in planking ⅝″ thick and over are counterbored and plugged (Figure 6-3) with plugs of the same wood as the planking, while the heads of screws in thinner planks are set slightly below the surface and then the heads are puttied over so the fastenings will not be visible on the finished hull. For many years white lead putty was used for this

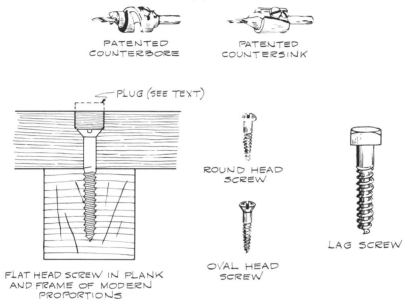

FIGURE 6-3.

purpose, but modern material like Famowood or Duratite, or even one of the polyester putty compounds is better. Marine hardware suppliers sell plugs of mahogany, teak or oak, or you can buy a plug cutter for a drill press and make your own from scraps of wood. The depth of counterbore for the plugs should be about one-third of the plank thickness. The plugs are dipped in thick paint, waterproof glue or varnish (the latter recommended for wood that is to have a natural finish), set in the counterbored holes with the grain parallel to that of the planking, and lightly tapped home with a hammer. If hit too hard the plug may be crushed and will swell later, possibly breaking the paint film or at least presenting an unsightly look. Give the bond a day or so to harden, then cut the plugs flush with the surface with a sharp chisel. Do not try to flush off the plug with one cut of the chisel. Rather take light cuts to determine run of the grain, then you will not chip off the plug below the surface of the plank and have to start all over again.

Holes for screws are started by first counterboring for the plug with a bitt and then boring the lead hole. These operations can be done with separate bitts or you can buy various sizes of a patented countersink that drills the lead hole followed by the countersink for the screw head, or a patented counterbore that drills the lead followed by the hole for the plug. See Figure 6-3. The latter is used most because it is unnecessary to countersink for a flat head screw that is to have a plug over it. A good sailboat planking job with narrow strakes of carvel planking sometimes causes crowding of the plugs near the ends of the planks where the plank width is least. This may be overcome by either carefully staggering the holes if the width of the frame will permit or by reducing the gauge of the screw just enough to use a plug of the next smaller size.

Hardware stores stock several types of wood screw pilot bits made for use in quarter inch electric hand drills and made for screws up to about 2″ No. 12. The two shown in Figure 6-4 are suitable for drilling and countersinking for flat head screws, drilling first a lead hole for the threaded part of the screw, then a hole for the shank, finishing with the countersink. In most cases the screw should be driven below the surface of the wood, so the bit shown on the left is best.

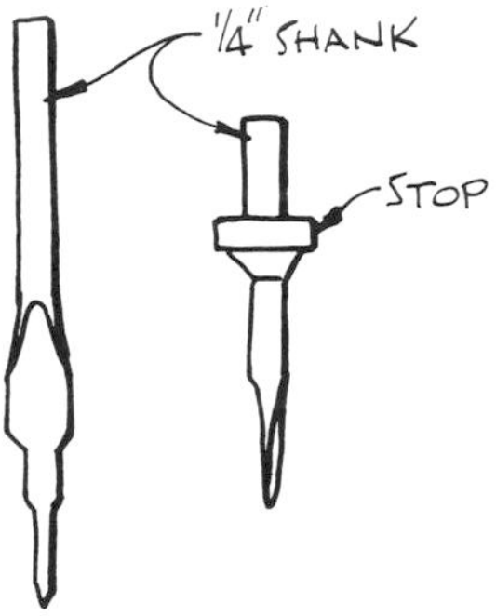

¼″ SHANK

STOP

FIGURE 6-4.

There are only a few places where round head screws are used in boats but they are of course the logical fastening for securing rigging tangs to masts since the thin metal of which a tang is made will not permit a countersunk hole. Oval head screws are only used in light joinerwork where fastenings must show, and for securing panels that are removed from time to time for access to such things as steering gear and other items located behind joinerwork. In these places oval head screws are used with finishing washers so the screw holes do not become too worn from repeated use.

For many years W. L. Fuller, Inc., 1155 Warwick Avenue, Warwick, R.I. 02888, has been supplying countersinks, counterbores, plug cutters and taper point drills to the boatbuilding industry. Ordinarily these items are difficult to find locally.

Lag Screws

Lag screws, sometimes called lag bolts, are large wood screws with a square head so they can be turned in with a wrench. Periodic tightening of a lag screw can wear the threads in the wood until the holding power of the screw heads is gradually lost, therefore lags are only used where through bolts are not possible or practical. A hole of the same diameter as the lag screw is bored for the length of the unthreaded shank and the hole for the thread should be sized the same as for a regular wood screw. Lag screws are made in galvanized iron, brass and silicon bronze.

Hanger Bolts

These are lag screws with the upper or head end of the shank threaded for a nut and are used principally for fastening propeller shaft stuffing boxes and stern bearings and for holding down engines to the beds. These parts are removed occasionally for repair or replacement and by backing off the hanger bolt nut the part may be removed and replaced without disturbing the screw in the wood. Hanger bolts are turned in with a wrench either by running the nut down to the end of the threads or by locking two nuts together on the threads. They are usually made of brass and silicon bronze.

Copper Nails

Copper nails are made in the form of common wire nails with flat heads. They are used almost exclusively as rivets for fastening frames to floors, stringers to frames, planking laps in lapstrake construction, and planking to frames where both the planking and frames are light in size. The hole for the nail should be drilled as tight as possible without splitting the parts or causing the nail to bend while it is being driven. Drive the nail all the way to draw the parts together, then an assistant must back up the head with an iron while driving a copper burr over the point of the nail. A burr is simply a washer and it is important that it be a driving fit over the nail or else it will dance all over the place when the rivet is being formed. The burr is driven up against the wood with a set which is nothing but a length of steel rod with a hole in the end slightly larger than the diameter of the nail. With nippers cut off the point of the nail so that a length is left for riveting equal to one to one and a half times the diameter of the nail. Again backing up the head of the nail with the iron, do the riveting with many light blows with the peen end of a machinist's hammer. Heavy blows will bend the nail inside of the wood. A bent rivet tends to straighten under stress, resulting in a weak, loose fastening. Light blows form the head and draw the wood together.

Copper rivets are excellent for light work but are rather soft. Screws should be used for fastening planking when the size of the frame will permit them. Nails are also thinner than screws for the same job, a point discussed under Wood Screws. See Figure 6-5 for sizes of copper nails.

Also made of copper are small square-cut "clout" nails. These are used in light construction such as canoe hulls with thin, flat frames, and for fastening the seams of lapstrake planking up to about ½ inch in thickness. Clout nails are driven through tight holes against a weighty block of steel or bronze held against the planking on the inside. This turns the nail points back into the plank and, when done by someone experienced, is a good fastening in light construction. The knack is acquired quickly with a little practice. When lapstrake planking, clout nailing is a one man job as opposed to the two men required to rivet common copper nails under most conditions.

Galvanized Boat Nails

As mentioned before, these are cheap fastenings and too much life cannot be expected from them. The nails are forged, have a peculiar button head, rectangular shank and either a blunt or a chisel point. In frames up to about 1¼ inch thick, chisel pointed nails are driven so the the points project about ½ to ⅜ inch through the frames and are clinched against the frame with the grain. To prevent splitting the frame the nail is driven with the chisel edge across the grain. A nail of acceptable quality will clinch without cracking either the nail or the zinc coating. Blunt pointed nails are used in heavier frames and are buried entirely within the frame. Whether or not counterbored for plugs, the heads of either type nail must be driven below the surface of the planking with a nail set and an attempt must be made to prevent cutting the coating of zinc by using a set shaped to fit over the entire head of the nail.

Threaded Nails

A relatively new type of fastening for a boat is a nail with a unique annular thread. As the nail is driven the grooves on the shank shape the wood fibers into countless minute wedges that grip the shank to resist withdrawal. See Figure 6-6. It is claimed that it takes 65% more force to pull this threaded nail than an unclinched galvanized boat nail, 31% more than a clinched boat nail, and 3% more than a wood screw. As these nails are available made of non-ferrous material the objection to nails because of corrosion are over-

NON-FERROUS NAIL SIZES

LENGTH	COPPER		ANCHORFAST & STRONGHOLD	
	SHANK DIAM.	APPROX. NUMBER PER LB.	SHANK DIAM.	APPROX. NUMBER PER LB.
5/8"	.065"	1380	.065"	
3/4"	.065"	1160	.065"	
	.072"	956	.109"	462
7/8"	.072"	808	.065"	825
			.109"	393
1"	.072"	704	.072"	775
			.109"	350
1 1/4"	.083"	424	.083"	525
			.109"	280
			.134"	
1 1/2"	.109"	208	.109"	210
			.134"	135
			.165"	90
1 3/4"	.109"	180	.134"	120
	.120"	144	.165"	76
2"	.134"	106	.134	105
	.120	130	.165"	68
2 1/4"			.165"	64
2 1/2"	.134"	86	.165"	58
2 3/4"			.165"	53
3"	.148"	56	.165"	48
3 1/2"	.165"	40	.165"	25

FIGURE 6-5.

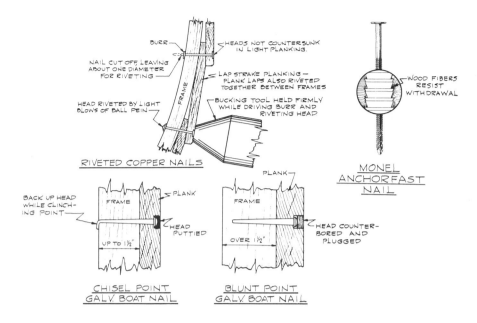

FIGURE 6-6.

come. Some boatbuilders have used these nails for their planking and figures show that some yards have reduced their planking labor by one quarter.

There are quite a few kinds of threaded nail on the market, including some made abroad. Tests have shown the importance of the thread form and one of the best is rolled on the nail by the people that make Anchorfast nails, Independent Nail & Packing Co., Bridgewater, Mass. The name Anchorfast is owned by the International Nickel Co., and is used only when the threaded nails are made of Monel. Anchorfast nails can be identified by an anchor stamped on the head of the nail. Independent also make nails of other materials and calls them Stronghold, but if Monel is not used it is recommended that second choice be limited to those made of silicon bronze. The Monel nails are stiffer than the silicon bronze, making them more resistant to bending when driving.

For fastening planking the diameter of the nails should be the same as the screws they replace, or else more of them used. Pilot holes as recommended by the manufacturer should be drilled for all but the smallest sizes. Pilot hole recommended is 50-70% of the nail diameter, depending upon the hardness of the wood, and about 80% of the nail length.

SCREW GAUGE VS. NAIL DIAMETER		
SCREW		NAIL
SHANK DIAM.	GAUGE №	WIRE DIAM.
.086"	2	.083"
		.095"
		.109"
.125"	5	.120"
.138"	6	.134"
.164"	8	.165"
		.180"
.190	10	
		.203"
.216	12	.220"
.242	14	.238"
		.265"
.268	16	
		.284"
.294	18	.300

FIGURE 6-7.

In Figure 6-5 are shown the sizes of Monel Anchorfast and Stronghold silicon bronze nails usually found in the stocks of distributors. Figure 6-7 is a comparison of standard nail and screw gauges as a guide for those wishing to substitute nails for screws, and in Figure 6-8 are tabulated nail sizes for various types of planking and decking. These sizes, of course, must be used with discretion as they do not necessarily apply to every case.

Miscellaneous Fasteners

There are few other fasteners that really are satisfactory for boats. Everybody is familiar with machine screws, which are nothing but bolts in the smaller

PLANKING & DECKING (NOT PLYWOOD)		
WOOD THICKNESS	NAIL SIZE LIGHT DUTY HULLS	NAIL SIZE HEAVY DUTY HULLS
1/2"	1 1/4" x .083"	
5/8"	1 1/2" x .134"	1 1/2" x .165"
3/4"	1 1/2" x .134"	1 1/2" x .180"
7/8"	1 3/4" x .165"	1 3/4" x .220"
1"	2" x .165"	2" x .238"

PLYWOOD PLANKING & DECKING		NAIL SPACING	
PLYWOOD THICKNESS	NAIL SIZE	ALONG EDGES	PLANKING BATTENS & DECK BEAMS
1/4"	7/8" x .109"	1 1/2" - 1 3/4"	3" - 4"
3/8"	1 1/4" x .109"	2 1/2" - 3"	4" - 5"
1/2"	1 1/2" x .134"	3" - 4"	4" - 5"
5/8"	2" x .165"	4"	5"
3/4"	2 1/4" x .165"	4"	5"

STRIP PLANKING (SEE TEXT)		
WOOD THICKNESS	NAIL DIAM.	APPROX. SPACING
5/8" - 3/4"	.083"	4"
7/8" - 1"	.109"	5"
1" - 1 1/4"	.134"	6"

FIGURE 6-8.

sizes, and these of course have a place where light fasteners are needed, such as for some deck mounted hardware and equipment, locker door hardware, etc. They are made of brass, plain or chrome plated, and stainless steel. Then there are production fasteners such as pop rivets for assembling thin parts of fiber glass boats, but this is not a method for the home workshop. In the same category is a really good fastener—Monel staples that are driven with an air operated tool. The staples come with a coating that improves the resistance to withdrawal to a remarkable extent. It is probably one of the fastest fastening methods suitable for boatbuilding and excellent for securing plywood parts.

Fastening Metal Fittings

To avoid galvanic corrosion fasten bronze underwater parts such as shaft logs, stern bearings, rudder posts, seacocks and propeller shaft struts with silicon bronze. On deck, fasten stainless steel trim and hardware with stainless steel, bronze fittings with silicon bronze, galvanized fittings with hot dipped galvanized fastenings, Marinium fittings with stainless steel or Monel, aluminum alloy fittings with stainless steel. Although not easy to find, use Type 316 stainless steel when you can get it.

Adhesives

We cannot leave the subject of fastenings without mention of adhesives because they have become very important in boatbuilding. One of the best glues for wood is the resorcinol resin type marketed as Elmer's Glue by the Borden Co., and as Waterproof Resorcinol Glue by the U.S. Plywood Corp. This glue is completely waterproof and is made by mixing a liquid resin and a catalyst powder and, when mixed and used to the manufacturers instruc-

FIGURE 6-9.   *Frame of a fine auxiliary yacht, illustrating uses of bolts mentioned in the text*

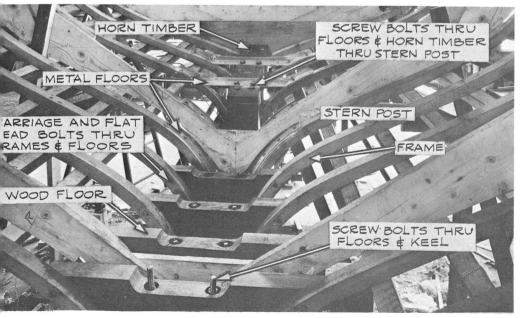

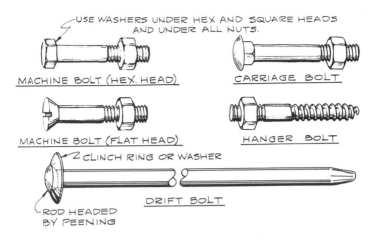

USE WASHERS UNDER HEX AND SQUARE HEADS
AND UNDER ALL NUTS.

MACHINE BOLT (HEX. HEAD)

CARRIAGE BOLT

MACHINE BOLT (FLAT HEAD)

HANGER BOLT

CLINCH RING OR WASHER

DRIFT BOLT

ROD HEADED
BY PEENING

FIGURE 6-10. *Bolts commonly used in boatbuilding*

tions, produces a joint that is stronger than the wood. It is easy to use, but working time and temperature must be watched, and the strongest joints result from plenty of clamping pressure.

Epoxy resin is also a strong, waterproof adhesive. It is commonly available in neighborhood hardware stores in tubes, and the resin and hardener is doctored by the marketer so that equal parts of each are squeezed out and thoroughly mixed prior to application. The cost of buying epoxy glue this way, however, is excessive unless just enough is needed for a small repair job. The boatbuilder needing a quantity of glue can buy the epoxy resin in gallons or by the five gallons, then the cost becomes more realistic, and the proportion of resin to hardener is nothing like the 1:1 tube variety so that mixing requires some measuring, but it is no more difficult than mixing resorcinol resin glue. One of the biggest troubles with epoxies is learning where to buy them and how to mix them. This dearth of information should improve with time.

For many years the hollow wooden spars for sailboats were made without fastenings of any kind except water *resistant* glue, not waterproof, the coats of paint or varnish being all that was needed to protect them from delamination. The so-called Plastic Resin Glue put out by U.S. Plywood is water resistant, easy to prepare by mixing the powder with water, and produces a joint as strong as the wood. This glue can be used for many purposes inside the boat where parts will not be immersed in water, and for spars by those who consider the dark purple glue line of resorcinol resin glue objectionable on a varnished spruce spar.

Chapter 7

LINES AND LAYING DOWN

HE FIRST actual step in building after a suitable design has been selected and plans procured from the naval architect is the reproduction of the hull lines and part of the construction plan to life size. To properly build a boat from plans the procedure of drawing to full scale cannot be avoided, a fact that has been repeated to the point of monotony in countless "how to build" articles, but the job is so important to the completion of a successful boat that instructions in boat building would be incomplete without a description of the work involved. The job is distasteful to some, even professional boatbuilders, but others find it fascinating work. Either way it is true that once the plans are on hand one becomes impatient until wood can be cut, but be assured that the camparatively few hours used to properly prepare for the actual building is time well spent and will never be regretted. The drawings are especially valuable when more than one boat is to be built from the same plans, or for the construction of a one-design class boat where the hull must conform to reasonably close dimensional tolerances.

Hull Lines

The work of enlarging the plans from the scale of the blueprints to full size is termed mold lofting, for it is from these drawings that molds are made for the shape of the hull and various other parts. Of course, to make the job more interesting the different lines which constitute the architect's lines plan should be understood, and to aid the beginner Figure 7-1 has been prepared. Some of the lines are obvious, because from reading the design sections of yachting magazines and from prowling around hulls under construction or stored in boatyards most of you are familiar with the first three lines drawn by the designer that really characterize a hull. These are the sheer line or edge of deck as seen from the side, the profile (the outline of the bottom and ends above the waterline as seen from the side at the same time the sheer line is viewed), and the deck line, a gull's eye view of the outline of the hull

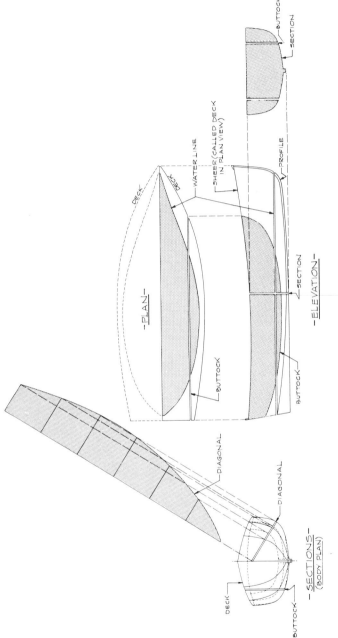

—PLAN—

DECK

DECK

WATER LINE

SHEER (CALLED DECK IN PLAN VIEW)

BUTTOCK

—ELEVATION—

SECTION

BUTTOCK

PROFILE

BUTTOCK

SECTION

—SECTIONS—
(BODY PLAN)

DIAGONAL

DIAGONAL

DECK

BUTTOCK

FIGURE 7-1.   *A solid block model sawn on planes to show location of hull lines drawn by architect to determine shape of boat*

as seen from above. Although these lines are important they are not sufficient for the builder to construct a hull. He also needs the shape of the boat between the three lines, and to provide points to define the hull shape between the three basic lines by providing points to which a builder can work the architect simply cuts the hull into pieces on planes that conveniently establish points for dimensions. These planes are called waterlines, buttocks and diagonals.

If a hull could be lifted straight up out of the water without the hole filling in with water, the shape of the edge of the hole would be the same as the shape of the boat at the surface of the water. This line is called the load waterline and is one of the important lines drawn by the designer. For further subdivision the architect then divides the depth of the hull above and below the load waterline into convenient spaces, and draws the edges of additional horizontal planes which, for the want of something better, are also called waterlines because they are parallel to the load waterline. Then there are vertical planes called buttocks, located parallel to the center line of the boat and conveniently spaced evenly outboard to each side of the center line. Finally, the edges of inclined planes are drawn and these are called diagonals because they are drawn diagonal to the horizontal and vertical planes. These planes, too, are conveniently established, meaning located to provide as many significant dimensioned points for the boatbuilder as is possible.

All of the aforesaid lines are fore and aft lines running the length of the hull, and although it has been mentioned above that these lines are drawn for the purpose of having points on the surface of the hull, actually no usable points have been established until vertical planes across the hull have been drawn to intersect the fore and aft lines. The outlines or shapes formed by vertical transverse planes intersecting the horizontal, vertical and diagonal fore and aft planes are called sections. A point on the hull is established wherever a section intersects one of the fore and aft lines, and by means of the many points of intersection it is possible for the builder to make molds for the exact shape of the hull as the architect has it designed.

Sections may be compared to slices of bread. All the slices through a loaf of rectangular sandwich bread look alike, whereas the slices through an old fashioned rye loaf, or a boat, are all different because the shape is ever changing from end to end. Molds for the construction of a hull are generally made at each section, and the sections are located on the lines plan by dividing the length of the hull on the water, called the waterline length into a number of ordinates called stations. This, of course, is done by the naval architect, not by the boatbuilder.

Figure 7-1 has been included to pictorially show waterline, buttock,

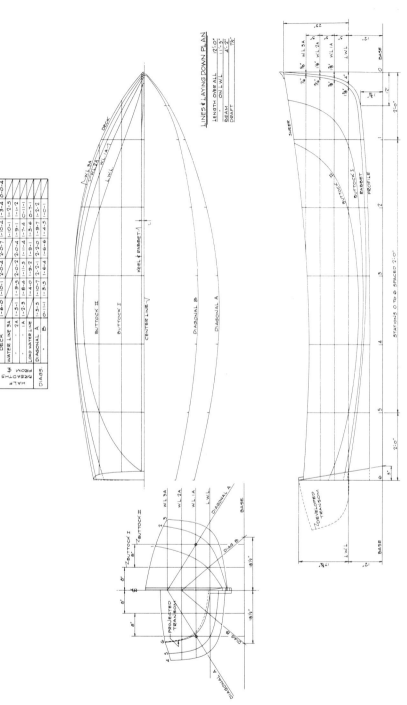

FIGURE 7-2. *Typical lines plan and table of offsets for a round bottom boat*

50

diagonal and sectional planes as though a solid block half model of a hull were sawn into pieces on the various planes. The shapes of the planes are shown by the shaded areas, and on the body plan it may be seen how a point on the hull is created wherever a buttock, diagonal or waterline is intersected by an athwartship sectional plane.

Figure 7-2 is the architect's lines drawing for the same hull shown in Figure 7-1, and on this plan are shown all the lines mentioned in the foregoing together with the necessary dimensions to reproduce them. (Incidentally, do not attempt to build a boat from these lines, as they are purely for illustration and have not been worked out for any specific purpose.) Note that spacing of waterlines, buttocks and stations are indicated as well as offsets for profile of stem, dimensions for profile angle of the stern board, and a table of dimensions for laying out all the fore and aft curved lines. Because of the nature of diagonals their location can only be indicated in section, that is, on the body plan.

Abbreviations

Before we go any further it should be pointed out that many sets of lines plans for hulls have abbreviations for words used thus far in this chapter and it is a help for the reader to be familiar with them.

Center line	C.L.
Water line	W.L.
Buttock	Butt. or butt'k
Base line	B.L.
Station	Sta.
Frame	Fr.
Deck	Dk.
Length over all	L.O.A.
Length of load water line	L.W.L.
Section	Sect.
Displacement	Displ.
Pounds	#
Longitudinal center of buoyancy	C.B. or L.C.B.
Center of gravity	C.G.

Offsets

An offset is simply another name for a dimension, and they are always taken from a straight line such as a base line for the elevation drawing or the center line in the case of the plan view of the lines. Dimensions are tabulated because it is obviously impossible to write them all on a lines plan and not have them become confused. To eliminate a multitude of fractional dimensions it has been made general practice to write offsets in feet-inches-eighths of inches. For example, 2-5-3 means two feet, five and three-eighths inches, and you will find that you will read them automatically once you have tried a few. Some architects pride themselves on the accuracy of their lines and offsets and read some dimensions to one-sixteenth of an inch, and this is shown in the offset table by a plus sign or ½ after the eighth numeral thus 2-5-3+ or 2-5-3½. The use of the offset table will be explained further along, but at this time it would be well to note that small boat lines are always drawn to the outside of the planking, and consequently when molds are made around which the hull is built the thickness of the planking must be deducted from the edges. The lines for steel framed ships and large wooden vessels having built-up sawn frames are drawn to the inside of the plating or planking in order to save the mold loftsman from deducting the thickness from the full-size drawing of every frame, all of which must be drawn when sawn or steel frames are employed because each frame is individually shaped before installation.

The hull lines discussed above are for a round bottom boat, the number of waterlines, buttocks and diagonals involved depending upon the size of the boat, while other hull types have fewer lines. Figure 7-3 shows an ordinary flat bottom rowboat having but four fore and aft lines, namely, the deck and sheer, and two views of a line called the chine, which is the corner at the intersection of the side and bottom. Also shown in the figure are the lines for a vee bottom boat having the same lines as a flattie plus the necessary addition of a keel profile. The sections of this particular boat consist of

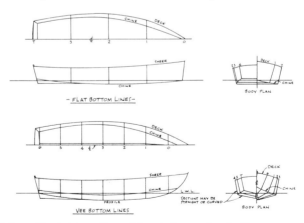

FIGURE 7-3. *Straight sectioned boats have simple lines*

straight lines. If they were curved, other points would be needed to draw the sections, therefore waterlines, buttocks and diagonals would be used to insure correct reproduction of the sections.

The Mold Loft

Although we have said that the builder's first step is lofting the hull, in reality the first thing is to find a place to do the job. The minimum space should be at least four or more feet longer than the boat in one direction, while in the other it must be equal to the distance from the base line to the highest point of the sheer, or top of cabin if there is one, plus some space on all sides for working around the drawing. Well equipped boatyards use a level wooden floor maintained for just this purpose, sanded smooth and coated with flat light gray or white paint. Such facilities at the disposal of an amateur are too much to ask, so the next best objective should be a level space such as a floor or platform where paper or plywood may be used to lay down the lines. So called building paper can be used, but is easy to tear and must be handled with care. The drawing supply people make a buff detail paper of acceptable quality, available up to forty-eight and fifty-four inches in width, in rolls of ten, twenty and fifty yards and priced reasonably. Some of the paper faced building panels are also all right, and so is plywood, as mentioned above, in standard size panels that may be arranged edge to edge to make any size desired. Whatever the material, if several pieces are used to make up the required size the pieces must be secured against movement.

Lofting Tools

The tools for lofting are simple and few. To draw sharp lines flat carpenter's pencils that can be bought in any hardware store are used, sharpened to a chisel point so a thin line may be drawn for a long distance. Colored pencils may also be used to advantage to make it easier to distinguish between different types of lines. For measuring a steel tape is ideal for long lengths, but an ordinary folding six foot rule will do, and the rule is also used to lay off many short dimensions. A large carpenter's square, either as manufactured or made by yourself out of three-eighths or one-half inch wood is needed for drawing lines perpendicular to another line, such as station lines in relation to the base and waterlines, but you may also erect perpendiculars with a regular or improvised beam compass as shown later. The adjustable bevel shown in Figure 3-1 will be found handy, as will a straight edge six or eight feet long which you can make yourself from a piece of thin wood. For the really long straight base and waterlines you should use either a mason's chalk line, penciling the line on the floor before it rubs off, or a length of light strong fish line which can be stretched tightly between two nails a quarter inch or so off the floor, spots marked in pencil directly under the cord at intervals of about three feet, and the line drawn in pieces by connecting the spots with the straight edge.

Battens

For laying down and fairing the long curved lines you must have straight, square edged pieces of clear white pine which loftsmen call battens. These should be at least two feet longer, preferably more, each end than the line to be drawn, therefore in the case of larger hulls it will be impossible to get them except at exorbitant cost. They may be in two pieces connected in the middle where the curve is least by making a tapered glued splice about 18 inches to two feet long, or the line may be pieced, making sure there is a fair overlap for the length of a couple of station spaces. A fair line is one without bumps which is always pleasing to the eye, and the best way to draw one is to use as stiff a batten as will go through all the points on the curve. A supple batten can be passed through all the points yet may not be fair, while a stiff one will tend to fair itself unless unduly forced. It is difficult to say just what size battens should be used, as the size depends so much on the length of the line and the character of the curve.

A batten ½ to ¾ inch thick by 1½ to 2 inches wide used on the flat is suggested for relatively easy curves like the sheer line. For certain curves it may be necessary to taper the battens at the ends somewhat, with all the taper cut on one edge. For curves in the plan view, the halfbreadth plan, something like ½ by 1 inch or 1½ inch used on the flat, possibly tapered at the ends, or ¾ inch square and untapered might be tried. Like a lot of boatbuilding operations, accumulated experience will aid materially in the selection of batten sizes. If you have a table saw, start with the battens on the heavy side until you get the hang of it, ripping the strips narrower as needed. Curves like sections, stem profile and similar shapes will be drawn with shorter battens, probably ⅜ and ½ inch square, and inasmuch as these curves sometimes have harder bends in the middle than at the ends, such as around the turn of the bilge, it may be they will have to be tapered in the middle in order to make a fair curve touching all the points.

Battens are held in place with finishing nails driven on both sides of a batten, not through it. Not necessary by any means, but very desirable from the standpoint of readily sighting the shape of a batten when sprung to a curve, is a coat of flat black paint. The contrast of the dark batten against the light colored floor or paper will help detect a line that is not fair.

The Grid

Principally to save space, but also as an aid in minimizing the distances one must crawl on hands and knees when mold lofting plans to full size, the lines of the boat are not drawn as arranged on the architect's plan. Instead, the halfbreadth plan consisting of deck line and waterlines is superimposed over the profile drawing as shown in Figure 7-5. By examining the table of offsets, Figure 7-2, it will be seen that dimensions for the waterlines, buttocks, diagonals, sheer and profile curves are laid out on the station lines and are measured above the base line and out from the center line. Therefore it is the straight lines that must be laid down in the beginning. This group of lines, called the grid, is shown in Figure 7-4. Begin by drawing a straight line that doubles both as the base line for the profile view and center line for the half-breadth plan. The spacing of the stations is laid off along this line and the stations drawn in perpendicular to it. Drawing of the perpendiculars may be done either with a set of trammel points, a regular beam compass or an improvised one, and is done as described below.

Mark a point A (Station 2 has been used as a practical example in Figure 7-4), then using the compass with A as a center strike an arc B equidistant to each side of point A. Lengthen the arm of the compass and, using each of the points B as a center, strike two intersecting arcs above the base line. From the intersection C draw a straight line through A on the base. The line CA is perpendicular with the base, making an angle of 90 degrees. This method may be used at each station or at only one, and the resulting right angle used to build a large square with which the remainder of the stations can be drawn in perpendicular to the base.

The spacing of the straight waterlines in profile is taken from the architect's lines plan and they are drawn in parallel to the base line. With the exception of the load waterline for reference it is not usually necessary to draw the profile view of the waterlines except at the ends of the boat. Therefore mark off the waterline spacing on the two end stations and again one or two stations from the ends and draw them in with a straight edge.

As mentioned above, the offsets for the curves are measured above the base line and out from the center line as the case may be. Some of the dimensions will be long enough that you will not be able to tell readily whether the end of your rule is exactly on the line or not. To be sure of this some builders nail a batten against the under side of the base line as shown in Figure 7-4 and the end of the rule is butted against it when making measurements. Instead of a batten a nail may be driven at each intersection of a station with the base. Either way will be found to be very helpful and, to say the least, easy on the knees.

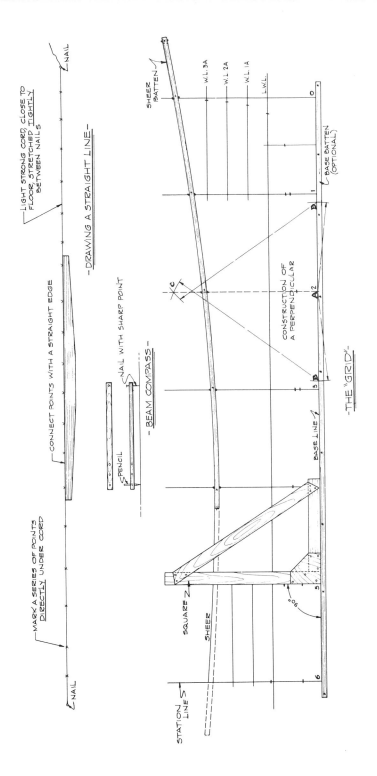

FIGURE 7-4. The grid for full size hull lines is laid out on straight lines on a suitable floor

56

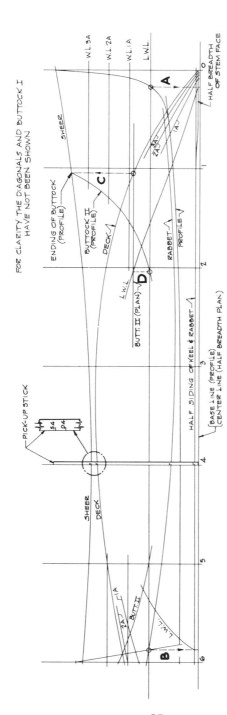

FIGURE 7-5. *Hull lines, as lofted full size, are arranged differently from an
architect's plan in order to save space on the mold loft floor*

57

Sheer Line

The sheer line or the deck line will be the first curved line to be drawn and faired. For the sake of argument we will select the sheer line, which reference to the table of offsets, Figure 7-2, will show is dimensioned above the base line. Starting at the bow, Station 0, the table reads 2-11-0 for the height of the sheer, so with the rule against the nail or batten measure up two feet, eleven inches above the base on Station 0 and make a mark. Move the rule over to Station 1, read 2-7-2 from the table and make a mark two feet, seven and a quarter inches above the base. The process is repeated similarly at all of the stations.

With all the points marked it is time to select a batten with which to draw the sheer line, placing it so it extends beyond the length of the boat at each end. With one edge of the batten against the sheer point on a station amidships, Station 3 in the case of the boat we are using as an example, drive nails to hold the batten in place. Now fasten the batten at Station 2, then at Station 4, alternating towards the ends of the boat until the batten is sprung to and fastened at all the points. The very ends of the batten projecting beyond the boat are sprung to extend the curve fairly and nailed. After the batten is secured for the entire length sight along it to see whether there are any unfair or lumpy spots in the curve. If so, pull the nails at the stations adjacent to the unfairness and note the result. If the batten moves very far from one of the points and still does not appear fair, then pull other nails and make adjustments, giving some here and taking there until the resulting line is pleasing to the eye. You may expect points to be out of line occasionally because the architect has drawn the lines to a small scale compared to the full sized job and errors are bound to creep into the work. However it must be remembered that the batten should be shifted as little as possible to obtain the required line. Keep the batten as close to the points as possible and still have the curve appear sweet and true without hard spots when viewed from either end of the line.

Deck and Profile

The deck line is faired in the same manner after first laying down the offsets measured out from the center line, then the profile and rabbet are drawn. The profile (bottom of keel) and the rabbet must be faired in to meet the relatively quick curves of the stem and stem rabbet, therefore they should be drawn extended beyond the point of tangency with the bow curves forward in order to make it simpler to draw them in to meet each other in fair lines. You will note this has been done in Figure 7-5.

Stem and Stem Rabbet

The stem profile as well as the stem rabbet, which will be explained later, are drawn with a thin batten as mentioned previously. When the spots for the stem curves have been marked in from the dimensions on the lines plan a nail is driven at each spot, the batten bent against the nails and other nails driven on the opposite side of the batten to hold it in place.

Body Plan Sections

If your particular plans give a half siding for the rabbet it should be drawn next, then work is started on the sections in the body plan . It is strongly recommended that a separate portable board be used for the body plan for convenience in moving around to suit the work and to avoid confusion of lines on the floor. Referring to the body plan for the lines in Figure 7-2, you see that the board or paper used for the sections must be somewhat wider than the boat and at least as high as the distance from the base line to the sheer at Station 0, the bow. Begin by drawing the base line, then draw the center line perpendicular to the base. The waterlines are put in parallel to the base, the buttocks parallel to the center line and the diagonals exactly as dimensioned on the lines plan. Needless to say, trouble will result if the waterlines and the buttocks on the body plan are not spaced exactly the same as they were laid out on the halfbreadth and profile plans.

Cut some narrow strips of straight wood anywhere from 1/16 to ⅛ inch thick for use in transferring to the body plan the deck halfbreadths and the sheer and rabbet heights from the already faired lines on the floor. Butt the end of the strip against the base line and mark the halfbreadths and heights on the stick, carefully identifying each one with a symbol and the station number. These measuring sticks are called pick-up sticks or battens and one is shown in the picking up position at Station 4 in Figure 7-5.

With the end of the pick-up stick at the base line of your body plan, mark on the center line of the plan the heights of the sheer and rabbet. Draw short horizontal lines at each rabbet point and draw in the width of the rabbet. Draw horizontal lines at each sheer height and with the pick-up stick against the center line of the body plan mark the deck width corresponding to each station. At each intersection of sheer and deck draw a small cross and label it with the station number. There are now two definite points on each section; one, the sheer height and deck width, the other the intersection of the rabbet height and width.

Now nail a batten against one side of the center line on the body plan and with the rule laid on a waterline and the end of the rule against the center line batten mark points for all the waterline halfbreadths from the

59

offset table and label each one. For instance, lay the rule on waterline 2A to the right of the center line and from the offset table under Station 1 mark off 1-1-2, put a little circle around it with a 1 next to it to show it is a point on the section at Station 1, then mark 1-9-1 for Station 2, and so on. Do the same with the offsets for the other waterlines, then place the rule on Buttock I with the end of the rule at the base and mark all the heights for Buttock I from the offset table. Follow with Buttock II, then lay the rule along the diagonal with the end of the rule again at the center line and lay off all the diagonal offsets along the diagonal lines. Move the batten to the right side of the center line and lay out all the waterline, buttock and diagonal offsets for the sections in the stern half of the boat. Needless to say, all the layout and transfer of measurements should be done with utmost care and accuracy and the time spent to this end will speed the job to completion faster than if the work is done in a slipshod manner.

Body Plan Battens

Nails are driven at all the spots on the sections, then taking one section at a time bend a batten around all the nails, using a batten long enough to extend six inches or so above the sheer point and beyond the rabbet at the center line as shown in Figure 7-6. Holding the sheer and rabbet points as definitely fixed by the previous fairing of these lines, examine the batten carefully and shift it if necessary to get a smooth true curve. Before doing any shifting remember that points established by lines crossing other lines at a

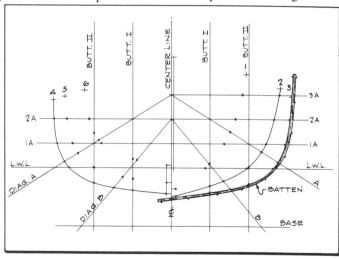

FIGURE 7-6. *The body plan is best drawn on a portable surface called a scrive board*

60

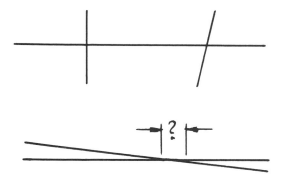

FIGURE 7-7.

right angle or nearly so are more accurate than those crossing at an acute angle. When two lines intersect at an acute angle it is difficult to tell precisely at which spot on a line the crossing occurs, consequently it is not easy for the architect to read the exact offset from his small scale drawing. See Figure 7-7. With this fact in mind it is readily seen that for the flat part of the bottom sections with nearly horizontal lines the best points are given by the buttocks because they cross the sections at almost right angles. The waterlines give the most unreliable points for the same parts of the sections but on the other hand they are the best for the topside sections. Another reason for points being out is due to the architect's scaling technique and as a result all the points on one line such as a diagonal may appear to be out the same amount. In such a situation these points may be ignored, the other points being held if they give a fair section or line.

Fairing Diagonals

Fair the diagonals first because they are laid out to cross the majority of the sections at a good angle. Lay a pick-up batten along a diagonal in the body plan, mark and identify all the points where it crosses the sections, then move the batten to the halfbreadth plan and mark each diagonal halfbreadth on its proper station. The diagonal is then faired, again proceeding as described for the sheer line. If the batten will not go through all the points and at the same time produce a fair line, the usual adjustments must be made. Bearing in mind not to make more changes than are necessary, the sections on the body plan are then corrected accordingly.

Ending Waterlines

When fairing the long fore and aft lines it is necessary to have them terminate correctly. The location of waterline endings is fairly simple. Considering the bow in Figure 7-5, the profile of the stem has been faired and drawn permanently. Each intersection of the stem profile with one of the waterlines is a definite point in the profile plan, and the corresponding point in the halfbreadth plan is found simply by projecting the intersection in the profile down to the line representing the half siding of the stem face in the half-breadth plan as shown at A in Figure 7-5. The endings aft are done exactly the same way, as indicated at B in the stern end of the same figure. It is obvious of course that in this particular design only the L.W.L. ends within the boat at the stern because the other waterlines cross the section at Station 6.

Ending Buttocks and Diagonals

Buttock endings are also quite simple. A short length of a buttock is drawn in plan to cross the deck line and then the point of crossing is projected to the sheer. The intersection with the sheer is the ending of the buttock in the profile view as shown at C in Figure 7-5. When drawing the waterlines and buttocks, fairing points in addition to those on stations are established at the intersection of waterline and buttock planes. D in Figure 7-5 illustrates how the crossing of the L.W.L. and Buttock II in profile projected to Buttock II in plan gives another point on the L.W.L. in plan. Points are developed elsewhere wherever a waterline and a buttock cross.

The determination of a diagonal ending at the stem is somewhat more difficult to understand, therefore the steps taken are shown in Figure 7-8 and should be self explanatory.

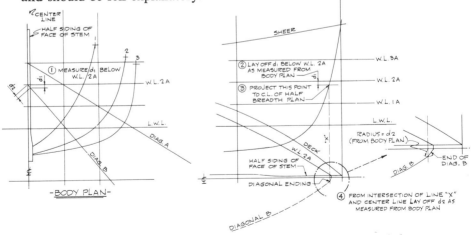

FIGURE 7-8. *Four steps in finding correct ending of a diagonal that crosses face of stem*

The preceding explanation of lofting a round bottom boat is modified for other types such as vee and arc bottom hulls, and generally speaking the latter are easier jobs. However all boats except double enders have one additional lofting problem in common and that is the development of the transom or stern board to obtain the proper shape.

Projected Transom

After the sections have been satisfactorily faired it is time to consider the development of the true shape of the transom or stern board of the boat, a plan that cannot very well be drawn in detail by the architect because of the scale of his drawings. In rare cases the transom is plumb vertical, and the section drawn at the transom station is actually the shape of the transom. More often the transom is set at an angle and the shape does not appear on the body plan. This is a good time to call attention to the transoms shown in the body plan of the twelve footer in Figure 7-2 and also the body plans in Figures 7-10 and 7-12, in all of which you will note a section labeled "projected transom". This is just what it implies. That is, the view of the transom outline as seen when standing astern of the boat looking forward, and the drawing, as such, is meaningless to the builder and need not be reproduced full size on the mold loft floor. The same is true of the plan view of the transom usually drawn on the lines plan, and as shown on the half-breadth plan of Figure 7-2. Such a view is also of no use to the builder as a construction drawing, although it may be used to obtain transom bevels.

Flat Transom Development

Development of the shape of the transom is sometimes puzzling to the builder, but there is nothing really mysterious about the work. The twelve footer has a flat transom of the simplest type, and the development of the correct shape is shown in Figure 7-9. The rake or angle of the transom in profile has of course been previously drawn from dimensions given on the architect's lines plan. For ease of illustration the center line for the developed transom has been drawn at the stern end of the lines in Figure 7-9, but actually this is not necessary and it may be located on a separate board or piece of paper.

The transom is just the same as another section except that it is located at an angle with the base line instead of perpendicular to it, and points on the transom are taken from the waterlines and buttocks the same as ordinary sections. It is merely a matter of picking up the waterline halfbreadths and

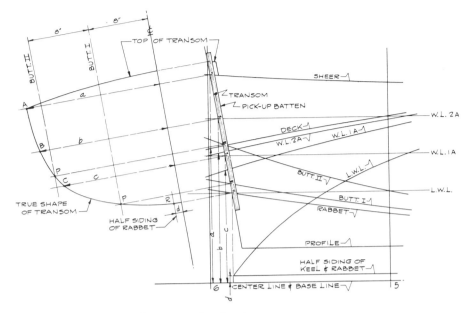

FIGURE 7-9. *Development of a flat transom*

buttock heights at the right places and transferring them to the development drawing.

If you have space for the transom drawing at the end of your lines, as shown in Figure 7-9, the development is exactly as indicated in the diagram. However, if you must locate the grid for the transom plan elsewhere there is one important point to remember throughout the development or you may end up with a stern board that will not fit as it should. On the profile drawing of the lines the waterlines are spaced 5 inches apart above the L.W.L., but due to the profile angle of the transom the distance between the waterlines drawn across the transom grid is obviously greater than 5 inches and when laying out the grid the spacing must be carefully measured along the profile of the transom.

In Figure 7-9 the center line for the transom grid has been drawn parallel to the rake of the transom, and then the intersections of waterlines and the sheer with the transom in profile are projected across the center line to complete the grid together with projections from the buttock and rabbet intersections. If the transom is flat, as it is in the design for the twelve footer, lay off the spacing of the buttocks the same as they are on your body and halfbreadth plans, and draw them in the grid parallel to the transom center line. Two points, **P**, are established on the transom development where the buttocks thus drawn cross the lines projected from the buttocks in profile.

64

Lay off d, the width of the rabbet, to locate another point, R.

Now project the intersections of the waterlines and buttocks with the transom profile down to the center line of the halfbreadth plan. The waterline halfbreadths a, b and c are picked up with a batten and laid off as points A, B and C on the corresponding lines in the grid. With all the points spotted, draw in the transom with a batten the same as you did the regular sections.

If you must draw the transom on a separate sheet, very carefully pick up the spacing of the intersections along the profile of the transom on a batten, as shown in the figure, and complete location of points as described above.

Curved Transom Development

A curved transom on either a sail or power boat is very handsome and, although the development is more involved than for the flat type, the work is worth while when finished appearance is considered. From the esthetic viewpoint a curved transom is not necessary on small craft generally up to twenty or twenty-five feet overall, but above this range the curved transom becomes a necessity, for good looks is an absolute must on a hull with an overhanging counter stern. This type is the most difficult to develop, due to the combination of the radius to which it is built and the angle of the transom in profile. The planks forming such a transom are bent to the arc of a circle with a radius perpendicular to the after side of the transom as seen in profile. A pattern for the shape must be made, and this is accomplished as though a cylinder were cut and rolled out flat.

A transom proportioned as shown in Figure 7-10 is developed principally with buttocks because they cross the edges of the transom more nearly at right angles than do the waterlines, and thus are the most accurate. By this time you are familiar with buttocks and must realize that those on the architect's lines plan are not the only ones it is possible to have on a hull. There are an infinite number, and they may be spaced as closely as needed to help you make proper templates for parts. The stern in Figure 7-10 has been purposely drawn with enough buttocks to develop the transom accurately, but ordinarily extra buttocks for development of the transom are added between those shown on the lines plan. Before the transom is attempted the hull lines have been completely faired full size, usually to a station beyond the transom. To be sure of the shape of his hull the architect designs to a vertical station at the extreme stern, and then cuts it off at the desired angle in profile and in a radius in the plan view as mentioned above.

There are undoubtedly other methods of transom development in use and sworn to by their advocates. However the system illustrated here will

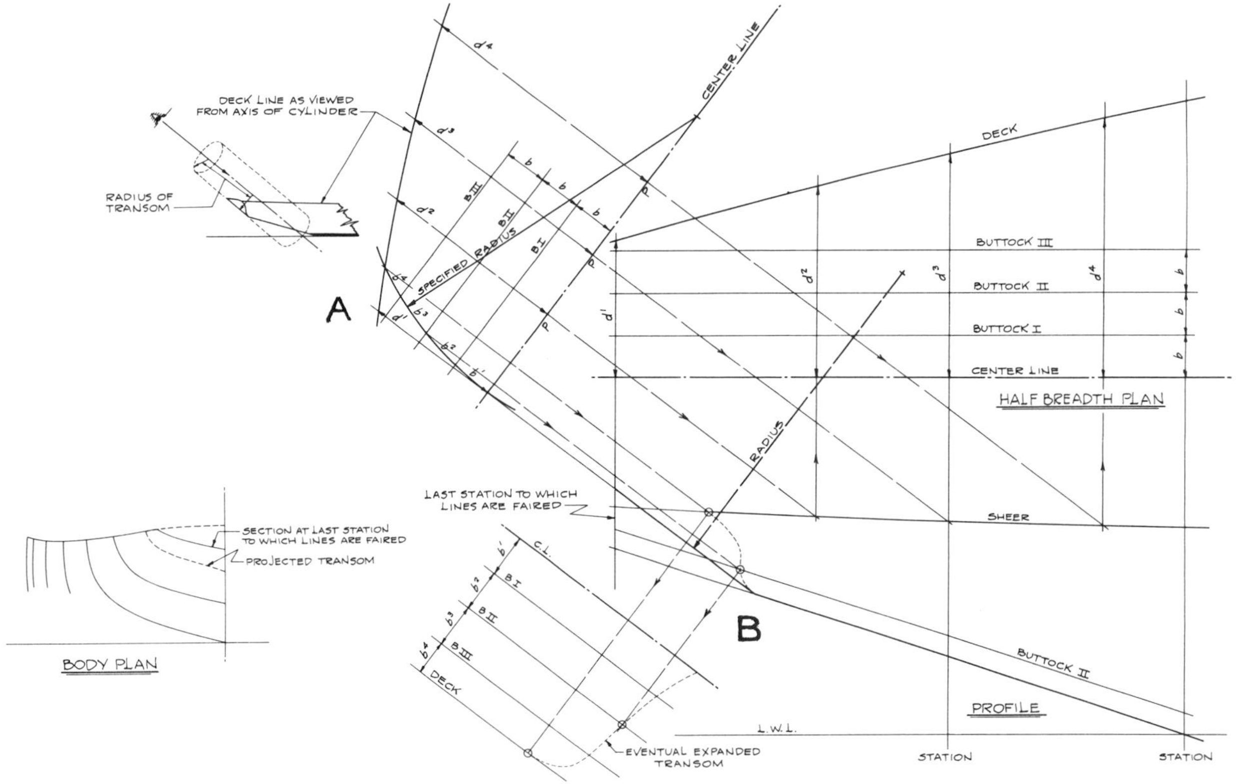

FIGURE 7-10. *Steps in the development of a curved transom*

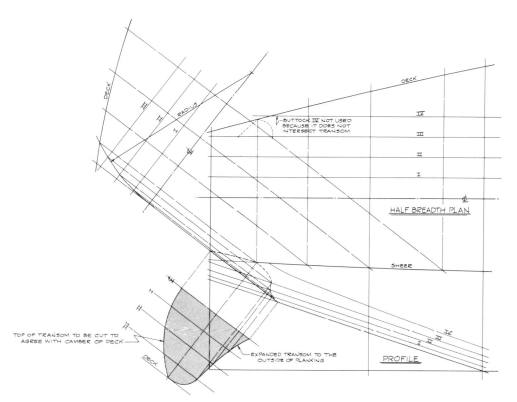

Labels visible in the figure:

DECK

RADIUS

BUTTOCK IV NOT USED
BECAUSE IT DOES NOT
INTERSECT TRANSOM

IV
III
II
I

HALF BREADTH PLAN

SHEER

DECK

TOP OF TRANSOM TO BE CUT TO
AGREE WITH CAMBER OF DECK

DECK

EXPANDED TRANSOM TO THE
OUTSIDE OF PLANKING

PROFILE

IV
III
II
I

FIGURE 7-11. *Complete development of curved transom started in Figure 7-10*

at least help the reader understand the principle. To avoid confusion the profile and halfbreadth plans of the stern in Figure 7-10 have been drawn separated and the transom radius made smaller than usual to clarify the drawing. Dashed lines show the projection of one view to another. After following the development of the flat transom in Figure 7-9, the use of the buttocks in Figure 7-10 is obvious with the exception of their spacing in the grid for the expansion.

Extend the after side of the transom in profile up clear of other drawings, Figure 7-10A, and draw a center line perpendicular to it. Tangent to the intersection swing an arc of radius as shown on the plans. This is the curve to which the transom planking will be bent when it is built. Draw the buttocks parallel to the center line, spaced the same as in the halfbreadth plan. Project the intersections of the buttocks with the arc down to cross the corresponding buttocks in the profile view. Now prepare the grid for the expanded transom, Figure 7-10B, spacing the buttocks out from the center line as measured *around the arc* instead of as laid out in the halfbreadth plan. These measurements give the true distances between the buttocks

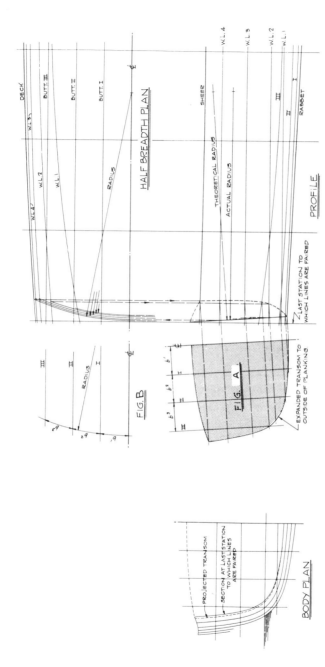

FIGURE 7-12. *Development of curved transom with little rake from the vertical*

68

when the cylindrical transom is rolled out flat. Project the buttocks in profile to the grid to obtain points on the edge of the transom as was done in the flat transom, Figure 7-9. For clarity only one buttock, buttock II, has been used as an example in Figure 7-10.

In order to find the point where the transom terminates at the sheer line, the deck line is drawn in Figure 7-10A as viewed parallel to the axis of the transom cylinder. To draw this view select convenient points (P) along the center line for fairing. Square them above the center line and also down to cross the sheer on the profile, and then the points of intersection with the sheer are squared up parallel to the stations and extended to cross the deck line in the halfbreadth plan. The widths of the deck at these points are lifted, transferred to Figure 7-10A, and a batten run through them. Where the curve crosses the arc is the corner of the transom at the deck. The halfbreadth of the point is measured from the center line around the arc and duly transferred to the grid.

Sailboat transoms often have considerable rake, like the one shown in Figures 7-10 and 7-11, but usually there is little angle to those on modern power cruisers. A small amount of rake may be neglected in the development of the transom, and the radius drawn directly on the halfbreadth plan of waterlines and buttocks as will be explained.

Powerboat Transom

A motor boat stern is shown in Figure 7-12. This is not typical of many present day boats in that the topside sections do not tumble home, and has been drawn purposely to avoid having waterlines that pile up on top of each other and make the transom development difficult to understand. Draw the profile angle of the transom and project every intersection of it with the profile view of a waterline or buttock up to the center line in the halfbreadth plan. Holding the specified radius constant throughout, swing an arc from each of the projected points on the center line (using the C.L. as center for the radius) until the arc crosses the line on the halfbreadth plan corresponding to the line in profile. Project the halfbreadth intersections with the arcs back down to the corresponding lines in profile and then across to the grid, Figure 7-12A. Of course it is important that the buttocks on the grid are spaced as measured around the arc, Figure 7-12B.

The development is the shape of the outside edge of the transom planking, but allowance must be made for the bevel on the edges which causes the transom to be larger on the inside than on the outside face, and when making the transom frame the planking thickness must first be deducted and then allowance made for beveling.

69

Chapter 8

MOLDS, TEMPLATES
AND THE BACKBONE

U PON COMPLETION of the full size drawing of the lines for the hull the builder is at last ready to start cutting wood, making frames for sawn frame boats or molds for a round bottom hull, and templates for the stem and other backbone parts.

Molds are made from the body plan, and because they are only temporary are made from lower grade lumber than that used for the boat parts. Any lumber except hardwood is suitable, the thickness of the molds varying with the size of the boat. A rough guide is ¾ inch for boats to sixteen feet, ⅞ inch for sixteen to twenty-four feet, and 1 or 1⅛ inch for thirty footers. As you will see further along, the molds are set up on the backbone or keel of the boat and strips of wood called ribbands are bent around the molds similar to planking except that ribbands have spaces between them. The frames for a round bottom boat are bent to shape against the ribbands. There are two schools of thought as to whether the frames should be bent inside or outside of the ribbands, but it will be observed as experience is gained that setting up the frame for the boat is simplified when the frames are bent inside the ribbands. When a number of boats are to be built alike it is advantageous to make a permanent mold, in which case the frames are bent outside and the mold removed for further use when the hull has been planked.

The lines for the twelve footer in Figure 7-2, like those for all small boats, are drawn to the outside of planking and of course the full size lines have been lofted accordingly. For construction with the frames bent inside of the ribbands the molds for the sections are made only after the thickness of the planking has been deducted. Similarly, frames for vee bottom boats are made only after the thickness of planking has been deducted.

It should be obvious after you have studied construction that to make a mold for a round bottom boat with the frames bent on the outside of the ribband, the thickness of the planking, frame, and ribband must be deducted from the sections that are drawn to the outside of the planking.

Countless boats have been built from molds made simply by deducting the planking thickness from the section lines by setting dividers equal to the plank thickness and setting off the thickness at frequent intervals along each section, then using a batten to draw new section lines to the supposed inside of planking as shown in Figure 8-1, *but only when the planking is thin is this method acceptable.* Let's try to simplify this. If a hole were drilled through the planking and a frame, and the thickness of the planking and the frame measured in the hole, *only if the hole were at right angles (normal) to the*

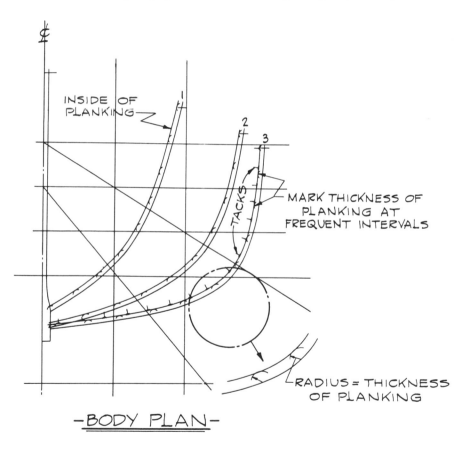

INSIDE OF PLANKING

MARK THICKNESS OF PLANKING AT FREQUENT INTERVALS

TACKS

RADIUS = THICKNESS OF PLANKING

—BODY PLAN—

FIGURE 8-1.   *One method of deducting plank thickness from the sections, but not accurate*

71

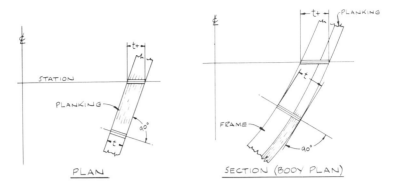

FIGURE 8-2.

surface of the hull will the parts measure correctly. This is shown in Figure 8-2, and bear in mind that normal does not mean that the drill will be parallel to any of the reference planes for the boat such as the horizontal waterline planes of the vertical station planes. Visualize drilling a hole normal to the surface of the planking on the bow of a boat that has a lot of shape—the drill will not be level nor will it be parallel to the plane of a section.

Unless the planking is thin it is best to take a little more time and make an effort to deduct planking thickness more accurately. There will be very little difference in the amidship area where in plan view the waterlines are running approximately parallel to the center line of the boat, but as soon as the waterlines break away sharply toward the center line at bow or stern it pays to be more accurate. To make the thickness deduction almost absolutely correct it should be done on the diagonals, even to the extent of adding diagonals in addition to those shown by the lines plan, but this is a chore that is not necessary in most cases. Rather than this procedure, at each station lay off the thickness parallel to the waterlines in the plan view of the lines, then pick up the thickness along the station line and transfer it to the body plan, laying it off normal to the section. See Figure 8-3. When this has been done at each waterline take a batten and draw through all the points to get the inside of planking. Once you have done this for a few points the work will be done quite rapidly.

When all the sections have been redrawn to the inside of planking the molds for a round bottom boat can be made. Figure 8-4 shows typical mold construction and Figure 8-1 shows how the shape of the section is transferred to the mold stock by pressing the lumber down against closely spaced tacks with their heads laid on the line to be reproduced. Turn the wood over, use a batten to connect the marks made by the tack heads, then work the board to the line. A mold is needed for each station.

72

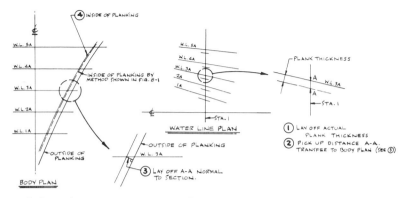

FIGURE 8-3.   *A more accurate method of deducting plank thickness from sections*

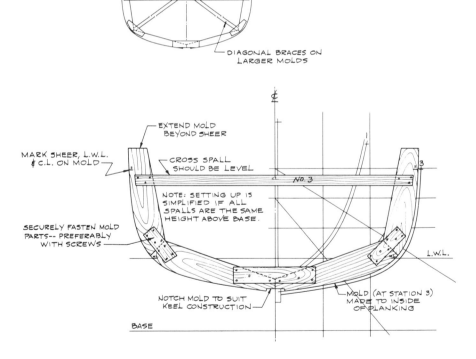

FIGURE 8-4.   *Typical mold construction. Molds must be well fastened and braced to retain shape when set up*

It is not practical to use boards wide enough to get an entire half mold out all in one piece. Therefore the mold is made in as many parts as necessary, laid out in any convenient manner to suit the lumber stock. Just remember that the mold must not be too flimsy. Normally the mold should be extended a half foot or so above the sheer line, but if it is planned to build the boat upside down, a logical method for small craft, the molds are extended to a straight base line above the sheer representing the building floor. Depending on the size of the boat, the inverted base line is made parallel to the waterline and at a height so the greater part of the hull may be planked from a normal standing position. The mold parts are laid on the sections on the body plan while carefully fastening them together with screws and butt blocks and, before the mold half is lifted from the plan, mark it at the deck line and L.W.L. for reference while setting up and building. Turn the first half of the mold over so the butt blocks are down and make a second half to match it. When assembled, the butt blocks will then all be on the same side of the mold. Connect the two halves with a block at the bottom, notched if required by the keel construction, and fasten a crosspiece, called a spall, at or near the deck line. Spalls on all molds should be level, and if all are located at the same height above the waterline or base the molds will be easier to align when set up on the keel or floor.

Stem and Rabbet

The stem assembly is drawn on the full size lines either as dimensioned on the construction plan or, lacking dimensions, the widths are scaled from the construction plan. In boatbuilding language the widths of the stem are the molded dimensions, whereas the thickness of the material for the stem is the sided dimension. Ideally, a stem for a small craft like a dinghy should be made from a natural hackmatack or oak crook as they were some years ago. A template of the stem would be taken to the dealer in this material to select a crook with a shape similar to the stem but, except for the island builders, nobody seems to bother with this any more.

Most often the stem is too large to get out of a natural crook, so an assembly of wood will be made up as illustrated in Figure 8-5 or the stem assembly can be laminated as mentioned elsewhere. For the amateur, who does not usually count labor, a lamination is often the easiest way out.

When an assembly of parts is used, templates of the parts are made, the lines being transferred with tacks as explained for the molds in Figure 8-1. Templates are usually made of easily worked softwood ¼ or ⅜ inch thick or of plywood or hardboard. Besides the shapes of the parts the templates must also have guide lines for rabbeting the stem assembly for the planking.

The profile of the rabbet line may or may not be dimensioned on the lines or construction plan, and even though it is shown it should be checked full size for accuracy and fairness. The width or half breadth of the rabbet is generally the same as the siding of the stem, and either retains a constant width throughout the length of the boat or swells in width toward amidship and then narrows again toward the stern.

It was mentioned before that countless boats have been built from molds made by not deducting the thickness of planking by the most accurate method, and so it is with the stem rabbet, and we will discuss this first and then explain how to lay out the rabbet by a more precise method that consumes but little more time.

Note in Figure 8-5 that the halfbreadth of the stem (the "half siding" or one half the thickness) has been drawn as well as the half siding of the face of the stem, and on each waterline halfbreadth the thickness of planking has been drawn to get the back rabbet and bearding lines to which the material must be cut. The nomenclature is shown on the section through the stem drawn on waterline 4A in the profile, Figure 8-5. Points to plot these lines on the profile are projected from the waterlines in the halfbreadth plan to the waterlines in profile and connected with a batten. The lines for the rabbet and the outline of stem parts are all transferred to the template material at the same time.

The templates are laid out on the stem material and arranged for a minimum of cross grain in the finished part. Cut and plane the parts to shape (if too heavy for your equipment have a mill do this for you) and lay them out on the full size lines to check the alignment of the joints in the assembled position. Mark the sheer line, all the waterlines and the center lines for the bolts, then bore the bolt holes and put the stem together with thick white lead or thiokol or other good bedding compound between the faying surfaces (the surfaces that touch each other) of the joints. Whether or not the bolt heads are countersunk and plugged, an extra precaution to make the bolt holes watertight should be taken by using a grommet. This is a piece of cotton wicking caulking long enough to go around the bolt a couple of times. Apply bedding generously to the wicking and wind it around the bolt just under the head just before the bolt is driven all the way home. After assembly of the stem, mark the center line of the boat on the stem and the width of the stem face each side of the center line.

Referring to the halfbreadth plan in the figure, make a template of stiff cardboard or thin wood for the rabbet at each waterline. Use the templates

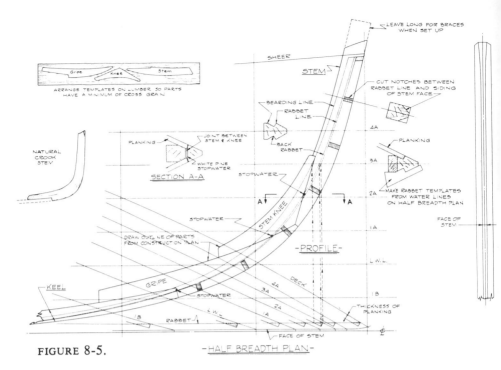

FIGURE 8-5.   −HALF BREADTH PLAN−

to cut a short length of the rabbet at the waterlines, then complete the rabbet by working away the material between the templated cuts on the waterlines. The rabbet may be cut with confidence if the full size drawing is *accurate* and complete. However even some professionals leave the rabbet just a little shallow and complete it when fitting ribbands at the time the boat is set up.

In many cases this is because from experience they have learned that their rabbet is not as accurate as it might be, and here is how you can make it more accurate.

In the beginning of Chapter 7 it was stated that vertical sections are drawn at intervals throughout the length of the boat to define the shape of the hull, but it should be realized that sections can be drawn through the hull at any angle, not only at the vertical planes at the stations and buttocks, the horizontal planes of the waterlines or the diagonal planes, and the designer often does this while drawing the construction plan to get the true, accurate sizes of parts like the stem assembly. Similarly to the previous explanation of the plank thickness deduction, only when a section is drawn normal to the part is full accuracy assured. Some say that lofting can be overdone, but it certainly pays to draw partial auxiliary sections at angles through the bow of the boat in order to more accurately cut the rabbet because the less dubbing is facing the amateur after he sets up the boat the better off he will be. It is at the bow that waterlines (used in Figure 8-5 for the rabbet) and but-

76

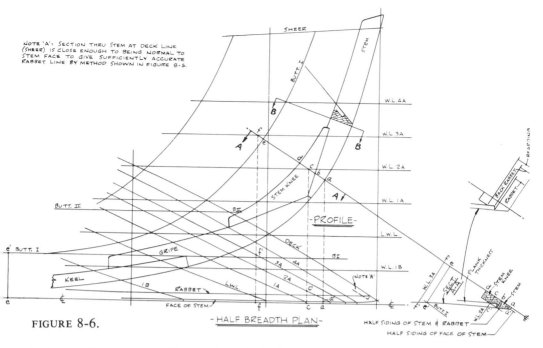

FIGURE 8-6.   - HALF BREADTH PLAN -

tocks are the most out of normal to the hull surface.

For the same reason the taking off of bevels from lines other than those that are normal to the hull surface, or nearly so, are not entirely accurate.

Figure 8-6 has been prepared to show how easy it is to draw sections through the stem. The sections should be spaced at intervals close enough so that there is no question about having enough of the plotted points for the rabbet, back rabbet and bearing lines (see Figure 8-5) to ensure a fair line. To save time and effort the sections should be drawn right on the lines profile, Section B-B of Figure 8-6, rather than separately as Section A-A was done in the figure in the interest of the explanation.

First a center line is drawn normal to the face of the stem, long enough to cross enough buttocks and waterlines to give a number of points so a batten can be set up to draw a fair section. For instance, the center line for Section A-A intersects two waterlines and a buttock. Then perpendiculars to the center line are drawn at the waterline and buttock intersections and at the joints in the stem assembly. Next the halfbreadths are picked up as shown in the profile and laid off on the perpendiculars to establish the points for the section to the outside of planking. The thickness of planking is set off, and this sets up the points for the rabbet, back rabbet and the bearing line.

Instead of making templates for the rabbet from the halfbreadth plan in the method shown by Figure 8-5, make them from the more accurate sections drawn on the profile as illustrated by Figure 8-6.

Stopwaters

Softwood dowels called stopwaters are fitted in joints in the backbone to prevent water from leaking into the hull along a joint. The location of stopwaters is important for full effectiveness and is shown in Section A-A ot Figure 8-5 and it is imperative that they not be forgotten wherever the rabbet crosses a joint in the backbone. Any durable softwood such as white pine or cedar will do and there are so few of them that they can be whittled out of scrap.

Vee Bottom Frames

A point in favor of vee and arc bottom hulls is that temporary molds are not necessary for their construction. Instead, the body plan is used to make frames that become a permanent part of the structure instead of expendable molds as required for round bottom boats. Typical vee and arc bottom hull frames are shown in Figure 1-1 and 1-2 in Chapter 1, but these sectional views do not reveal that the bottom and side pieces are not simply square edged. Rather they are beveled so the planking will bear against the entire thickness of the frames as shown in A of Figure 8-8 and Figure 8-10. In many cases the bevel is not the same at the sheer as it is at the chine. This makes for more work, but this is the nature of boat hulls. The character, or curvature, of the deck line and chine, etc., determines the amount of bevel. At Section B-B of Figure 8-8, where the deck line and chine are approximately parallel to the boat center line it can be seen that there is practically no bevel needed. Forward and aft of B-B though, as the deck and chine curve in toward the center line, the frames must be beveled.

For a simple boat with straight sections like that shown in Figure 8-8 the bevels can be measured as indicated, the side frame bevels at deck and chine in the halfbreadth plan and those for the bottom frames at chine and keel in the profile. The bevels are cut in a straight line between deck and chine and between the chine and keel respectively. If the frames have some curve the bevels at major points as described above are just the same, but those for the side frames at points between the deck and chine are taken from the waterlines in the halfbreadth plan, and those for the bottom frames at points between the chine and the keel are taken from the buttocks in the profile. Bevels for the notches in which the keel, chines and clamps are fitted are taken off similarly or cut later when the boat is set up. At that time battens for fairing the frames are run in and bevel adjustments made by planing the frames.

To determine bevels with more accuracy, however, and this is very important to time saving in the larger hulls with a good number of frames, the

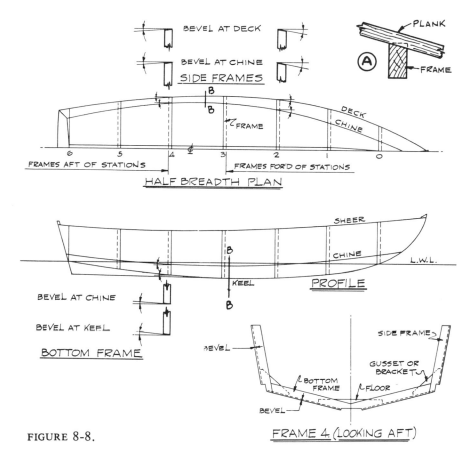

FIGURE 8-8.

bevels should be measured *normal* to the surface, much like the deduction for planking thickness previously discussed, and this can be done by the method shown in Figure 8-9. The square can be made up by the builder and applied as shown to measure the bevels. These should be marked right on the body plan in degrees for reference, then marked on the actual frame material for reference when band sawing to shape and bevel at the same time. The bevels should be taken along diagonals laid out to be as close to normal as possible to all the frames crossed.

Bevel Board

Instead of using a protractor to measure a bevel each time you take one off, make yourself a simple bevel board as shown in Figure 8-9a. Use a piece of plywood about 3½ inches wide and mark off angles from zero to about thirty degrees. Slide the adjustable bevel along the left edge of the bevel board until it lines up with one of the angles and read it off.

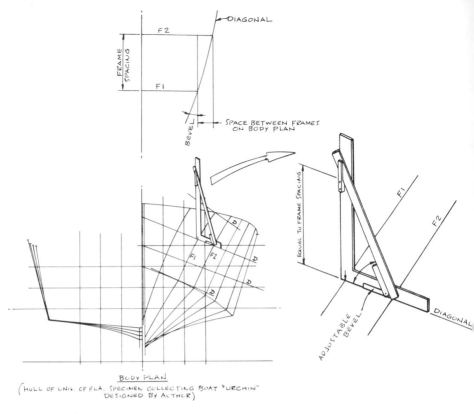

FIGURE 8-9.

When a bevel is marked on a piece of stock to be sawn there must be a designation of whether the bevel is *under* or *standing,* marking the piece UB or SB as shown in the figure. This is most important, and after a few pieces have been ruined the principle will be understood.

Transom and Transom Bevels

As will be seen later, what may be called the upright parts needed before the boat is set up are the station molds, the stem and the transom. The molds and the stem have been explained and the development of the transom shape illustrated. Besides the shape of the transom, the bevels on the edges where the side planking laps must be considered. It has been shown that the developed shape of the transom is to the outside of the planking, and depending upon the type of construction may or may not be the actual size of the finished transom. The simplest method is to let the side planking overlap the transom and cut it flush with the after side. In this case the plank thickness is subtracted from the edges of the transom. The best practice, however, is to make the transom to the outside of planking and rabbet the edge for the planking. Both methods are shown in Figure 8-10.

80

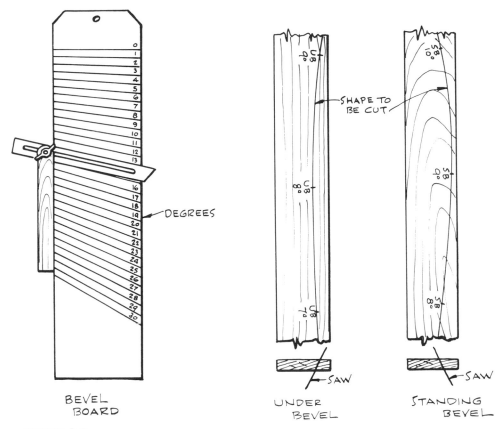

BEVEL
BOARD

UNDER
BEVEL

STANDING
BEVEL

FIGURE 8-9a.

Figure 8-10A shows that the inside of the transom is larger than the outside, except at the top edge where the shape depends upon the construction details, because the boat narrows from amidships to the transom. Consequently, like the frames of a vee bottom boat, the edges of the transom must be beveled to allow the planks to lie flat. The bevels are taken from the full size lines as shown in the figure, those for the sides from the waterlines in the halfbreadth plan, those for the bottom from the buttocks in the profile drawing. But once again it should be remembered that this is not the most accurate way to take the bevels off because it should be done normal to the surface of the hull by the method shown in Figure 8-9.

Small boat transoms are generally made of wide boards with the edges splined or doweled and waterproof glue, and are made sufficiently thick to properly fasten the hull planks to the edge. They can also be made of marine plywood with cheek pieces around the edges to take the plank fastenings. Larger transoms like Figure 8-10C are made the same thickness as the

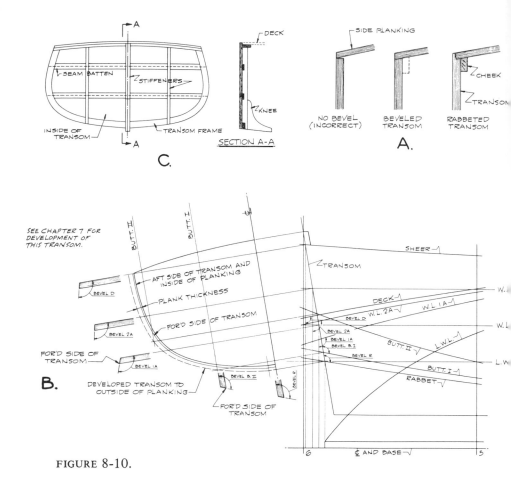

FIGURE 8-10.

hull planking or thicker, and have a frame or cheek pieces on the inside edges to take a share of the plank fastenings. There is usually a vertical member on the center line where a wood or metal knee is used to connect the transom to the keel or horn timber. For the sake of appearance the seams of transom planks are not caulked. If single planked the seams are usually backed with battens.

Wide transoms have a series of vertical stiffeners outboard of the center line. Sometimes these are spaced to take the ends of engine stringers.

Most transoms do not have enough radius to prevent the planks from being bent cold. Otherwise they can be soaked with hot wet rags or steamed so they will bend to the transom frame.

Keel and Deadwood

There are quite a number of keel construction methods, varying with the type boat and preference of the architect, and sometimes with the custom of a particular locality. The types most likely to be encountered by the amateur are illustrated in Figures 8-11 and 8-12. Needless to say, for longevity only sound timber should go into the backbone members. White oak is the usual material for keel and other backbone members, but other wood is used as dictated by local practice.

FIGURE 8-11. *Typical small boat keels*

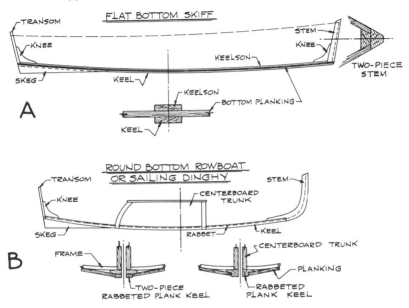

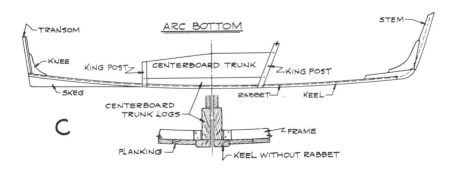

The flat bottom skiff construction in Figure 8-11A is very common. Building the boat upside down, the forms are notched for the keelson, then the bottom is cross planked and the keel fitted on top of the planking. Sometimes twin keelsons are used, one on each side instead of a single one on the center line. Before fastening the keel a slot for the skeg is cut on the center line aft. Boats with straight stems frequently have two piece stems, as shown, to avoid rabbeting. The side planks are cut off flush with the inner stem, then the outer stem is fastened to the inner with composition between the two.

The rabbeted keel in Figure 8-11B is typical construction for a great many boats. The shape of the rabbet at each station is taken from the sections in the body plan and templates made for use when cutting. As for the stem in Figure 8-5, cut the rabbet at each station, and then cut away between the stations to make a continuous fair rabbet for the planking. The amateur will find it easier to make the two piece keel, fastening the pieces together over the molds after first beveling to form the rabbet. Between the pieces there should be thick white lead or other composition to exclude water. All backbone joints are so treated.

A few of the one-design class sailboats use a keel without rabbet like that in Figure 8-11C. This is all right, but because the garboard plank (the one next to the keel on each side) is not fastened to the keel, care should be taken to attach the frames strongly to the keel. If the frames butt at the center line, the floor timbers connecting the frame halves must be well fastened to the frames and keel. In way of the centerboard slot in the keel the bed logs should be thick for good fastenings through the keel.

Powerboat Keels

Figure 8-12A is typical of many modern powerboats. The keel is usually the same thickness throughout and is cut to shape from a template made from the full size profile, and then a batten is bent to place on top to form a back rabbet for the planking. The rabbet is cut the same as for the little boat in Figure 8-11B. The horn timber aft is rabbeted. A bronze shaft log with packing gland is installed for water-tightness where the shaft leaves the hull. The bottom of the keel may be cut away or continued aft and fitted with a skeg to support the bottom of the rudder.

Although not as extensively seen as formerly, the wooden shaft log in Figure 8-12B is worthy of mention. A two piece log is shown in the section and is easier for the amateur to make than a log in a single piece, because the shaft hole in each half can be worked out and the grooves for the splines can be cut on a small table saw or with a plow plane. The purpose of the splines is to swell and prevent leaks in the same manner as stopwaters, and they are

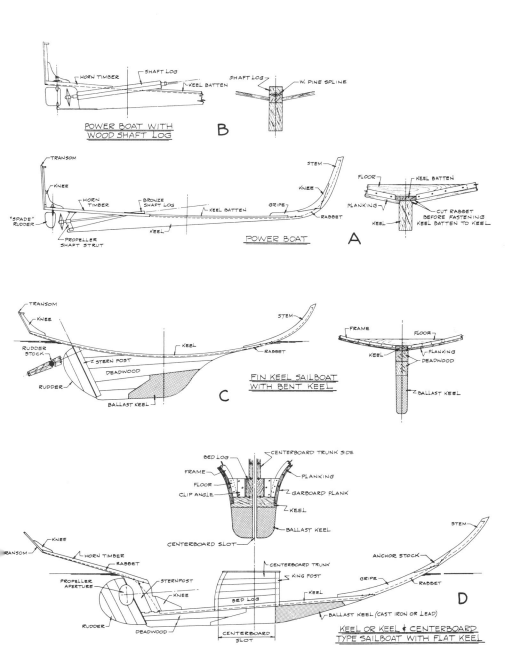

FIGURE 8-12. *A few of many possible backbone structures for power and sailboats*

85

made of softwood such as white pine. It is all right to cut the splines with bolts so long as the bolt holes are tight. The splines swell against the bolts and function just as well as when not cut. The shaft hole in a one piece log is bored with an auger and may be troublesome for the inexperienced because a jig must be devised that will prevent misalignment of the hole. The chances are against finding a commercially made auger of sufficient length. Therefore, have someone cut the shank and add the needed length by welding in a piece of rod. It is very important that the shaft hole be lined with a light copper tube or lead pipe to exclude water from the wood around the hole. The ends of the tube are flanged under the bases of the stern bearing and stuffing box.

Fin Keel Sailboats

Fin keel sailboats up to about thirty feet overall may have bent keels like Figure 8-12C. Indeed even larger boats have had this type construction, with keels thick enough to need steaming to bend the keel to shape. Probably the easiest way to build a boat of this type is upside down, the keel being bent down over the molds and the fin keel added after the hull is turned over.

Attention must be given to the sequence of the bolting in order to properly fasten the fin. The ballast keel bolts usually extend from the casting through the deadwood, keel and floors, although sometimes they are terminated between frames where they pass through the keel. The deadwood is carefully shaped as called for by the lines, and although it requires hard work by hand a lot of effort should be put into the deadwood to make it smooth and fair, not only for the sake of appearance but also to offer a minimum of resistance as the boat moves through the water. The aft edge of the sternpost is gouged out to take the rudder stock and the rounded forward edge of the rudder. Even after it is installed, the forward edge of the rudder can be painted by alternately swinging it hard over to each side, but it is impossible to paint the concave edge of the sternpost. To prevent accumulation of marine growth the after side of the sternpost is sheathed with light copper sheet brought around on the sides just enough to fasten it with tacks.

Large Sailboat Keels

The backbone in Figure 8-12D is typical of most keel sailboats or combination keel and centerboard sailboats upward of twenty feet waterline length. The keel in these boats is a thick plank of the same thickness from end to end, but varying in width throughout the length. It is rabbeted for the planking as shown in the section. The vertical position of the keel in the hull structure is drawn in on the full size profile, then the heights of the keel at the stations it crosses are transferred to the corresponding sections in the body plan to obtain the half widths of the keel at the stations. A center line is drawn on the piece of lumber to be used for the keel, the station spacing picked up and laid off from the full size profile (the station spacing along the keel is greater than the spacing along the base line because the keel is at an angle with the base), and the halfbreadths of the top of the keel are picked up from the sections and laid off on the keel stock. Draw the outline of the keel with a batten. After the keel is sawn to the shape of the top edge, draw a center line on the under side of the keel, making sure it aligns with the one on top, and similarly lay off the halfbreadths of the keel bottom. The outline of the bottom will give the constantly changing bevel to which to cut the sides of the keel. The rabbet at each section is then templated as a guide for cutting, as mentioned heretofore.

Gripe and Horn Timber

The gripe is the piece that connects the keel to the stem. A member called the horn timber connects the keel or sternpost to the transom in some types of power and sailboats, and both the gripe and horn timber are very similar to a stem. The rabbet for comparatively horizontal parts like the horn timber is taken from the sections in the body plan. Knees are used to fasten the various backbone members to each other. Much of the backbone construction work is made clear by construction sections on the architect's plans.

Backbone Bolting

After all the backbone members are shaped, but prior to fastening together, it is recommended they be given two coats of a wood preservative. These preparations are inexpensive and well worth the investment for their rot preventive qualities. The liquid should also be poured down the bolt holes before fastening. Through bolts and drift bolts, described at length in Chapter 6, are made and fitted as shown on the construction plan for the boat, and the fastenings must be studied for sequence so the assembly will go together properly. It will be seen as you go along that some of the bolts which actually are backbone fastenings must be delayed because they pass through floor timbers (Figure 8-12A, C) that are not made and fitted in the structure until later. All parts being bolted together must have thick white lead or other composition in the joints so that no crevices are left for water to seep through or collect in the joints and possibly start to rot the timbers. Under the washers of through and drift bolts it is advisable to wind a few turns of cotton wicking soaked in paint before the bolts are finally driven home. Very often this treatment will prevent leaks that otherwise would be troublesome or at least annoying. Wicking is stringy cotton available in balls at marine suppliers and does not resemble the familiar woven lamp wicking. The stopwaters mentioned elsewhere are fitted after the parts have been bolted.

Scarphs

It is not always possible to obtain pieces of wood long enough for keels, deadwood, bilge stringers, clamps and shelves. Fortunately sufficient lengths may be found for keels more often than the other parts, even though an extensive search is required. The backbone is enough work for the builder without having to splice the keel, particularly the type shown in Figure 8-12D. When it cannot be avoided the long members are pieced out by means of through bolted joints called scarphs. Nowadays these joints in wood are often waterproof glued for good measure. If not glued the joint should be made up with the usual thick white lead or heavy paint. Bolts are staggered when thickness of lumber permits. Figure 8-13 illustrates three types of scarphs commonly in use, and it should be noted that all have nibs to prevent one part from slipping by the other when under strain. The joint shown in A is the very common plain scarph and is extensively used for stringers and clamps. The hooked scarph, B, is sometimes employed in backbone members. Just as effective and easier to make is the key scarph shown at C, which is simply a plain scarph mortised to take a tightly fitted rectangular key, preferably of durable wood like white oak or black locust. In large timbers the key is sometimes made of two wedges driven from both sides at the same time and cut off flush with the sides of the timbers. The wedges are made with a taper of about one-half inch to the foot.

The scarphed joints and their fastenings are carefully planned and shown on the drawings by the architect. A rough rule for the scarph length is six times the depth of the timber, while the keys and nibs are made up to one-fourth of the depth. If the inexperienced builder should not be able to locate a piece of wood large enough for the keel, the designer or a competent boat builder should be consulted for the layout of scarphs most suitable for use with the available material.

Tenons

The mortise and tenon joint is sometimes called upon to lock adjoining members with grain perpendicular to each other. The joints between the vertical sternposts and the keel in Figure 8-12D are typical. When the wood is not too thin the tenon is made blind, that is, only part way across the pieces, and therefore it is not visible when the parts are fitted together. In either case the joint must be made as snug as possible and put together with white lead on the mating parts.

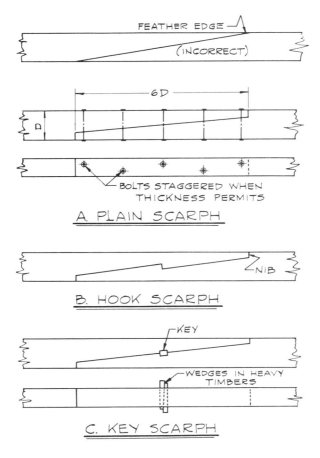

FEATHER EDGE

(INCORRECT)

6D

D

BOLTS STAGGERED WHEN
THICKNESS PERMITS

A. PLAIN SCARPH

NIB

B. HOOK SCARPH

KEY

WEDGES IN HEAVY
TIMBERS

C. KEY SCARPH

FIGURE 8-13.   *Common scarphs for joining long members such as keels,
clamps and stringers*

89

Chapter 9

SETTING UP

ITH THE backbone and molds made, the builder is ready to set up the boat preparatory to framing the hull. Just as much care and accuracy should go into the work of setting up as went into the mold loft work and construction of the backbone. Continued attention to detail at this stage of the game will pay dividends in time saved later. The method of setting up depends upon the size, type and construction of the hull, but in general most small craft are best built upside down, a method that has much merit.

Upside Down or Right Side Up?

Although the majority of boats, excluding small stock boats produced on a mass basis, are constructed right side up, it would be impractical to copy this routine in building a boat like a flat bottom skiff when it is so easy to fasten the bottom planks with the hull inverted. By the same reasoning, flat sectioned boats like vee and arc bottom hulls are also set up and built upside down. The same is true of small lapstrake boats that are usually planked over the molds, with the frames bent inside the planking after it has been completed. In this case the fitting of the lapped plank seams is very much simplified with the hull upside down. Small strip planked hulls, on which the planking is started at the keel and worked toward the sheer, are best built right side up because it is much easier to nail downhand, and if it has been decided to bend the frames of a round bottom boat on the inside of the ribbands as mentioned under *Molds* in Chapter 8, the boat should be built right side up in order to readily bend the frames. Any other method would be impractical. In other instances the finished hull will be too heavy or bulky for the amateur to turn over, and therefore should be built upright.

Building Under Cover

Considering that weather can be a drawback if it should be cold and windy or rain during your precious spare time for boatbuilding, your hull should be

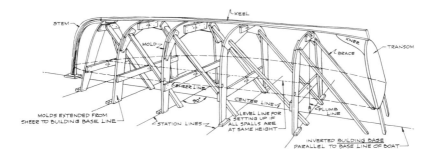

FIGURE 9-1. *Typical setup for building a small hull upside down, shown before installation of ribbands*

built under cover if possible. A building also permits work to be done evenings under lights, and provides convenient means of overhead bracing of molds and backbone to the roof rafters. A good solid floor is ideal whether or not it is level and smooth. On the other hand an outdoor construction site can be made to serve well, as many amateur builders have found from experience, although the task of bracing the frame is somewhat more difficult.

Building Upside Down

Using the little twelve footer as an example of a boat to be built upside down, a center line is first drawn in on the floor, the station spacing laid off along the center line, and the station lines squared off from the center line. See Figure 9-1. As previously described, the molds for upside down building are extended beyond the sheer to an arbitrary inverted base line parallel to the base line of the boat and located above the highest point of the sheer by an amount calculated for convenient working height. The molds forward of amidship are set up on the aft side of the station lines, and those aft of amidship set up on the forward side of the station lines. The reason for this system will be obvious when the ribbands are applied. If the molds are set on the wrong sides of the station lines the ribbands will be forced out of their proper position due to the shape of the hull, as shown in the sketch, Figure 9-2.

Use a plumb line to align the center line of a mold with the boat center line on the floor, and also use the plumb line or a level to align the upper part of a mold in a fore and aft direction. Fasten the molds to the floor with blocks and brace them securely against fore and aft movement. You will remember that it was pointed out in Chapter 8 that it would be helpful if the mold cross spalls were fitted at the same level on all molds and it is now that this fact is realized. If the building floor is not perfectly level the line of the spalls can be used to determine where shims must be fitted between the floor and the ends of the molds to bring them to the proper height.

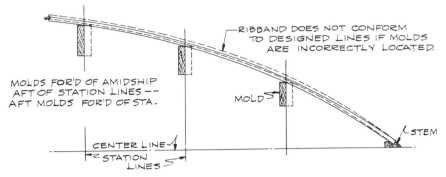

RIBBAND DOES NOT CONFORM
TO DESIGNED LINES IF MOLDS
ARE INCORRECTLY LOCATED.

MOLDS FOR'D OF AMIDSHIP
AFT OF STATION LINES ––
AFT MOLDS FOR'D OF STA.

MOLD

STEM

CENTER LINE
STATION LINES

FIGURE 9-2.

It must be emphasized that the utmost care should be taken to align the backbone and molds properly. An extra hour or two spent on this job will be appreciated when the ribbands are fitted, frames bent, and planking made and installed. The boat will not be the same on both sides if the setting up is not done accurately. There are more straight lines in a boat than meet the eye in the finished product. The center line and base line, water lines and station lines are all straight, and as such enable the builder to erect the backbone and molds with the use of vertical and horizontal lines just as the designer laid out his lines plan and construction drawings. Shores and braces of sufficient number must be fitted to prevent movement of the structure in any direction. The braces may be of low quality lumber of any kind.

To continue setting up the twelve footer shown in Figure 9-1, the keel with stem, transom and knee attached is dropped into position over the molds and screw fastened to blocks on each mold. Secure the head of the stem to the building floor with blocks to hold it in position. Brace the transom, after making sure it is raked to the correct angle and square across the boat. When the keel was made the station lines were marked on it, and if everything has been done accurately the marks on the keel should coincide with the molds. If not, the frame is not properly aligned and must be corrected. One aid that can be employed is to use a batten longer than the hull and bend it around the molds as a test fairness. Test and adjust until the batten touches all the molds without forcing. The forward end of the batten should be laid in the stem rabbet and the batten should test fair when tried anywhere from keel to the sheer. The ribbands should not be installed until the molds have been aligned to your complete satisfaction.

Building Outdoors

When building boats outdoors there are many arrangements that are workable, but probably the most satisfactory for upside down building is a pair

92

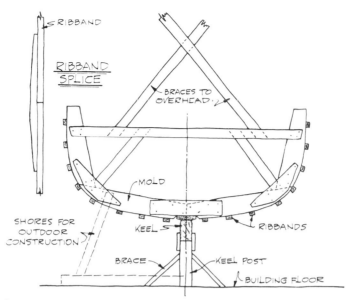

RIBBAND

RIBBAND
SPLICE

BRACES TO
OVERHEAD

MOLD

SHORES FOR
OUTDOOR
CONSTRUCTION

KEEL

RIBBANDS

BRACE

KEEL POST

BUILDING FLOOR

FIGURE 9-3.

of substantial timbers longer than the boat secured to the ground on both sides of the center line and made level. The cross spalls on the molds are fastened to the parallel timbers. Crosspieces are fastened between the timbers to take the stem head and transom braces. For building right side up outdoors, timbers are placed on the ground athwartship at stations and staked solidly against movement. Keel supports are built up with blocks to the proper height, and lateral shores are used to hold the mold sideways. See Figure 9-3.

Building Right Side Up

Center line and station lines for a boat to be built right side up indoors are drawn as described before and a post erected at each station. The posts must be securely nailed to the floor and braced against movement as shown in Figures 9-3 and 9-4. The heights of the posts are carefully measured from the full size profile and checked with the keel template. Posts are only used for relatively narrow keels like those for motor boats or to shore the stems of sailboats. The latter may be built on their flat keels and the ballast keel casting and deadwood added after the hull is planked, or the complete backbone may be finished before setting up, like the auxiliary in the photograph, Figure 9-5, in which are shown husky keel blocks properly used to take substantial fastenings to the floor to prevent shifting of the structure, and also to

93

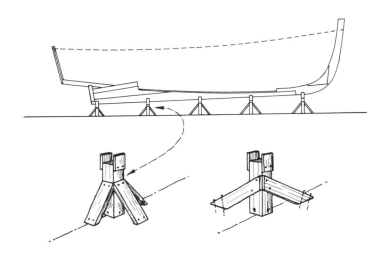

FIGURE 9-4. *Common forms of keel posts. Any similar arrangement may be devised*

take the considerable finished weight of a boat of this type. Quite frequently motor boat keels are held down on the posts with turnbuckles set up near each end of the keel between eye bolts in the keel and floor. Such fastening prevents the hull from being raised off the posts when planking is forced into place with shores and wedges, as this action tends both to lift the hull upward and to tilt it to one side.

Ribbands

The ribbands are applied only when the backbone and all molds have been set up accurately and properly braced to hold the parts rigidly in position. Ribbands were briefly mentioned under *Molds* in Chapter 8, when it was pointed out that they are long strips of wood bent around the molds in order to provide a form against which to bend the frames to correct shape in the hull between the molds. The function of molds and ribbands should be perfectly clear from the excellent photograph, Figure 9-6, a rare treat because it is not cluttered up with scaffolding. As considerable pressure will be used to clamp the frames to the ribbands, it is best they be of moderately hard and strong wood such as fir or yellow pine. Boats vary to such an extent that there is no general rule for size of the ribbands. They must be stiff to retain the hull shape when the frames are bent against them, but not so heavy that they are hard to bend and hold in place or force the molds out of alignment. As a safeguard against distorting the shape of the hull the ribbands are applied alternately port and starboard. Ribbands are generally bent on the flat of sizes like 1¼ by 1½ inches and spaced about 10 inches apart, or 1½ by 2 inches spaced about a foot apart. A sample should definitely be tried around the molds before getting out the stock for all the ribbands.

The proportion of ribband sizes may be seen in Figures 9-6 and 9-7 where the former, a hull for a moderately heavy cruising auxiliary, has been framed. A comparison of the ribband sizes for the boats in the two pictures indicates that the racing sloop will have relatively light frames. The ribbands should be in single lengths if possible, otherwise they should be spliced as shown in Figures 9-3 and 9-6. This type of splice tends to eliminate unfair flat spots in the ribband, but as a further precaution against hard spots the splices should be located where bends in the ribbands are easiest.

Husky ribbands and close spacing will contribute toward a fair boat. Put them on by fastening the middle first and, working toward the ends,

FIGURE 9-5.   *Stern view of backbone of a Rhodes designed ketch. Note the husky blocks under deadwood of this auxiliary, shores to prevent side movement of backbone, and transom bracing to overhead*

95

securing the ribbands to each mold with screws having washers under the heads. Screws will permit the ribbands to be removed easily as the planking is fitted. The top ribbands should go on first, fitted parallel to the sheer and a few inches above it. The rest of them should be run in fair lines similar to strakes of planking and as illustrated in Figure 9-6. Where the frames will be bent to the sharpest curves the ribbands are spaced closer than where the frames will be fairly flat.

Photograph by Morris Rosenfeld

FIGURE 9-6. *View from the stern quarter of a double ended auxiliary after frames have been bent inside the ribbands. Attention is directed to the excellent bracing of molds and sternpost. The appearance of the ribbands is pleasing as well as practical, and the third and fourth ribbands above the keel are correctly spliced*

Careful mold loft work and setting up will make running ribbands an easy job, and will eliminate the task of trimming and shimming molds to get the ribbands to touch all molds and still remain fair. If considerable trouble is encountered fairing the ribbands it will pay to check the sections by bending a batten into position like a frame on the inside of the ribbands to see if it touches all of them while bent in a fair curve. Running the ribbands is the last job before framing is started, and the hull in this condition usually is the cause of excited anticipation on the part of the builder, for now the shape of the hull may be appreciated.

Vee Bottom Hulls

It should be understood without mention that hulls other than the round

Photograph by Morris Rosenfeld

FIGURE 9-7. *The men at right are fitting ribbands prior to framing a racing sloop. Note mold braces to rafters of building and strongback on top of mold cross spalls on center line of boat*

bottom type must be set up, aligned and made rigid with the same care. There is no point in doing an accurate job of laying down and mold making unless the setting up and the following work do not follow the same standard. Refer to Figure 10-13 for a fine example of meticulous workmanship in a framed hull ready for planking.

FIGURE 9-8. *First mold to be set up is carefully checked for alignment. Other molds stacked in background*

98

Chapter 10

FRAMING

THERE ARE two basic systems for framing a hull, transverse and longitudinal. Transverse is the most common and, due to being located athwartship or across the boat, led to the expression "ribs". Transverse frames for round bottom wooden hulls are either bent from one piece, Figures 1-2 and 1-3, laminated from two or more pieces bent on top of each other, sawn from natural crooks of wood, or "double sawn" from boards and made up of two layers with staggered joints. Small to moderate hulls usually have the bent frames, although in places where material for bent frames is non-existent, such as islands in the Bahamas, the frames are sawn from crooks or double sawn according to both the size of the boat and the supply of crooks. See Figure 10-1. Sawn frames for vee bottom and arc bottom hulls are shown in Figures 1-1 and 1-2. Some designers and builders use a combination of sawn and bent frames for their vee bottom hulls.

For the longitudinal framing system in general, transverse frames are used to shape the hull, but are spaced further apart than in the transverse system, then fore and aft longitudinals are used to build up the necessary framing strength. This system can get quite complicated for construction in wood, but is well suited for metal boats of welded construction.

In this book discussion is limited to the two types of framing suitable for the size craft likely to be built by the amateur, bent frames and sawn vee bottom frames. Before undertaking a craft with other kinds of more complex framing the builder should be certain before starting that he is aware of what is involved.

Vee Bottom Frames

The lofting and construction of frames for a vee bottom boat should be understood from the figures referred to above and an explanation in Chapter 8. The frames are made from the full size sections and must be beveled on the edges so the planking will bear properly. The process of picking up bevels is explained in preceding chapters.

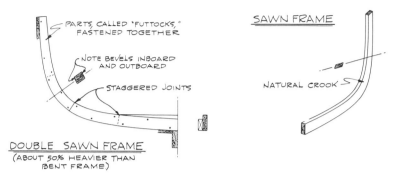

FIGURE 10-1. *Sawn and double sawn round bottom frames are not easy for the amateur builder*

Bent Frames

The bending of frames for a round bottom boat seems to disturb the peace of mind of an amateur contemplating the construction of such a hull, but a trial will dispel this fear. It is recommended that the builder start with a fairly small boat with light frames in order to gain experience and overcome the mental hazard that is the principal obstacle to frame bending. We all know that any piece of dry wood may be picked from the lumber pile and sprung to a curve of large radius, but the plastic condition present when wood is both wet and hot is needed to bend the curves in frames. The material most commonly used for bent frames in the United States is white oak because of its durability and strength, and elm is extensively used in Canada and abroad. Although responsible agencies have proven that oak with a moisture content as low as twelve per cent is suitable for bending if handled properly, it is recommended that the amateur use unseasoned wood because it is usually free from surface checks, heats rapidly, and needs only heat to bend rather than the addition of moisture required by dry wood.

The frame stock should be as straight grained as possible and, although not ordinary procedure, this is sometimes achieved by splitting a plank with the grain and then sawing out the frames parallel to split the edges. The stock is prepared about a foot or so longer than the finished length of the frame. It is best to bend the oak on the flat of the grain (Figures 6-3 and 10-2) for not only will it bend easier this way but the tendency to split when plank fastenings are driven is minimized. Specifications for some boats call for a flat frame of size such as one by one and three-eighths inch bent on the flat. From the standpoint of theory a frame is a transverse strength member, and is best when the dimension across the hull is relatively great. If this were carried too far it would be impossible to bend the frame so a good compro-

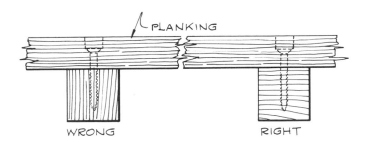

FIGURE 10-2. *Frames are bent on the flat of the grain*

mise is to make the frame square, for then it is just as strong crossways as fore and aft and in practice it may be quickly turned on its other edge if it does not readily bend in the direction first attempted.

Steaming Arrangements

You have probably seen the local boatyard steam box in action. The source of steam does not have to be elaborate when one boat is to be built. It may be generated in an old hot water boiler from a house, a large kettle, or any similar device rigged so a wood fire may be built under it and the steam piped to the box. The supply of water must be ample for the period of time you plan to work. Watch this point because the water goes fast.

The steam box is made of wood, made as steam tight as possible by caulking with cotton if necessary, and large enough for a half dozen frames and some room to spare. It is possible that the garboard and one or two other planks will need steaming to bend them in place, so make the box large enough for this job. There must be a door at one end, opposite to the end with the steam supply pipe, and the cracks are packed with rags to prevent steam leaking out. Needless to say, the box is located close to the boat because bending calls for fast work to make the shape before the frame becomes too cool. Handle the frames with cotton work gloves. A rough rule for steaming is one hour per inch of frame thickness. A few trials will have to be made to get the hang of it.

Light frames are sometimes made supple in boiling water by placing them in a length of pipe set at an angle with the ground and a fire built under the lower end. This scheme works well because with water in the pipe there is little danger of unduly drying the frames. Strings should be tied to the frames with which to pull them out and the upper end of the pipe is stuffed with rags to retain the steam. Typical steaming arrangements are shown in Figure 10-3. Others on the same order may be improvised by the builder.

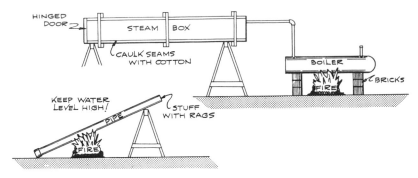

FIGURE 10-3. *Devices for heating frames*

Bending the Frames

Frames may either be bent to shape in the boat against the ribbands or bent on forms and fitted to the boat cold. The former is by far the easier method, and unless the frames for your boat are relatively heavy or the hull extremely shapely this system should be followed. Guided by the frame layout on the construction plan, first mark the frame positions on all the ribbands and at the keel, marking both edges with a thin batten the same width as a frame, and making sure the marks are made square across the boat at right angles to the center line. Start framing amidships where the bends are likely to be easy, and your experience will accumulate as the work progresses toward the ends where sharp bends are likely to be encountered.

Take a frame out of the steam box, as rapidly as possible cut the heel of the frame to fit the keel and nail it in place, then start the bending by pulling inboard on the head of the frame as you progressively force the frame against the ribbands with hands or feet, all the while twisting the frame to lie flat against the ribbands. By pulling the head inboard the frame will bend more than enough, and it then can be flattened and forced into position against the ribbands. A gadget like Figure 10-4A may be employed to aid in twisting the bevel should it give trouble.

If plenty of hands are available the frame can be clamped to the ribbands as you bend it, otherwise clamp it at the topmost ribband, give it a downward wallop on the head if necessary to have it touch all the ribbands, then temporarily toe nail it to the ribbands so that your clamps will be ready for further duty on the next frame. You will soon learn that the bending must be done quickly once the frame has been removed from the steam box. If possible two men should work on the bending while a third tends the box. When the boat is designed with frames in one piece from sheer to sheer

102

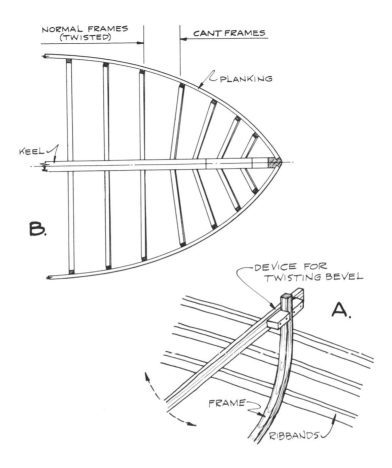

NORMAL FRAMES
(TWISTED)

CANT FRAMES

PLANKING

KEEL

B.

DEVICE FOR
TWISTING BEVEL

A.

FRAME

RIBBANDS

FIGURE 10-4.

there absolutely must be two men bending, one on a side, each working from the keel toward the sheer in order to do all the bending before the frame cools.

In many boats all the frames may be bent right in the boat as described above. However the frames in full-bowed hulls and those along the horn timber aft of the waterline in hulls like sketch D of Figure 8-12 are often troublesome due to twisting the bevel in them in their short length. It is permissible to depart from bending at right angles to the center line in the extreme bow and to allow the frames to lie naturally against the planking so they slope forward from keel to sheer. These are called cant frames and are shown in Figure 10-4B. The same is true of stern frames in a double ender.

103

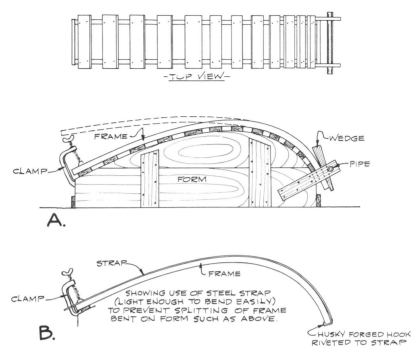

-TOP VIEW-

FRAME

WEDGE

CLAMP

PIPE

FORM

A.

STRAP

FRAME

CLAMP

SHOWING USE OF STEEL STRAP
(LIGHT ENOUGH TO BEND EASILY)
TO PREVENT SPLITTING OF FRAME
BENT ON FORM SUCH AS ABOVE.

B.

HUSKY FORGED HOOK
RIVETED TO STRAP

FIGURE 10-5.

Frames Fitted Cold

In the interest of fair lines in the counter, as the stern overhang in Figure 8-12D is called, the frames are either bent over a mold outside of the boat, as described later, or oversized stock is used to bend the frames with too much curve, after which they are removed, straightened to the proper curve, then beveled to lie against the ribbands. The inner edge is finally beveled to correspond to that on the outside of the frame so that stringers and clamps to be installed later will fit properly. These cold-fitted beveled frames are similar in cross section to the double sawn frame illustrated in Figure 10-1. The excess curvature first bent into the frame is accomplished by padding the ribbands with short lengths of wood in way of the frame location. Curvature can be taken out of frame after it has cooled and set, but none may be added. Framing of the counter stern should be very carefully done to avoid hollows and bumps.

If cold fitted frames cannot be avoided, one or two forms similar to Figure 10-5A must be made over which to bend the frames. To get an idea

of the curves required for the forms, bend a piece of soft iron rod or lead wire against the ribbands like a frame in position and use it as a guide to build a form. The frames must always be bent to more curve than necessary, and the form can be padded to vary the shape. When ready to bend, the end of the frame is slipped under the pipe shown in the figure and wedged, then the bending is done with a steady pressure. Leave the frames on the form at least over night, so they will cool and set properly and not lose too much shape when removed. When there is excessive curve the frames can be straightened with a rig device like Figure 10-6 on a bench or corner of the shop building. Reverse curves can be made on the form by bending one curve at a time, allowing the first bend to set well, and then nailing braces across the curve to hold the shape while the reverse is being bent.

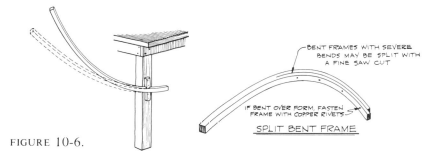

FIGURE 10-6.

The tensile stresses in the outer fibers of the frame while bending will tend to split the edge when the curve is sharp, but someone long ago found that a metal strap on the outside of the frame was a very successful way of combating this breakage. The strap shown in Figure 10-5B is typical of the simple scheme involved and will be found very handy. The tendency to split is also present when bending sharp curves against ribbands. If you find some bad ones, a strap similar to that illustrated may be devised to do the same job. In most cases the strap need only extend somewhat more than the length of the hard bend, such as around the turn of the bilge of a motor boat. After some practice you will be able to judge which bends may give trouble, like those in the S frames forward of the counter of boats like Figure 8-12D, and the frame stock may be split with a fine saw cut as shown in Figure 10-6 to permit the bend to be made easily. As a matter of fact this is easier than using a strap when the frames are bent right in the hull inside of the ribbands. When the frames are bent outside of the ribbands a strap is not difficult to use. If splitting is resorted to the frame should be fastened in way of the cut as soon as possible.

Floor Timbers

One of the most important members of the hull frame is the so called floor or floor timber. These pieces of flat grained material, usually oak, are the strength connection between the frames and backbone. Without floors severe strains would be imposed on the garboard planks, the planks against the keel that fit into the rabbet, and their fastenings along the rabbet and it is to be expected that the hull will not remain tight. Floors are generally placed alongside every frame to be sure each frame is securely fastened to the backbone, but there are certain exceptions to this rule. You will see plans for some power boats and light centerboard sailboats with floors located at only every other frame, but most boats of the cruiser type, whether sail or power, do not omit any of them in the interests of safety.

Floors are made from planks set on edge on top of the backbone members and drift or through bolted depending upon their location in the boat. Fastenings to frames are either bolts or copper rivets. The bolts through the keel are always two in number where the width of the backbone permits, otherwise one is driven and good practice calls for three or four fastenings to the frame on each side. Floors are shown in Figures 1-1, 1-2, 1-3, 6-1, 8-8 and 8-12D and are clearly visible in Figures 6-1, 6-9, 9-5, 9-8 and 10-8. The latter picture well illustrates the bolting of frames to the floors.

It should be noted that floors have already been fitted to the backbone shown in Figure 9-8 although the boat has not yet been framed. This method is common practice for the professional builder, but would be recommended to the amateur with reluctance because the mold loft work involved might well try his patience to the breaking point. With this system each floor must be preshaped from a full sized section drawn at each frame, and correct bevels cut on three edges before the floor can be bolted in position. In vee bottom hulls the floor is an essential part of the frame but the shape is obtained simultaneously with that of the frame being built, and because the frame spacing is greater there are not so many of them to make.

The thickness of floors should be as specified on the plans and is usually the same as the frames in vee bottom boats. In bent frame hulls most of the floors are the same thickness or slightly less than the thickness of the frame, while those under the mast steps and engine beds in both type boats are made heavier to take the extra strains and fastenings through the adjoining parts at these points. Floors in way of ballast keels are bored for bolts through the keel casting and are sided equal to the ordinary floors plus the diameter of the bolts.

Like all joints in a well built boat, it is imperative that floors be carefully fitted. They are made to have full contact with the frames, and where the frames twist in the ends of the boat the floors are beveled off to fit tightly as shown in Section A-A in Figure 10-7a. Due to the curvature of the hull toward the center line forward and aft of amidship the twist in the frames will be toward the ends, consequently the floors are placed on the forward side of the frames forward of amidship and on the aft side of the frames from amidship to the stern. An occasional floor may be located otherwise for one reason or another at the option of the designer.

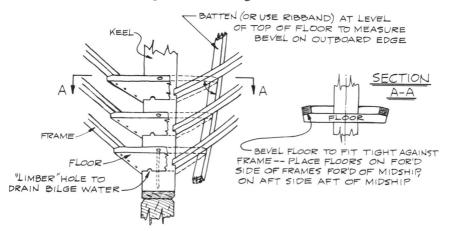

FIGURE 10-7a.   *Beveling and fastening of floors are important*

The bottom edge of a floor is beveled to fit the member it rests upon, and many professionals prefer to notch them a half inch or so over the keel to aid in preventing movement of the parts when the hull is stressed. Limber holes are cut on the bottom edges of floors before installation (Figure 10-7A) so rain or bilge water cannot be trapped between the floors and will drain to the low point of the bilge for removal by pumping. The outboard edges of the floors are beveled so the planking will bear against them. This bevel may be obtained from a ribband in the vicinity, or a short batten may be sprung around the adjacent frames for the same purpose.

Longitudinal Strength Members

Although fore and aft stringers and clamps may not be fastened in place before the hull is all or partially planked, they may be considered part of the hull framing because they are used whether or not the boat is decked. Stringers and clamps are planks on edge, fitted on the inside of the frames, and because they strengthen the hull considerably should fit neatly and be carefully fastened so they will do the most good. They are made of hard pine or Douglas fir, and sometimes oak where weight is not objectionable. Not only to save weight but also to make installation easier the clamps and stringers, in hulls other than the smallest, are tapered in width from a maximum amidships to about one-half the width at the ends of the boat. Stringers and clamps are clearly shown in the photograph of the workboat in Figure 10-8. If material is not available to install these pieces in single lengths they may be pieced out with scarphs as described in Chapter 8 and as shown in Figure 8-13.

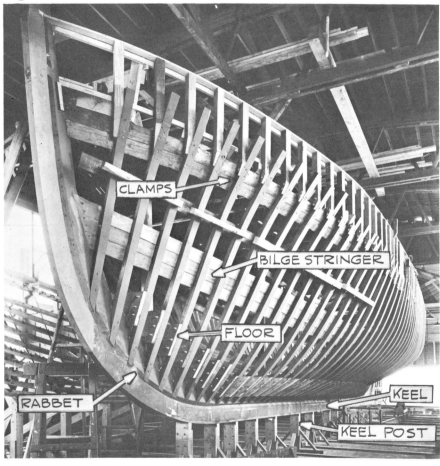

FIGURE 10-8. *This illustration of a workboat after framing shows why bent frames are often called ribs. Rosenfeld photo*

Bilge Stringers

Bilge stringers are used in all round bottom boats except the smallest, and in power boats there may be several on each side of the hull. Stringers give valuable support if a boat should run aground and lay over on her side. Because of the chine location, bilge stringers are not found in vee bottom boats. Usually there is one stringer on each side made up of one or more strakes, and when multiple the strakes are wedged tightly together. The bilge stringer is fastened to each frame with staggered flat head wood screws except in heavy construction where bolts are used. In some boats the screws are counterbored and plugged where they will be visible in quarters, and the upper and lower inboard corners of the stringers are sometimes chamfered or beaded on a machine for appearance by professional builders. The stringers should be located as closely as possible to the position shown on the drawings, run as far fore and aft as is practical and, depending upon the relative thickness of the piece, sprung or shored in place for fastening.

Sheer Clamps

The sheer clamp is located on the inside of the frames as shown in the sketch illustrating general types, Figure 10-9, and in Figure 10-10, especially drawn to show that in decked boats the upper edge of the clamp is set down from

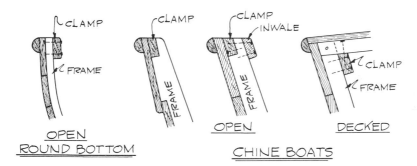

FIGURE 10-9. *Sections showing sheer clamps*

the sheer line a distance equal to the thickness of decking plus depth of the deck beams. It is important to keep this point in mind or else the sheer line will not be at the right height. The clamps are bolted to the frames for maximum strength, and this means that if the amateur should go ahead and completely plank the hull before installing the clamps the bolts would have to extend through the planking, possibly interfering with the plank fastenings.

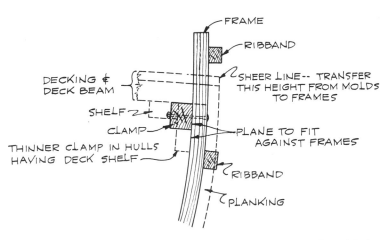

FIGURE 10-10. *In decked hulls the top edge of the clamp is placed below sheer as shown*

There are two ways of getting around this, although we are a little ahead of our story because planking will be discussed in the next chapter. One way is to fasten the upper two planks in place temporarily until planking is completed. The molds are taken out of the hull, the two planks taken off for fitting and bolting of the clamps, then replaced and fastened for good. The other method is to transfer the sheer heights from the molds to adjacent frames, then cut away enough of the molds to install the clamps before planking. The uppermost ribbands are depended upon to hold the frames in position during this work. The molds, of course, cannot be used for another boat without some rebuilding. The clamps are run from the transom to the stem, the outside faces are planed to fit snugly against the frames, and except in straight sided boats this is always necessary if the clamp has much depth (Figure 10-10). Like the bilge stringers, the lower inside corners are sometimes chamfered or beaded for looks.

Clamps in vee bottom hulls are installed and fastened when the frames are set up, and with the chines are used to hold the frames in alignment. Because of the depth of vee bottom frames the clamps are more often screwed than bolted.

Engine Stringers

In order to distribute the weight of the engine, and also to aid in elimination of hull vibration, engine stringers are found in all properly designed motor boats. Sometimes of oak, but more often of wood like fir or yellow pine, the

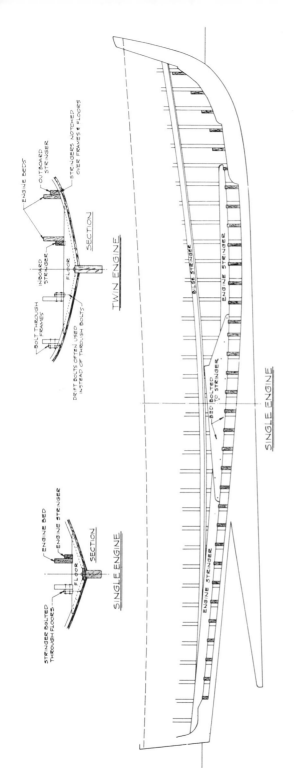

ENGINE BEDS
OUTBOARD STRINGER
STRINGERS NOTCHED OVER FRAMES & FLOORS
INBOARD STRINGER
FLOOR
SECTION
BOLT THROUGH FRAMES
DRIFT BOLTS OFTEN USED INSTEAD OF THROUGH BOLTS

TWIN ENGINE

ENGINE BED
ENGINE STRINGER
FLOOR
SECTION
STRINGER BOLTED THROUGH FLOORS

SINGLE ENGINE

BILGE STRINGER
ENGINE STRINGER

BED BOLTED TO STRINGER

SINGLE ENGINE

ENGINE STRINGER

SINGLE ENGINE

FIGURE 10-11.   *Engine stringers and beds in powerboat hulls*

111

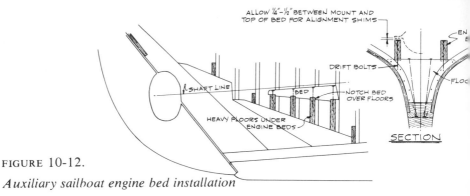

FIGURE 10-12.

Auxiliary sailboat engine bed installation

stringers are run as far fore and aft as possible. To accomplish this they are occasionally pulled toward the center line in the forward part of the boat to permit them to extend further and still remain on top of the floors to be securely fastened. This applies to both stringers in a single engined boat and to the inboard stringers in a twin engined craft. The outboard stringers for twin engine installations are usually too far out to catch the floors and are set on the frames. They are run straight and cannot be as long as the inner members due to hull shape. It is desirable to have the stringers in single lengths but if necessary they may be scarphed, and the joints should be planned to avoid conflicting fastenings.

The stringers are notched ⅜ to ½ inch over the floors and frames, through or drift bolted to the floors. Outboard stringers not resting on floors are through bolted to the frames. See Figure 10-11. The center line of the propeller shaft is laid out from the drawings and the engine stringers spaced equally to each side, the distance being figured from the horizontal center to center distance of the engine holding down bolts and allowances made for the thickness of the engine bed material.

Engine Beds

In motor boats the engine beds are bolted to the engine stringers, Figure 10-11, and may or may not be notched over the floors. If enough bolts are used to transfer the engine thrust to the stringers notches are not necessary.

The present custom of having the engine in an auxiliary as far aft as possible does not lend itself to the installation of stringers, and in this case the beds are notched over the floors and drift bolted to them. See Figure 10-12. In all boats the installation diagram for the engine must be consulted for the vertical position of the bottom of the bolt lugs in relation to the center line of the propeller shaft in order to determine the top edge of the beds. Anywhere from ¼ to ½ inch is allowed between the lugs and the beds for the insertion of hardwood shims when the engine is aligned with the propeller shaft unless the engine is fitted with mounts that have a vertical adjustment.

112

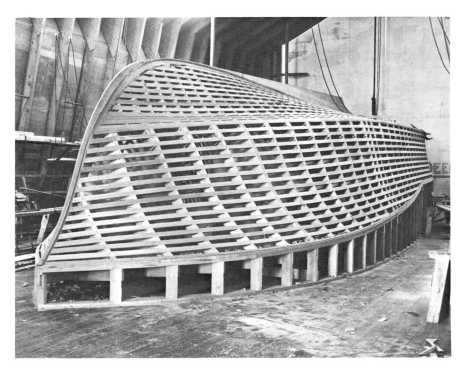

FIGURE 10-13. *Framed hull for a Gulfstream 42 built by Deebold & Adams Boat Works, Atlantic City, N.J. Photo courtesy of William G. Hobbs Yacht Sales*

113

Chapter 11

PLANKING

T HE CONVENTIONAL type of planking is often the most difficult part of boatbuilding for the amateur, and always one of the simplest for the professional. The beginner has trouble laying out the width of the planks and the run of the planking seams, while the expert does not seem to give it much thought due to accumulated experience and first hand teaching. The stumbling of an amateur is understandable, because it is not easy to learn planking from a book or even to explain the subject in words. It is strongly suggested that time be taken to study the planking on boats in yards, and especially of the type you will build. Through the ages a good many methods of planking have been devised, but only the most common will be discussed here.

The individual planks are called strakes, and for appearance most systems require nicely proportioned planks, shaped so the lines of the seams are pleasing to the eye from every direction. Seams open and shut a little due to shrinking and swelling and for well kept appearance, especially on the topsides above the water, the strakes should not be too wide or the seams will become unsightly as well as difficult to keep tight.

Carvel Planking

It will be well to discuss smooth planking at first (Figure 11-1) as this method is the most common, and much of what is said about carvel planking a round bottom boat will apply also to other methods.

It is not recommended that an amateur attempt his first boat with planking less than ½ inch thick. Carvel planking is made with the seams tight on the inside and open on the outside to receive the cotton caulking which makes the planking watertight. The bevel on the seams is called "out-gauge" (11-1A) and should be made so the opening on the outside is about 1/16 inch wide per inch of plank thickness. The planking material should be ordered somewhat thicker than the specified finished dimension to allow for

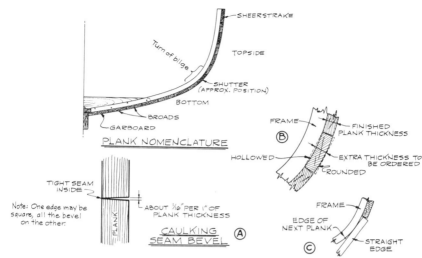

Labels in figure:
SHEERSTRAKE
Turn of bilge
TOPSIDE
SHUTTER (APPROX. POSITION)
BOTTOM
BROADS
GARBOARD
PLANK NOMENCLATURE

FRAME
FINISHED PLANK THICKNESS
HOLLOWED
EXTRA THICKNESS TO BE ORDERED
ROUNDED
(B)

TIGHT SEAM INSIDE
Note: One edge may be square, all the bevel on the other.
ABOUT ⅟₁₆" PER 1" OF PLANK THICKNESS
PLANK
CAULKING SEAM BEVEL (A)

FRAME
EDGE OF NEXT PLANK
STRAIGHT EDGE
(C)

FIGURE 11-1. *Carvel planking*

planing and sandpapering, also for hollowing the inside face of planks on sharp turns (Figure 11-1B). Most of the hull planking will not need more than an extra ⅛ inch for finishing, but that on the turns may require more. A straight edge held on a frame will determine the amount, Figure 11-1C.

Butts in Planking

Some small boats can be planked with strakes running the entire length but inasmuch as the usual available lengths of planking material are from twelve to twenty feet in intervals of two feet the strakes will ordinarily be in two or three pieces butted end to end. From the standpoint of strength the location of butts is important, and a plan should be laid out before starting to work, taking into consideration the material at hand. Rather than try to visualize the butts on the frame of the boat, it is much easier to make a rough diagram as a guide.

Figure 11-2 shows a satisfactory way of laying out the butts, and you will note that no two of them should be in the same frame space without three strakes between, and adjacent strakes should not have butts without three frame spaces between them. Butts are made midway between a pair of frames, the joint being backed by an oak or mahogany block as thick as the frame and wider than the strake of planking sawn to length to fit between the frames, planed on the outside to fit snugly against the planking, and the outboard corners chamfered to drain water that otherwise may be trapped on top of the block. Using a butt block thinner than the frame requires shorter fastenings than those for the normal planking.

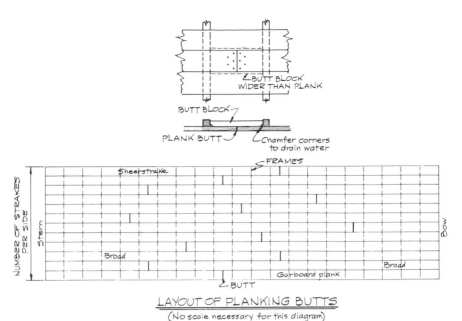

LAYOUT OF PLANKING BUTTS
(No scale necessary for this diagram)

FIGURE 11-2.

Planking Procedure

Let us consider carvel planking a simple round bottom boat like the twelve footer used to illustrate loft work in Chapter 7. The normal procedure for the amateur will be the sheer strake (Figure 11-1) first, then the garboard, the two adjoining broad strakes, and the bottom planking to the turn of the bilge, then alternately one plank under the sheer strake and one on the bottom, with the shutter, as the last plank is called, coming about midway between the bottom planking and the sheer. Because it is difficult to clamp the shutter it should be a plank that is fairly straight, without twist, and not requiring steaming to bend it.

The first consideration is the total number of strakes to be used, determined by the widths amidships at the longest frame. The garboard will be the widest, and the widths will decrease toward the turn of the bilge until the topside strakes become the narrowest and all about the same width. The sheer strake can be a little wider than the rest of the topside planks because of the rub rail often used.

As to exactly how wide to make the planks on a given boat, here is where your inspection of other boats can be a help. For a general guide to proportion, say 6 to 8 inches for the garboard, diminishing on the bottom to 4½ inches for the topsides and 5 to 6 inches for the sheer strake. These sizes are not hard and fast, but it should be remembered that for good appearance the topside strakes should not be over 4½ inches wide amidships. Cut a thin batten, bend it around the amidships frame, mark the length from the keel rabbet to sheer, and lay out the plank widths. Naturally these widths apply only at amidships, as the frame girths at ends of the boat are less, and the planks must taper in width toward the ends. Again for appearance, the taper of the planks should be uniform.

On the amidships frame lay off the width desired for the sheer strake and run a full length batten around the frames for the purpose of obtaining the bottom edge of the plank. The width of the plank should be tapered a little at the bow and stern and the batten must be fair. When satisfied with the appearance of the line, mark the edge of the plank at the ends of the boat and on all the frames and remove the batten. Of course it is understood that the top edge of the plank is the sheer line, from which is deducted the thickness of decking, if any.

Spiling

In small boatbuilding the planks are not given any "edge set", that is, sprung edgewise into position, and the job is to cut a plank that will fit properly without springing edgewise when bent around into place. The shape is obtained with the aid of a spiling batten, a piece of soft wood somewhat longer than any individual piece of planking, about 4 to 6 inches wide and 3/16 inch or less in thickness. Several pieces of this stock should be on hand because you will mutilate them with use. The batten is clamped or tacked to the frames, making sure it lies flat against the frames for its entire width and is not sprung edgewise, and with the upper edge a little below the top edge of the plank to be made. This does not mean that the edge of the batten will be parallel to the plank edge. If it is, you are probably springing the batten on edge and the plank you make will not fit. The whole idea of the spiling batten is to have it placed like the plank to be made and so determining the *difference* in shape between the edge of the batten and the edge of the plank. For greater accuracy on hulls with a lot of sheer a batten with a curved edge should be made if the batten should lie more than a couple of inches from the plank marks.

To use the spiling batten, take your carpenter's pencil compass and set the legs with a gap about a quarter inch more than the greatest space between the edge of the batten and the plank marks on the frames. With one leg of the compass on the plank mark, make a point on the batten square down from the line of the top edge of the plank. See Figure 11-3. Repeat at every frame and the ends of the plank, labeling the points with frame numbers and identifying all points for the particular plank with a numbered or lettered circle so

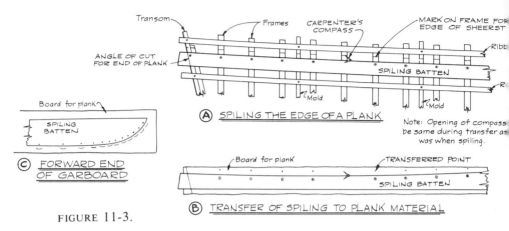

Transom

Frames   CARPENTER'S
COMPASS

MARK ON FRAME FOR
EDGE OF SHEERSTR

ANGLE OF CUT
FOR END OF PLANK

Ribb

SPILING BATTEN

Board for plank

SPILING
BATTEN

Ⓐ SPILING THE EDGE OF A PLANK

Mold   Mold

Note: Opening of compass
be same during transfer as
was when spiling.

Ⓒ FORWARD END
OF GARBOARD

Board for plank

TRANSFERRED POINT

SPILING BATTEN

Ⓑ TRANSFER OF SPILING TO PLANK MATERIAL

FIGURE 11-3.

they will not become confused with points for other planks later on. Do not change the opening of the compass while spiling any one plank. Mark across the batten the cut for the butt, the stern ending, or the stem rabbet, as the case may be. Now take the batten off the boat and lay it on the board that is to be used for the plank (Figure 11-3B). Still not changing the compass opening, reverse the procedure and this time, with one leg of the compass on a point on the batten, mark points on the board, but before making any actual marks test with the compass and shift the batten until the points will be as close to the edge of the plank as possible in order to not waste width, then tack the batten against movement.

Mark all the points and the endings of the plank. Remove the spiling batten and run a fairing batten through all the points and draw the edge of the plank with a pencil. Do not worry if the shape of the line is peculiar. If the spiling has been done correctly the plank will fit in place when bent around the frames. Now at each frame on the boat pick off the width of the sheer strake that was previously laid out with a batten and marked on the frames. At the corresponding frame marks on the board lay out the plank widths and run a batten through them to draw a line for the lower edge of the plank. If the boat is decked, allow a little extra on the upper edge for the crown of the deck, then saw out the plank. Plane the upper edge for the crown and the lower edge square, then clamp the plank in place and unless there is something obviously wrong it can be used as a pattern for the same plank on the other side of the boat. After that it can be fastened in place. Bear in mind that the butt end of a plank has to have outgauge for caulking, same as a plank edge. Incidentally, always use a block of wood between the plank and a clamp so scarring from pressure will not occur.

118

Garboard Strake

The garboard plank is very likely to be the most troublesome, but once it is fitted in place the remainder will seem all the easier. This plank is in a class by itself in regard to shape due to the contour of the rabbet line. In order to have a nice fair upper edge on the garboard plank from which to start the tapering of the remaining planks, the garboard might be wider at the forward end than at amidships. This is not unusual and is because the plank is twisted into place at the forward end, and if it were to be tapered narrower forward than amidships the upper edge might dip down. This is the general rule, although it depends entirely on the hull form.

To get out the garboard a spiling is taken for the lower edge by the method described above, with the exception that the spiling batten should be cut so that it is close to being an actual pattern for the plank. This is especially true at the stem, where the end of the garboard is well rounded at the place it fits in the rabbet. The spiling marks must be close together where the curve is pronounced and are made square out from the rabbet. When transferring the spiling to the board for the plank, draw an arc with the compass (Figure 11-3C) instead of just a point, and when using a batten to draw the edge of the plank run the batten so it is tangent to the arcs.

Lay out the width of the garboard at the amidships frame and, like you did for the bottom edge of the sheer strake, run a batten on the frames for the top edge of the garboard. The width of the garboard and the two broad strakes at the ends should be such that any excessive curvature is removed, then the remainder of the strakes will be fairly straight when they are flat before being bent. This straightening, however, should not be overdone or there will be too much upward curve at the forward ends of the remaining strakes. As stated before, the garboard will probably be as wide, or a little wider forward as it is amidships, but the test is to sight the batten you have placed and see that the line it makes is fair and pleasing in appearance from wherever you look at it. In all likelihood the width at the transom will be a little less than amidships. As before, mark the edge on all the frames, remove the batten, and take a spiling of the edge. Saw out the plank, plane the top edge square, and plane the edge against the rabbet so it is open a little on the outside for the seam to receive caulking.

The forward end of the garboard will probably need steaming to get it in place, and it is possible that this will be the only plank on the boat that will. While the plank is steaming, assemble at hand plenty of clamps, wedges and material for shores to the floor. When ready, fit the forward end of the plank in the rabbet first and clamp it, then as quickly as possible bend the plank in place while it is still limber. Get the plank flat against the frames with shores to the floor. Cut a shore a little short, toe nail it to the floor, and drive a wedge between the top of the shore and the plank. If the bottom edge does not lie properly in the rabbet, clamp a piece of oak to the frames above the plank and drive wedges against a block on the plank edge to move it sideways. Never drive a wedge directly against the edge of a plank or the edge will be crushed. Fasten the plank in place if the fit is satisfactory. If it is not, there is nothing to do except to let it cool, when it can be removed and the fit corrected, and if you are lucky it will not need more steaming for replacement. Don't be discouraged, for in a normal boat the garboard is the most difficult to fit, and it may even cost you some wasted material before you produce one that is right.

Broad Strakes

The next plank to go on is the one next to the garboard, called the first broad, and a spiling is taken of the edge against the garboard. A batten is run for the upper edge as described, the width amidships being taken from the batten with the predetermined plank widths at the amidships frame. Now you have got to decide how to taper it so the remaining planks will be straight and easy to make. Start by tapering it in proportion to the space between the garboard plank and the sheer strake. This is done by counting the number of strakes shown on your amidships planking layout batten, and at every third or so frame, called the spiling frames, divide the distance between the top edge of the garboard and the bottom edge of the sheer strake by the planned number of strakes. At this time mark on the frames only the width of the first broad. Now run the batten and look at the line from all directions. It may be it will want to be wider at the forward end in order to straighten it or to give a more pleasing appearance when viewed from forward. If so, make it a little wider but don't overdo it. When the line satisfies, mark the frames, remove the batten, take a spiling for the top edge, and saw and plane the plank to shape. The next two or three planks are lined out with the same system, so that when the turn of the bilge is reached the remainder of the planks to the sheer strake may all be of uniform width and taper.

Width Scale for Remaining Planks

The planks between the last of the bottom planks and the sheer strake may be lined out by dividing into equal spaces the girth to be planked at each spiling frame, but the work is easier with what is called a planking scale made with a batten about ⅛ by 1 inch. Mark on the batten the greatest space still

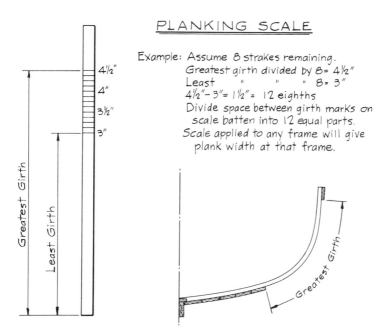

PLANKING SCALE

Example: Assume 8 strakes remaining.
Greatest girth divided by 8 = 4½"
Least   "   "   " 8 = 3"
4½" – 3" = 1½" = 12 eighths
Divide space between girth marks on
  scale batten into 12 equal parts.
Scale applied to any frame will give
  plank width at that frame.

FIGURE 11-4.

to be planked, which will be near the middle of the boat, and also the shortest space wherever it may be. Measure the greatest girth with a rule, and on something besides the batten arithmetically divide the distance by the number of strakes still to go on. Let us say the answer is 4½ inches, therefore call the corresponding mark on the scale 4½ inches. Do the same with the shortest girth and, assuming the answer is 3 inches, call the corresponding mark on the scale 3 inches. Now find the number of eighths of an inch there are between the two girth marks on the scale, twelve in this case. Divide the space on the scale between 3 inches and 4½ inches into twelve equal spaces and label them so each one represents ⅛ inch. See Figure 11-4. You will see that the scale when bent on any frame will give the width of the strake at that frame. It only takes a few minutes' time to make a planking scale, and with it you can go along and note the plank widths on as many of the frames as you like for reference when making the remainder of the strakes. From now on it is unnecessary to run battens, but each plank must be spiled. However, if you find that the seams are not coming out as they should, it is best to run a batten to straighten things out and then redivide the remaining space once again.

The ribbands are only removed as they become an interference to making a plank. To keep the hull from becoming distorted do not put more

121

planks on one side of the boat than on the other. As you fit a plank make a mate for the opposite side, and do not forget that the planks are not truly opposite. In other words, due to hollowing, for instance, the planks on opposite sides are not exact duplicates and may be compared to a pair of shoes.

Hollowing and Rounding

Hollowing of planks, Figure 11-1B, is best done with a wooden plane having a rounded bottom. After a plank is hollowed to fit the curve of the frames, mark the finished thickness on the edges with a marking gauge and roughly round the face of the plank before fastening in position. This will save work later.

Stealer Planks

The typical auxiliary sailboat hull, with the greatest girth to be planked located at a frame well aft of amidships, requires short planks known as stealers. These generally start at the rabbet in the sternpost and end at varying positions forward of the sternpost, depending upon the number of stealers and the shape of the hull. A study of such a hull will show that these short planks are necessary to straighten the remaining planks as the turn of the bilge is reached. The photograph, Figure 11-5, of a hull built over a permanent mold, in the process of being turned over, clearly shows the shape of the stealers along the keel. (Referring to remarks in preceding chapters, the deadwood and ballast keel will be fitted to the hull in Figure 11-5 after it is right side up.) Often, to avoid plank ends that are too pointed to take a fastening, stealers are nibbed into their neighbors, Figure 11-6A. In this

FIGURE 11-5. *Note stealer planks used to straighten the remaining strakes as the turn of the bilge is reached*

122

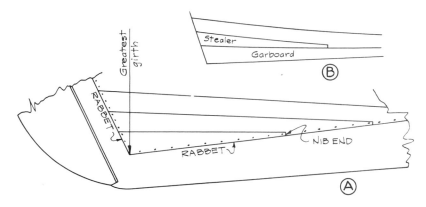

FIGURE 11-6. *Stealers are short planks necessary when greatest planking girth is well aft*

particular type of planking (Figures 11-5 and 11-6A) there is no garboard running for the length of the keel rabbet, but it still is possible to have one as illustrated in Figure 11-6B. There are numerous possible variations, and it is strongly urged that a study be made of the planking on a boat similar to the one being built for whatever pointers can be picked up before beginning the job.

Plank Fastenings

The type fastening will of course be as specified on the plans or according to your own choice. Normal planking is secured with three fastenings per plank at each frame where the width of the plank will permit, such as throughout the bottom, and two at each frame in the narrow topside strakes. The fastenings are staggered to the extent allowed by the width of the frames, and planks that cross floors have an additional fastening or two driven into the floor. The butts are fastened with five in each plank end as shown in Figure 11-2. Butts in larger size auxiliaries are frequently bolted. Drilling for fastenings and plugging are discussed in Chapter 6.

After planking, the hull is ready for preliminary smoothing, done by planing with a jack plane and using long strokes to smooth off high areas. With a shorter smooth plane you are liable to plane hollow areas in the planking. Rubbing the hull up and down with palm and finger tips will reveal high spots that are not readily seen with the eye.

Caulking Carvel Planking

Before further finishing, the plank seams are caulked to make them watertight. This is a very important step in hull building, because by caulking too

123

hard it is possible to pull the plank fastenings and force a plank away from the frames. Just the right amount of caulking adds considerable stiffness to the planking.

The entire job of correct caulking is a skilled art, and if the amateur plans to employ professional help with his boat at any stage of construction here is a good place to do so. Don't let this discourage you from tackling the job, however.

When the plank thickness is ⅝ inch or under, a strand or two of cotton wicking may be rolled into the seams with a caulking wheel or driven with a thin edged making iron. Thicker planking has regular caukling cotton in the seams, obtainable at marine supply stores in one-pound packages made up of folds of multiple strands about a foot or so long. On a clean floor unfold the bundle to the full length of the strands, then separate the strands. They break easily, so handle them with care. Now take two strands at a time and roll them in a ball. Also make a couple of balls from single strands for use in narrow seams and plank butts or for adding a piece to a double strand for use where the seam is wide. Keep the cotton clean, else you will have to pick wood chips and pieces of trash off the strands as you use them.

If the seam at any point should not be open enough to take the caulking a dumb iron is driven in the seam to spread it wider. Careful fitting of the planking will reduce the work with a dumb iron to a minimum. Start at one end of a seam and tuck an end of the cotton strand in the seam, leaving a little sticking out to drive into the seam at the end of the plank, then gather the cotton in a small loop with the caulking iron and drive it in the seam with a making iron. Normally you will use one with a blade $1/16$ inch thick at the working edge, but for wider seams you may need another iron about ⅛ inch thick. Next to the first loop drive a second, and so on down the seam. The trick is to make the size of the loop just right so the bulk of the cotton is correct for the width of the seam, and this will necessarily vary if the seams have not been made uniform. After you have driven a few feet of loops go back to the beginning and drive the cotton in the seam far enough to make room for the seam composition that is put in later. This is being done by the caulker in Figure 11-7.

The cotton should definitely not be driven all the way to the bottom of the seam. When finished being driven it should be in the middle of the seam depth, formed in a tight rope-shaped strand which should make a slight depression for itself in the plank edges. Heavier blows with the caulking mallet will be needed in hardwood planking like mahogany. So you see that good caulking calls for a combination of cotton bulk, determined not only by the thickness of the strand but also by the size of the loops, and the amount of mallet pressure to make the strand force a depression in the plank edges at the right depth. If the cotton is too lightly driven it will be forced out of the seam by the swelling of the planks when wet. Don't forget to caulk the butts. Caulking tools are shown in Figure 11-8.

Smoothing

After they are caulked the seams are painted with thickish paint, using a narrow seam brush made for the purpose. Wipe off the paint that gets on the outside of the planking while doing the seams. When the seams are good and dry the hull is again smoothed with a plane, set for a finer cut this time to get the remainder of the high spots, all of the while rubbing the palm of your hand diagonally across the planking to find the bumps and hollows. If not smoothed perfectly at this time the unfair portions will show up when paint is applied, and then the hull must be left as is or a part of the job done over. Sandpaper the hull after planing, gradually using finer grit until the

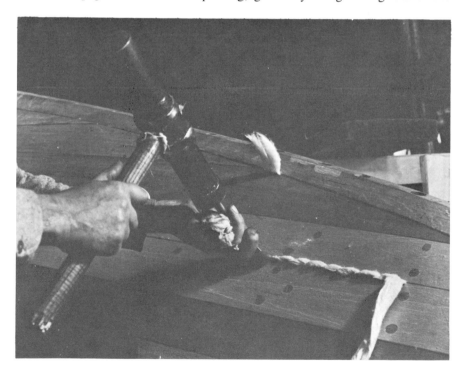

FIGURE 11-7. *Caulking is looped just enough to properly fill seam. Too much caulking can harm planking*

125

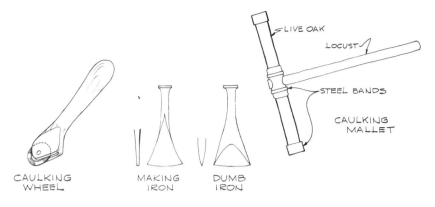

FIGURE 11-8. *Seam caulking tools. Cotton is rolled into seams with the wheel when planking is ⅝ inch thick or less*

job is as smooth as you want it. Garnet paper is better than sandpaper, more expensive but cuts faster and lasts longer. A fine finish can be obtained by diagonal scraping if you are skilled with this tool. Give the hull the first coat of paint and carefully fill the seams with hull seam composition made for this purpose.

More About Caulking

The caulking described above is the old standby method and is as good today as it ever was, but modern materials permit a different filling compound for the seam and even permit the cotton caulking to be omitted. So many old hands have sworn that the caulking of the cotton tightens the whole hull structure and, indeed, caulked boats have been so satisfactory for so long that the writer would stay with the method using cotton for that reason and also the matter of expense. These new compounds are high in cost and less of it will be needed if the seam is partly filled with cotton.

It is our understanding that absolutely clean bare wood in the seam is required for proper adhesion of the modern compounds. This is no problem with a new hull but certainly would take a lot of work to prepare the seams of an old boat. The cotton and seam sides are not painted in the old fashioned way, but some woods such as teak and Douglas fir, and perhaps yellow pine, have an oil that impairs adhesion and consequently need coating with a special primer made by the manufacturers of the polysulfide compounds. Check the makers' recommendations carefully in regard to seam priming. The polysulfide compounds are a two-part mix, the silicones are not.

Hull Painting

For preservation while the boat is being finished the hull can be given a priming coat of paint. A few remarks about materials are in order. Take our word for the fact that house paints will not do for boats. Good paint is cheap insurance, so use only marine paints to protect and beautify your hard work. Most of the marine paint firms have descriptive booklets which tell you how to do a good paint job from start to finish, and it is recommended that you stick to the rules. There are different systems, all of them good nowadays, and instructions should be followed carefully. The only suggestion we have that may not be found in a paint company booklet is to cover the entire inside of the framework and planking with two coats of a wood preservative and nothing else, except where visible in quarters. Where you do want to paint later the preservative acts as a primer.

Lapstrake Planking

Sometimes called clinker planking, this method is very different from carvel planking. In the first place, because of the stiffness of the planking it is possible to plank over the molds, the frames being bent in place when planking is complete. Secondly, inasmuch as one plank laps over the next, the planking must start at the garboard and proceed upward to the sheer strake without any change in order. The nature of the planking prevents efficient smoothing after completion, so each plank is planed before final installation, but a light final sanding may be done after planking and before painting.

The strakes are lined out and spiled the same as a carvel planked job, but the width of the laps must be taken into account when laying out the widths of the planks. Lapstrake planking is used principally for small boats where light weight is preferred, for this method of planking is very stiff due to fastening the edges of the laps, and thinner material can be used, resulting in a saving of weight. For this reason the method is utilized for boats that are hoisted out of the water like yacht tenders and lifeboats, and for high speed fishing skiffs and sport cruisers where weight is important.

The section in Figure 11-9 shows how the upper edge of each plank is beveled so the next one is tight against it for the width of the lap. The bevel varies from one end of the plank to the other due to the shape of the sections. Figure 11-9A shows how the bevel may be gauged with a rule at any frame or mold. Your plans should call for a specific width of lap, but the minimum is about ¾ inch on planking as thin as ¼ inch, and a little wider as the plank thickness is increased. It is helpful to scratch the lap width on the plank with a marking gauge or mark it with a pencil as a guide when beveling. At each mold or spiling frame the correct bevel is cut on the plank for the length of an inch or so, then the job becomes bench work to cut the bevel for the entire length of the plank, using the short cuts as guides.

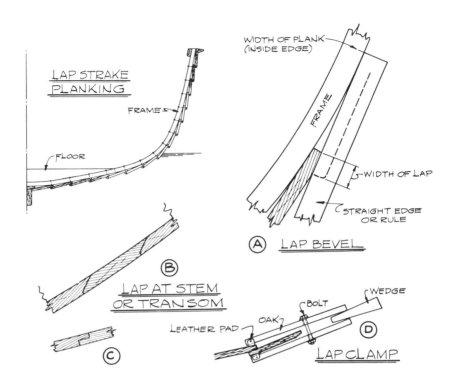

LAP STRAKE PLANKING

FRAMES

FLOOR

WIDTH OF PLANK (INSIDE EDGE)

FRAME

WIDTH OF LAP

STRAIGHT EDGE OR RULE

(A) LAP BEVEL

(B) LAP AT STEM OR TRANSOM

(C)

WEDGE

BOLT

OAK

LEATHER PAD

(D) LAP CLAMP

FIGURE 11-9. *Lapstrake planking details*

At the ends of the boat the planks must be flush where they fit in the stem rabbet or against the transom. This is done by beginning about two feet or so from the plank end and changing the bevel to a beveled rabbet (Figure 11-9B) in order to avoid a feather edge on the outside. Some builders prefer a tapered half lap joint, finishing off at the very ends of the planks with an equal lap like Figure 11-9C. This can be done quickly and neatly with a Stanley rabbet plane with the gauge set for the width of the plank lap. Naturally all beveling of laps must be carefully done or leaky seams will result, but it is surprising how rapidly this part of the work goes along when experience is gained. Always remember that while the shape of any one plank is the same on both sides of the hull the bevels are opposite. In other words, the planks are made right and left hand.

If the lapstrake boat is being planked over the molds the frame spacing is marked off on the keel and extended up on each plank as it is fitted in place. Between the frames the laps are copper riveted (Figure 6-6) as each one is made and placed in position. The frame marks are guides for bending in the frames after completion of planking, after which the planks are riveted to the frames at each lap. The lap rivets should be spaced about 1½ inch apart in ¼ inch planks, up to about 3 inches in ¾ inch planks. At the stem and transom screws are used to fasten the ends of the planks. Before fastening the plank ends in the stem rabbet the lapstrake experts generally lay a length of cotton wicking in the rabbet, bedded in thick white lead, to eliminate caulking at the rabbet. Unlike carvel planking the plank ends are fitted tightly in the rabbet without outgauge. This is not recommended for the amateur builder.

The throat depth of ordinary C clamps is not great enough to clamp the laps, and builders have devised the clamp shown in Figure 11-9D, a half dozen or so of which will be needed to hold the planks while riveting the edges. If the boat is lapstrake planked over frames in the conventional manner the planks are clamped to the frames same as smooth planking.

Batten Seam Planking

This planking system is so called because the seams are backed on the inside by battens to which the planks are fastened along the edges as shown in Figure 11-10. Although it is possible to plank round bottom boats in this manner the best application is to vee bottom hulls. One of this country's largest producers of vee bottom stock cruisers uses seam batten construction, and the method has been popular with amateurs because lining out the plank edges is fairly simple. The frames may be spaced relatively wider because the planking is stiffened by the battens.

Marine batten seam glue is applied to the battens just before fastening the planks to eliminate caulking the seams, although the seam between the garboard plank and the keel is caulked as usual. The batten seam glue is not well named because, unlike ordinary glue, it remains pliable indefinitely.

To plank a boat by this method the vee bottom hull is set up with chines and clamps fitted and fastened in place, then the seam battens are clamped to the frames, located by dividing each frame into a number of equal parts, the spacing depending on the width of the available planking material. The plank widths may be greater than with carvel planking, say an average of 6 inches amidships. The battens are sighted for appearance, and when they have been adjusted if necessary to have them look fair, the top and bottom edges are marked where they cross the frames, stem and transom frame. With the battens removed notches are cut so the battens will be flush with the inside of the planking when fitted. The battens are fastened in each notch with one or two flat head screws.

A plank is clamped so it overlaps the battens and pencil lines drawn along the edges of the battens from the inside. Thus the shape is obtained,

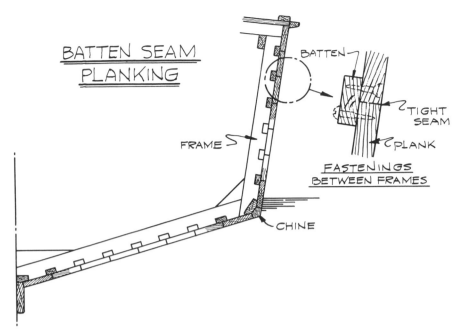

BATTEN SEAM PLANKING

BATTEN

TIGHT SEAM

FRAME

PLANK

FASTENINGS BETWEEN FRAMES

CHINE

FIGURE 11-10. *Typical section through batten seam construction*

but remember the net width of the plank is to the middle of the battens, and half the batten width must be deducted from each edge of the plank. If the frame spacing is very wide and there is no clamp against the planking at the sheer, as in the boat in Figure 11-10, the sheer line may be preserved by spiling the top edge of the sheer strake from a fairing batten sprung around the frames. Screw fasten the planking to the frames and to the battens along the edges.

Double Planking

The purpose of double planking is twofold. The method insures watertightness without periodical recaulking, and a sleek finish is relatively easy to maintain. Double planking is expensive because the planking job is really done twice, notwithstanding that each layer of planking is thinner than normal and easier to apply. The total thickness of planking is the same as single planking, but weight can be saved over a single planked mahogany job by making the inner layer of the double planking of a good lightweight wood like white or Port Orford cedar. On the other hand, some of the saving of weight is offset by an additional quantity of metal used to fasten the two layers together between the frames. The garboard plank is usually made single so that it can be replaced easily if necessary, while the sheer strake and the first broad are single thickness and rabbeted for the outer layer as shown

130

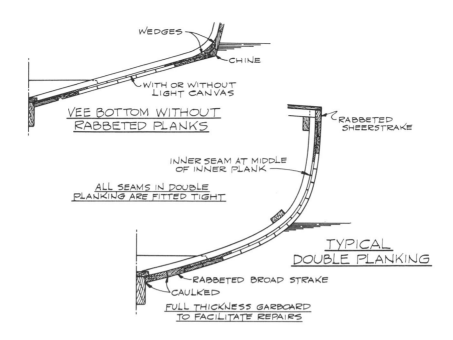

WEDGES

CHINE

WITH OR WITHOUT
LIGHT CANVAS

VEE BOTTOM WITHOUT
RABBETED PLANKS

RABBETED
SHEERSTRAKE

INNER SEAM AT MIDDLE
OF INNER PLANK

ALL SEAMS IN DOUBLE
PLANKING ARE FITTED TIGHT

TYPICAL
DOUBLE PLANKING

RABBETED BROAD STRAKE
CAULKED
FULL THICKNESS GARBOARD
TO FACILITATE REPAIRS

FIGURE 11-11. *Double planking details*

in Figure 11-11. The seams of the inner layer are arranged to come at the middle of the outer strakes.

The planking is lined out and spiled the same as a regular carvel job, for actually there is no difference except for two layers, and of course the width of the outer strakes is the primary consideration. The inner strakes are sufficiently fastened with small screws to hold them in place, and when the outer strakes are fitted the fastenings to the frames are the same as for single planking. Before each outer strake is fastened it is first coated on the inside with a double planking compound. All seams are fitted tightly together without outgauge, as no caulking is necessary. Between frames the layers of planking are fastened together from the inside with screws along the edges of the inner strakes and also along each side of the middle of the inner strakes to fasten the edges of the outer strakes. The fastenings from the inside are round headed screws with washers under the heads. The whole job is very strong because the two layers are so completely tied together. Naturally the outer layer must be thick enough to take the screws from the inside. An example of layer thickness proportion would be a ⅝ inch outer layer against ⅜ inch inner planking, making a finished total of 1 inch of wood.

Sometimes light canvas is used between the planking. This is done by stretching it over the inner layer before the outer is started, which means that the entire inner layer must be completed before starting the outer. It seems to be general practice to use canvas only on bottoms that do not have rabbeted planks as shown in Figure 11-11. Almost without exception such a bottom would be on a vee bottom power boat, and on this type boat with flat bottom surface the canvas is easy to apply. When using canvas the inner planking is painted with a coat of thinned double planking compound before stretching the cloth and the outer planks are coated on the inside as they are applied with the compound at full consistency. The paint companies make double planking compound and will gladly tell how to use it. The planking is fastened the same as on a round bottom boat.

Plywood Planking

Plywood can only be bent in one direction, necessitating hull lines specifically designed with curves consisting of portions of cylinders and cones. Just because a hull is of vee bottom form does not mean it can be planked with plywood, although it is possible to bend panels on some of the vee bottom boats which were designed before the advent of waterproof plywood. Be sure to use plans that have been made for plywood construction, or make sure before starting an older design that panel planking is possible.

Often the standard plywood panels will not be long enough for you to plank in one piece from one end of the boat to the other. If so, either special panels must be ordered or else the regular panels are butted end to end. These joints should be detailed on the plans and consist generally of a good sized butt block. The joint is not only waterproof glued but also well fastened with screws or rivets.

The plywood should be fastened in place by just enough screws to hold the panel while fitting. When the fit is satisfactory the panel is removed and then, depending on the specifications for the boat, either marine or waterproof glue is applied to chines, rabbet, frames, etc., and the plywood bent on again, using the few screws again to hold it. Working as fast as possible because of the glue, the remaining screws, of which there are a great many, are driven. Work from the middle of the panel towards the ends, drilling for screws and countersinking the heads slightly below the surface of the panel so the heads can be made invisible with marine surfacing putty.

Some builders use plywood instead of solid lumber for the inner layer of a double planked hull, even when there is considerable curvature. They apply the plywood in as large pieces as will bend on the hull and in this way save labor over the usual double planking method.

132

Molded Plywood

Only a few years ago thousands of hulls, mostly small but some up to about thirty feet in length, were produced commercially by laying up alternate layers of narrow wood veneer and glue over a male mold for a hull or cabin structure. After the final layer was in place the mold, with layup, was placed in an autoclave and subjected to heat and pressure to cure the glue in a minimum of time. The process is not suited for amateur building because there is too much work involved in mold making to turn out a single piece, but many builders made molded plywood hulls available for the amateur boatbuilder to complete. These hulls were tough and capable of taking considerable abuse. Many are in existence today and with care will last indefinitely. Some amateurs attempted and had good results with "cold molding" by laying up veneers over a framework and bonding with adhesives that cure at room temperature. Unlike planking with panels of plywood, the molded construction permits almost any desired curvature and the work of planking is very light. Molded plywood is seldom used now because of production methods made possible by fiber glass.

The first layers of veneers for molded plywood planking are laid up at about 45 degrees to the center line of the mold, the second layer at 90 degrees to the first, the third 90 degrees to the second, etc., and are secured with enough brass staples to make the strips lay flat on the mold while the glue is curing. When the hull is removed from the mold all of the staples that held the first layer are protruding on the inside and are cut off with nippers and made flush with a disc sander.

Diagonal Planking

This is a variation of molded plywood used for planking vee bottom hulls and consists of two, or three at the most, layers of planking much thicker than veneers. The greater thickness of the strakes is possible because of the shape between the keel and chine and the chine and the sheer is less than there would be with strakes extending from keel to sheer as in molded plywood planking. A solid mold is not used for diagonal planking as for molded plywood. The hull shape is formed instead by the frames of the boat—keel, chines, steer clamps and the transverse frames, and in some cases by longitudinal battens similar to seam batten construction. In fact the principle of a seam batten type hull framing is suitable for double or triple diagonal planking except that far fewer battens are required for strength. The skin formed by glued diagonal planking is remarkably strong.

133

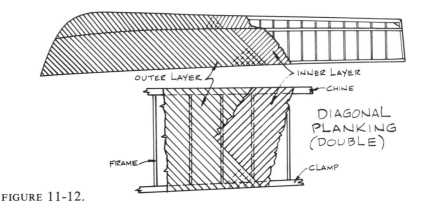

OUTER LAYER

INNER LAYER

CHINE

DIAGONAL
PLANKING
(DOUBLE)

FRAME

CLAMP

FIGURE 11-12.

The planking material is made of uniform width, 2 inches to 4 inches depending upon the size of the hull, and laid up about 45 degrees to the keel to start, then succeeding layers at 90 degrees to each other. The first layer is secured to the frames crossed and at the ends with glue and screws or nails; also the edges of the first layer of strakes are glued to each other. In short, the planks are glued to all parts of the frame and to each other.

The shape of the bottom and the topsides in the area of the bow tends to change the angle of the planks too much out of parallel with those amidships. To correct this a number of strakes are tapered in width as required to bring the planks back approximately into line. The angle is not critical, but the planks must cross a number of frames in order to form the hull shape.

The second layer is glued to the first and also edge glued and fastened in place with screws to the keel, chines, clamps and frames. Then, to provide clamping pressure between frames the intersections of the inner and outer strakes are clout nail riveted as discussed in the chapter on fastenings. The clout nails are finished off with a punch to sink the heads below the surface of the planks. After the adhesive has cured the planking is smoothed by sanding.

When layers of planking are each ⅝ inch or more thick the fastenings between the layers are best wood screws.

This type planking, illustrated in Figure 11-12, is ideal for covering with synthetic cloth and resin.

Strip Planking

Although planking a hull with narrow strips has enjoyed popularity in certain areas for many years, it has picked up since the introduction of synthetic cloth and resin covering for hulls. Nailed and glued strips are dimensionally

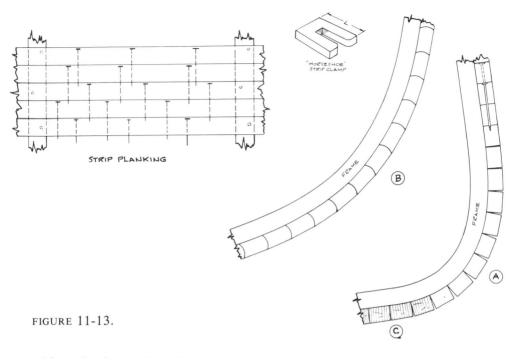

STRIP PLANKING

"HORSESHOE" STRIP CLAMP

FRAME (B)

FRAME (A)

(C)

FIGURE 11-13.

stable to the degree desirable for such covering. Strip planking is reasonably easy for the amateur, the shape of the hull dictating just how many complications will be encountered, because unless girths of the hull from keel to sheer are the same throughout the length of the hull, and normally they will not be by any means, there is usually more to completing a hull with this kind of planking than just nailing one parallel sided strip to another just like it. It is easy to understand that when the girths vary something must be done to compensate for this just as with carvel planking.

Sections through strip planking are drawn in Figure 11-13. Strips are usually no less than one half inch thick and the width varies from the same as the thickness to one and one half times the thickness. The amount of curvature regulates the amount of beveling required, Figure 11-13A. The original of this section was drawn full size by the writer to show the open seams around the turn of the bilge if the strips were not beveled. The smaller the boat the greater the relative curvature to be reckoned with. The most popular adhesive for strip planking is waterproof resorcinol glue and this is not noted for its gap filling ability and the makers call for fairly good clamping pressure for proper cure, therefore the strips should be neatly fitted. This has not been tried by the writer but strong opinions have been heard

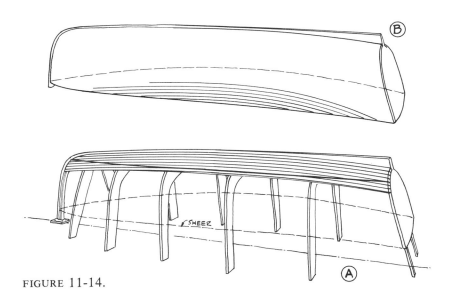

FIGURE 11-14.

that seams open on the outside, saving much beveling in the case of some hulls shapes, can be tolerated by using an epoxy adhesive thickened with Cabosil until the mix is such that it will not run out of the joints. It would be simple enough to make up a few test samples to try the technique and the strength of the joint.

Some builders run the strips through a shaper to hollow one edge and round the other to eliminate beveling as shown in Figure 11-13B. If this method is used and the hull form requires tapered strips the latter are best beveled from square edged stock.

There is one decided advantage to using square strips and this is the selection of grain. Due to the natural expansion and contraction of wood, and possibly to avoid a washboard appearance in the future, the strips are best laid with the grain as shown by Figure 11-13C.

If the strips are not long enough they must be scarphed. You can make yourself a sort of miter box for doing this or the cutting can be done on a table saw. Scarph length should be about five times strip thickness, and it is best to glue up the strips in advance of springing them in the hull.

The nails should be approximately two and one quarter times the width of the strips. Choice of material for nails is a matter of economics. If cost does not count either Monel Anchorfast or Stronghold silicon bronze nails are the first choice but when getting down to pennies it is all right to use hot dipped galvanized common wire nails because they are buried in the wood, not exposed to water. The spacing and number of nails should be just sufficient to clamp the strips tightly in place while the adhesive cures. Nail heads are set slightly below the surface of the wood with a nail set. Fred Bates has a good scheme for keeping the strips aligned while nailing with horeshoe clamps cut from three quarter inch plywood. Make a dozen or so, varying the depth L, with width of slot slightly more than the strip thickness.

Some like to drive the nails at an angle to the strip for a locking action. Every other strip should be fastened to the frame with a nail or screw.

Some of the best workmanship ever turned out planking with strips was done by Ralph Wiley in his yard on the Eastern Shore of Maryland. A few of his strip planked deep keel sailboats seen by the writer were planked with mahogany strips about 1¼ inch square. The parallel sided strips extended from the sheer and ran to well below the water line where Wiley then tapered the strakes suitably and worked the edges to bevels for perfect glue fits. The

Carvel planked 72 foot shrimp boat showing desirable narrow strakes of planking. Ring Power Corporation. Photo by Floyd Cagle

planking was of course started at the keel and advance planning done to determine where the tapering would stop and the parallel sided strips take over. In the opinion of the writer, beveled strip planking thicker than ⅞ inch is just too much of a job for the first attempt of the amateur.

Before tapering frightens unduly, let us look at a layout for strip planked hulls of simple form practiced by Fred Bates, designer-builder of Damariscotta, Maine, that eliminates tapering. Referring to A in Figure 11-14, planking strips are laid starting at the keel and temporarily held in place, not permanently fastened. Then a distance equal to a number of strip widths is laid off from the sheer at each frame or mold, a line drawn on the strips by springing a batten through the points. The strips are carefully marked for exact location, then removed and cut to the line, and permanently replaced with glue and fastenings. The remainder of the hull is planked with parallel sided strips to the sheer.

A number of Phil Rhodes' sailboats were built by a Great Lakes yard using all parallel sided strips, no tapered strips, all the way from keel to sheer, letting the strips run out as shown in B of Figure 11-14.

Still another version of strip planking seen by the writer was a hull on which the strips were laid on diagonally. Looking down into the hull from above the appearance was herringbone. This might be termed single diagonal strip planking.

Chapter 12

DECK FRAMING

HE DECKING of a boat is laid on beams which not only function as supports for the deck but also hold the sides of the hull together. This is important in all boats designed to be decked and especially so in sailboats. There are many small types of both power and sailboats that are not decked for one reason or another, and these hulls must be designed strong enough to do without the deck structure. In many such hulls the seats or thwarts do double duty as hull stiffening.

Clamps and Shelves

The deck beams must be of good size and strongly connnected to the hull if they are to contribute proper strength. They are fastened at their ends to the clamp in small boats and to the frame heads as well (Figure 12-1A and B). As hulls increase in size an additional stiffening member called a shelf, or deck shelf, is fitted on each side of the boat. These shelves are generally of the same material as the clamps and their position against the clamps on the flat provides a greater landing for the beam ends. When shelves are used, the ends of the beams are fastened through them instead of the clamps. In small craft screws are used as fastenings, but as size is increased and the parts permit through bolts they are always used instead of screws. Bolts have an extra advantage of being able to be tightened if necessary, whereas screws through beams are not accessible once the boat is decked. Shelves are bolted to the clamps between frames to lessen the concentration of fastenings in the vicinity of the deck beams (Figure 12-1B), and are sprung in place on edge in single lengths when possible or in several pieces joined by scarphs, with the joints located elsewhere rather than amidship. The inner edges of the shelves may be left square but the outer edges are planed to fit snugly against the clamps. To have the deck beams bear on their entire width the shelves must be fitted with a pitch to correspond to the camber of the deck beams. The best way to get the edge bevel is temporarily to set a few deck beams

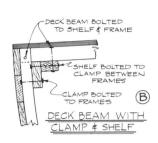

DECK BEAM BOLTED
TO SHELF & FRAME

SHELF BOLTED TO
CLAMP BETWEEN
FRAMES

CLAMP BOLTED
TO FRAMES   Ⓑ

DECK BEAM WITH
CLAMP & SHELF

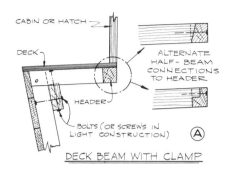

CABIN OR HATCH

DECK

ALTERNATE
HALF- BEAM
CONNECTIONS
TO HEADER

HEADER

BOLTS (OR SCREWS IN
LIGHT CONSTRUCTION)   Ⓐ

DECK BEAM WITH CLAMP

FIGURE 12-1.

in place so the bevels may be measured every few feet, or at least at every station, and correctly planed on the edges of the shelves. See Figure 12-2A.

When the clamps and shelves are bolted together they act as a single member shaped like an angle, and to get every bit of benefit out of them the two sides should be fastened together at the ends of the boat. Just abaft the stem this is done with what is called a breast hook fitted between the shelves and bolted to them. The hook is often sawn out of a natural wood crook, either oak or hackmatack. Just as good as a connection is a piece of oak laid on top of the shelves and through bolted (Figure 12-3A). A piece of plywood or metal plate used the same way is also suitable.

At the stern the connection to a flat transom takes the form of quarter knees (Figure 12-3). These are sawn from crooks and located on top of the shelves (or against the clamps where no shelves are used) and against the transom cross framing at the under side of the deck and bolted in place. With a curved transom the connection is more difficult, as in this case the knees are not only cut to the proper camber but are curved to fit the transom as well. Unless you are a trick and fancy mold loftsman who can work out the intersection of the deck and the transom it will be well to make these pieces by the cut and try method. The shape of them in plan view is easy because it will be shown on the deck framing plan for your boat and the width will be sufficient to take the fastenings for the ends of the decking. It is best to install the deck beams for five or six feet ahead of the transom, or even more if convenient, and at intervals of every three or four inches each side of the center line clamp a batten on top of the beams with the aft end of the batten just touching the transom on the inside. Make a mark on the transom at the under side of the batten each time it is set and when all the points are connected a line through them will be the under side of the decking as well as the top edge of the quarter knees, which is what you are most interested

140

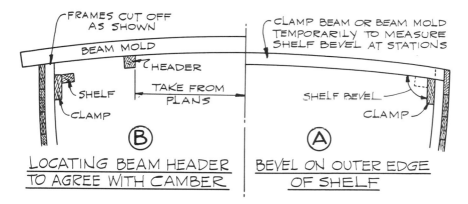

B LOCATING BEAM HEADER TO AGREE WITH CAMBER

A BEVEL ON OUTER EDGE OF SHELF

FIGURE 12-2.

in at this time. The battens are also used to measure the bevel needed to shape the top and aft edges of the knees. These pieces are really quite a job for an amateur, shaped as they are in every direction.

Deck Beams

The deck beams are made of oak or ash where maximum strength and durability are desired, and of spruce where light weight is a consideration. There is a beam at each frame, and the edges are crowned or cambered across the boat for strength and so the deck will quickly shed the weight of water which comes aboard at times. Where the camber is not unusually excessive the beams are sawn to shape, a method especially good when boards with curved grain are obtainable. When there is heavy camber, such as is often found in cabin tops, the beams are either steamed and bent to shape or a combination of bending over-width stock to approximate form and then sawing exactly to shape is undertaken. Another method which has much merit because of the resulting strength is to laminate the beams of three or more pieces bent over a form and glued with one of the waterproof adhesives. Beam construction is shown in the sketches, Figure 12-4A. Most of the beams will have the same thickness or siding, but at hatches, masts and ends of cabin trunks there will be heavier beams about three-quarters again as thick as the regular beams. See Figure 12-3.

Although it is customary to show the beams and frames on the plans as indicated in the deck framing (Figure 12-3), the enlarged sketch (Figure 12-3E) shows how the beam ends are beveled to fit against the frame heads. The frames are twisted because they are flat against the planking which curves toward the center line at the ends of the boat. Due to a combination

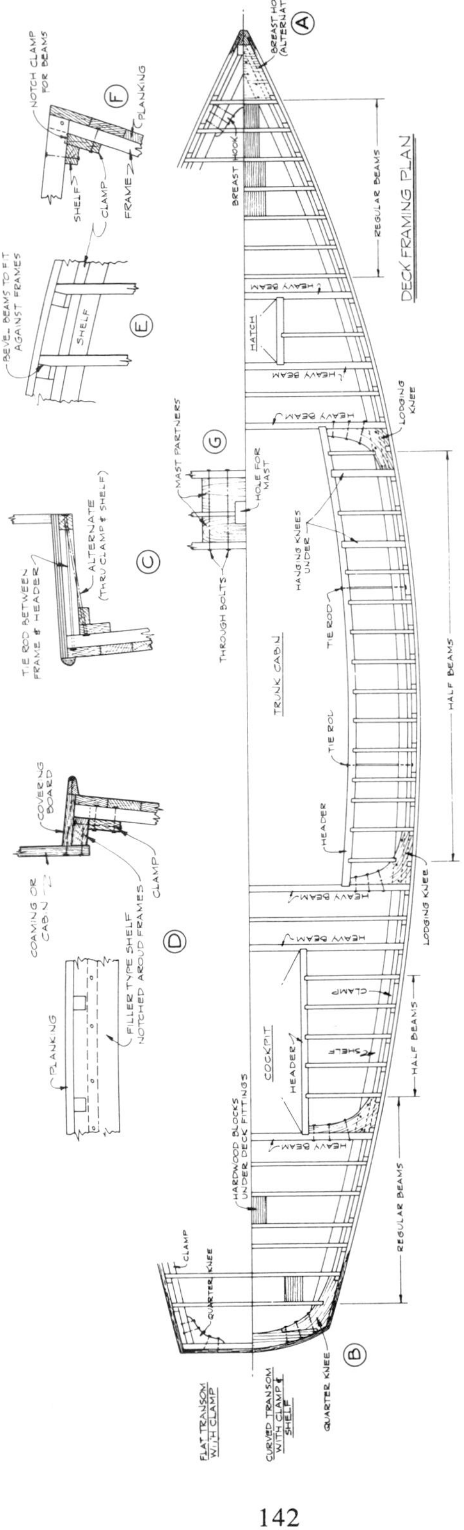
DECK FRAMING PLAN
BREAST HOOK (ALTERNATE)
A
BREAST HOOK
REGULAR BEAMS
HEAVY BEAM
HATCH
HEAVY BEAM
HEAVY BEAM
LODGING KNEE
HALF BEAMS
HANGING KNEES UNDER
TIE ROD
TIE ROD
HEADER
TRUNK CABIN
LODGING KNEE
HEAVY BEAM
HEAVY BEAM
CLAMP
HALF BEAMS
SHELF
COCKPIT
HEADER
HEAVY BEAM
REGULAR BEAMS
HARDWOOD BLOCKS UNDER DECK FITTINGS
CLAMP
QUARTER KNEE
QUARTER KNEE
B
FLAT TRANSOM WITH CLAMP
CURVED TRANSOM WITH CLAMP & SHELF
NOTCH CLAMP FOR BEAMS
SHELF
CLAMP
FRAME
PLANKING
F
BEVEL BEAMS TO FIT AGAINST FRAMES
SHELF
E
MAST PARTNERS
HOLE FOR MAST
THROUGH BOLTS
G
TIE ROD BETWEEN FRAME & HEADER
ALTERNATE (THRU CLAMP & SHELF)
C
COVERING BOARD
COAMING OR CABIN
CLAMP
D
PLANKING
FILLER TYPE SHELF NOTCHED AROUND FRAMES

FIGURE 12-3.

of deck camber and flare of the hull sections the inboard corner of the clamp must be cut away so the beams will land on a flat surface instead of a point. This is sketched in the section, Figure 12-3F.

Deck Beam Camber

The desired camber of the beams will be as given on the plans or in the specifications and is stated in so many inches in a given length, which for practical purposes should be the length of the longest beam. To make a pattern for the beams, or beam mold as it is called, the procedure in Figure 12-4B is followed, or the camber may be laid out easily with a mechanical method as shown in Figure 12-4C. The way shown in Figure 12-4B is self explanatory and is suitable when only one camber curve is needed, but C is faster and very useful should you run into a curvacious cabin top where each beam must be laid out individually with different camber. Three nails are driven in the board, one at each end of the beam length and one at the top of the beam at the center line of the boat. Then two straight edged battens, each longer than the required beam by at least two feet, are placed snugly against the nails as shown and tacked together rigidly enough to hold the angle between the battens. The middle nail is removed and a pencil held in place of it at the intersection of the battens. Draw the camber curve by sliding the batten assembly from the center line to one end of the beam and then to the other, always holding the battens in contact with the nails at the ends.

Half Beams and Headers

At the sides of openings in the deck the beams are short (Figure 12-3) and are termed half beams. At the ends of the opening there are the strong beams before mentioned and at the edges are fore and aft headers into which the half beams are notched and fastened as shown in the sections in Figure 12-1A. The old timers always dovetailed the half beams, and although this practice is still followed today the connection is more often made the easier way as shown in the sketches. The headers must be elevated to coincide with the camber of the beams, and the procedure is to make a couple of beam molds, clamp them in the space between the strong beams, then pull the header up to the mold, all the while springing the header to its planned dimensions from the center line of the boat. See section, Figure 12-2B.

In power boats and small sailboats with very narrow side decks the normal half beams are sometimes replaced by a shelf fitted on top of the clamp. The shelf in this case is simply a filler piece as thick as the deck beams, notched around the frame heads, on which is laid the decking or a covering board. This kind of shelf extends only for the length of the narrow side deck, the usual clamp being fitted from bow to stern. See Figure 12-3D.

Deck Tie Rods and Lodging Knees

When the decking consists of planks rather than large pieces of plywood the deck framing is stiffened with tie rods installed at intervals between frame heads or clamps and the headers (Figure 12-3C). These fastenings also take some of the load off the connections between header and half beams. As additional stiffening there may be "lodging" knees in the deck frame to provide strength at ends of large openings in the deck or at masts. These knees are sawn from hackmatack or oak crooks and are planed on top to conform with the deck camber. They are bolted or riveted to the beams and shelf or clamp. See Figure 12-3.

Deck Blocking

Wherever there are fittings on deck such as cleats and tackle blocks there are blocks fitted between the beams to take through fastenings. The blocks provide more wood for the fastenings to bear against and distribute the load to the beams in the case of a pull in line with the deck, such as that on a mooring cleat, and they distribute the load over a greater area of decking when the pull is upward. The blocks can be of oak, mahogany or plywood, planed on top to conform to the deck camber and sawn to a tight fit between beams. Whenever possible the blocks are best if through fastened to the beams with long bolts. Blocks are shown in the deck framing, Figure 12-3.

Mast Partners

The deck framing plan in Figure 12-3 is for a sloop with the mast stepped through the cabin trunk, the top of which will have large blocks called mast partners fitted between beams. These blocks are always as thick as the depth of the deck beams between which they are fitted, and they are always made of hardwood and through bolted. The supplementary sketch, Figure 12-3G, is typical of mast partners whether located in the trunk top or the main deck.

All comparatively large deck frame surfaces such as blocking or lodging knees are coated with thick white lead or other bedding as the decking is laid to keep out water should there be a leak in the vicinity.

Hanging Knees

Forces on the side of the boat at sea and from the mast in sailboats have a tendency to collapse the hull, similar to a man standing on a packing box

144

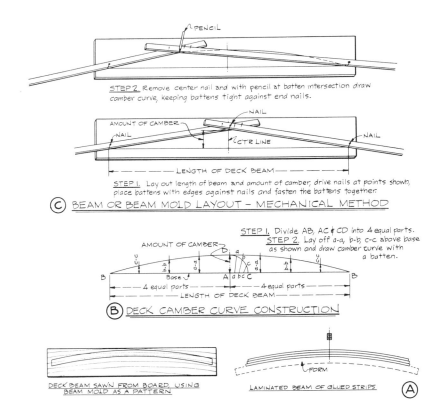

STEP 2. Remove center nail and with pencil at batten intersection draw camber curve, keeping battens tight against end nails.

AMOUNT OF CAMBER
NAIL
NAIL
NAIL
C'T'R LINE

LENGTH OF DECK BEAM

STEP 1. Lay out length of beam and amount of camber, drive nails at points shown, place battens with edges against nails and fasten the battens together.

Ⓒ BEAM OR BEAM MOLD LAYOUT – MECHANICAL METHOD

STEP 1. Divide AB, AC & CD into 4 equal parts.
STEP 2. Lay off a-a, b-b, c-c above base as shown and draw camber curve with a batten.

AMOUNT OF CAMBER

B   Base   A a bc C   B
4 equal parts   4 equal parts
LENGTH OF DECK BEAM

Ⓑ DECK CAMBER CURVE CONSTRUCTION

DECK BEAM SAWN FROM BOARD, USING BEAM MOLD AS A PATTERN

FORM

LAMINATED BEAM OF GLUED STRIPS   Ⓐ

FIGURE 12-4.

from which the ends have been removed. These forces try to hinge the hull structure at the deck corner and are only one of the reasons why properly sized and located fastenings are important if long hull life is to be expected. Brackets called hanging knees are fitted for strengthening in the sideways direction. Like lodging knees they are made of natural crook oak or hackmatack and are through fastened insofar as possible. Metal in the form of flanged plates, plates and angles or castings is being used for knees to a great extent and has the advantage of not splitting with age as wood is liable to do. Hanging knees are generally used in pairs at the masts and singly at the ends and midlength of long deck openings. Figure 12-5 shows typical wooden hanging knees at the mast of a sloop with the mast stepped through the cabin trunk.

145

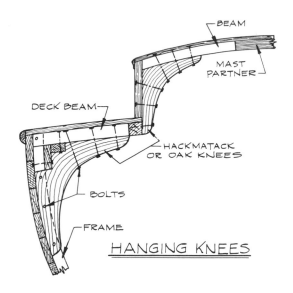

BEAM

MAST PARTNER

DECK BEAM

HACKMATACK OR OAK KNEES

BOLTS

FRAME

HANGING KNEES

FIGURE 12-5.

Modern Construction

The foregoing description of parts such as quarter knees, lodging knees and hanging knees is for old fashioned construction of a sound type as practiced in many areas of the world today when building boats with decks laid of caulked strips that do not provide much horizontal strength when compared to the plate steel deck of a large ship. It should be realized however that modern materials for small craft such as marine plywood for decks provide enormous stiffening due to the nature of the material, and when this is used properly there is no need for parts like lodging knees. Likewise, marine plywood bulkheads properly located can eliminate the need for hanging knees.

In any case, be guided by the plans for your boat. The designer should provide details of the structure in way of masts when panel material is used to take advantage of weight and labor savings.

146

Chapter 13

DECKING

I N GENERAL there are really only two basic kinds of decking for wooden boats. The first, and this can be the lightest kind, is the deck that is covered with a fabric to make it watertight. This type deck can be built up in various ways or made of marine plywood. The other type is the so-called laid deck made of narrow strips and thick enough to be caulked like planking for watertightness. Depending upon the viewpoint, each has an advantage, either economic or esthetic, and the two types can be combined. Regardless of what kind of deck your boat is to have, remember that it serves the double purpose of providing strength and watertightness. Both contribute to safety, the latter to comfort and rot prevention as well.

Tongue and Groove Deck

Tongue and groove boards make a cheap deck because the width of the material, anywhere from four to six inches, permits the deck to be quickly built with the boards parallel to the center line of the boat as in Figure 13-1A. Very often these decks are made of non-durable material, unseasoned in the first place, and quick to rot if the deck covering leaks. The straight run deck is not as strong as other types and tongue and groove has the disadvantage of a tendency for the thin upper edge of the groove to warp between where it is fastened (Figure 13-1B). The only proper covering for a tongue and groove deck of wide boards that will come and go easily with the moisture in the air is the old fashioned canvas duck. The groove warping shows through the canvas as ridges and the canvas life is shortened by wearing along the ridges.

Unless the boards are laid in single lengths there must be joints in the decking, and these should be scattered as much as possible. For strength and to prevent curling the butt ends must be well fastened, and it is not practical to make such a butt on a deck beam. Instead the ends are fastened to blocks between the deck beams similar to planking butt blocks.

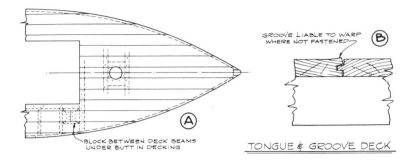

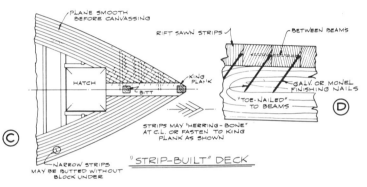

FIGURE 13-1.

Most tongue and groove decks are fastened with galvanized common nails, and these have a way of working upward with age and help to poke holes in the canvas to make it leak. Galvanized wood screws are cheap and much better but cost more to drive. Better still are bronze threaded nails.

A tongue and groove deck really does not have much to recommend it except low cost, and in time this is doubtful.

Strip Built Deck

The strip built type of decking shown in Figure 13-1C is strong, rather quickly laid, and suitable when the deck is one-half inch thick or better. The strakes are usually square, or perhaps just a little wider than their thickness, and for maximum rigidity they are sprung with the curve of the deck edge. It is best to cut any laid decking from rift sawn boards and lay it with the edge grain up, for this way there will be a minimum of shrinking and swelling across the width of the deck (see Figure 4-3). Galvanized finishing nails

148

are used for fastening and are satisfactory because they are hidden and not exposed to sea water. The fastidious, of course, can substitute nonferrous Monel or bronze nails at many times the cost and eliminate all misgivings.

The strakes are fastened to each other between the beams and toe nailed to the beams as shown in the section, Figure 13-1D. It is good practice to set the nails slightly below the surface of the wood. Around the edge of the deck the outermost strip is fastened to the edge of the sheer strake of planking. The deck is planed off smooth when finished.

If a strip built deck is built with glued seams like a strip planked hull (Chapter 11) it will be even stronger when constructed properly with well fitted seams, and a covering of canvas or other fabric can be omitted if desired. The deck can be painted instead.

Plywood Deck

A main deck or cabin top of marine plywood is strong, light and quickly laid. The arrangement of the pieces of plywood must be planned with care for maximum strength of the deck and for minimum waste of material, taking into consideration openings in the deck for hatches, cockpit and cabin, together with the size of the panels available. In the previous chapter the function in construction of lodging knees under the deck at openings and at masts to minimize horizontal racking was mentioned. Following the same reasoning the plywood should be cut so seams do not come at the ends of large openings in the deck as shown in Figure 13-2. The butts should overlap as shown in the sketch, and joints should be located between the beams where the panel ends can be securely screw fastened to a butt block underneath.

Joint locations are not so important if the plywood is waterproof glued to the deck beams because this adds considerably to the horizontal strength.

The deck panels should be fastened around the edges and along the deck beams with closely spaced flat head screw or annularly threaded nails. Countersink the fastening heads slightly below the surface and cover them over with a surfacing putty, non-oil base if the deck is to be covered with fabric and resin.

Fir plywood is best covered either with canvas or, better by far, fabric and resin such as is known as fiber glassing, but the fabric does not necessarily have to be glass fiber. At this writing glass is the favorite, but other cloths have been developed and undoubtedly there are more to come.

When a plywood deck is specified to be ¾ inch in thickness or more the curvature due to camber and sheer might make laying the deck in a single thickness either very difficult or even impossible. As soon as it is obvious

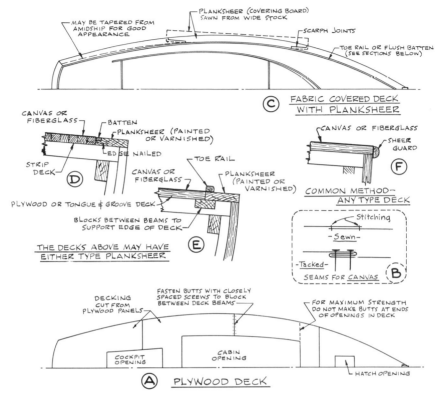

FIGURE 13-2.

that the flat panels will not conform to the surface the job must be done by using a double thickness, such as two layers of ⅜ inch or ½ inch plywood, and they should be waterproof glued together for the most strength.

Canvas Covering Decks

Canvas for covering should be bought wide enough to go over the entire deck in one piece if possible, allowing enough width to turn down over the edge of the deck. If a suitable width cannot be had, get a sailmaker or other canvas worker to sew two strips together so there will be a seam down the center line of the boat. When unable to use sewn canvas, tack it on the center line with a double fold. Seams are shown in the sketches in Figure 13-2B.

The weight of the canvas varies from eight ounce for small boats to ten and even twelve ounce for decks that are liable to get considerable wear.

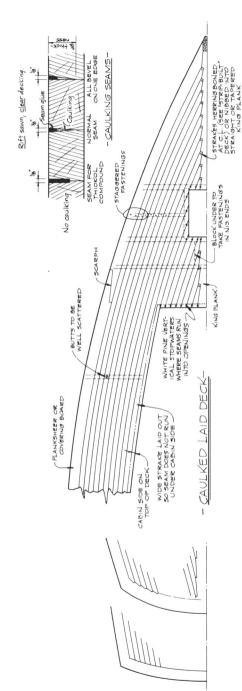

Rift sawn, clear decking

¾" thickness

SEAM FOR THIOKOL COMPOUND

NORMAL SEAM

ALL BEVEL ON ONE EDGE

- CAULKING SEAMS -

No caulking

Seam glue

Caulking

STAGGERED FASTENINGS

SCARPH

STRAKES HERRING BONED AT C.L. (SEE "STRIP-BUILT" DECK) OR NIBBED INTO STRAIGHT OR TAPERED KING PLANK

BLOCK UNDER TO TAKE FASTENINGS IN NIB ENDS

KING PLANK

WHITE PINE VERT- ICAL STOPWATERS WHERE SEAMS RUN INTO OPENINGS

BUTTS TO BE WELL SCATTERED

PLANKSHEER OR COVERING BOARD

CABIN SIDE ON TOP OF DECK

WIDE STRAKE LAID OUT SO SEAM DOES NOT RUN UNDER CABIN SIDE

- CAULKED LAID DECK -

FIGURE 13-3.

151

Although there are canvas cements on the market it is recommended that you use plain marine paint applied to the deck immediately before laying the canvas. Make sure the paint is smooth so there will be no lumps to show under the canvas. Also be sure the canvas is clean for the same reason. Select a dry day for the laying, or else the material may be shrunk by moisture and stretch later, resulting in a loose covering.

First stretch the canvas fore and aft along the center line. All stretching should be done as tight as possible and is at least a two man job. It is better accomplished by rolling the ends of the canvas around sticks so that more area can be worked on than can be handled with just your two hands. Pull the canvas down over the edges of the boat and secure it with tacks where they will be hidden by moldings. Tacks should be copper or Monel, never steel or even galvanized, and very closely spaced in order for them to hold the pressure.

After the ends, start working amidships, pulling from opposite sides of the boat and tacking as you go along until the canvas is completely fastened around the edges. Where the canvas covers openings for cabin and hatches, cut it about four inches inside of the openings, stretch tightly, and temporarily tack it to headers and beams, because it will be turned up inside deck structures later as they are added to the boat.

When the canvas has been completely fastened it is not a bad idea to apply the first coat of flat paint. Believe it or not, one of the best methods is to wet the canvas to further shrink and stretch it just before painting. Do this with a scrubbing brush and paint the surface before the canvas is dry. At any time later one or two more coats of flat paint can be added, then a final coat of deck paint. Too much paint, sometimes unknowingly applied in an effort to get a slick glossy surface, will start to crack early and will also crack the canvas.

"Fiber Glassing" Decks

Quite a few words were used in the explanation of canvas covering docks because there are quite a few areas where more modern and superior materials are not available. Nowadays the common practice for covering wood is to use cloth of fiber glass or polypropylene ("Vectra") laid with extremely weather-resistant resin such as polyester or epoxy. These are types of resins and there are many, many variations of each type. Due to the constant development of new materials, both fabrics and resins, we are not going to name names or suggest procedures, but strongly recommend that you consult with a reliable supplier of these materials in the marine field for the latest advice. There are few issues of the boating journals that do not carry advertisements of these firms that are only too glad to advise and supply you. Two things are guaranteed—that you are in for a lot of power and hand sanding, and that the finished job is well worth the effort.

Fiber glass decks are painted after being sanded smooth, a fiber glass primer being used first.

If the cabin sides and such items as hatch coamings are to be finished bright the decks should be covered before the installation of the deck joiner-work; otherwise, when everything is to be painted, the most leakproof method of keeping water out below is to build the cabin, etc., and turn the fabric up against it for an inch or two and "feather" the edge of the covering by taper-ing it with the sander so it is not visible in the finished job.

The fabrics are also available in tape form, narrow strips that are great for covering joints in the exterior woodwork to be painted to strengthen them and make watertight.

Decks With Planksheer

A variation of the completely canvas covered deck can be laid with a var-nished or contrasting colored covering board around the edge of the deck as illustrated by Figure 13-2C. This piece is called a planksheer, is sawn to shape from wide boards and the segments joined with scarphs. To obtain the shape of the planksheer lay the board on the deck as shown by the dotted lines in the figure and mark the edge of the planking on the under side. Then draw a parallel line for the width unless it is tapered planksheer, in which case it is best to cut the outer edge on all the pieces needed, assemble them on the deck, and draw in the tapered width with a batten.

When the deck is sufficiently heavy the joints are edge bolted, otherwise they are screw fastened from the top to a butt block underneath the deck. In some cases where the planksheer is fairly narrow it is steamed and bent to shape on edge. The canvas is stopped at the edge of the planksheer in either of two ways. The inner edge of the planksheer can be rabbeted (Figure 13-2D) the canvas run down into the groove and tacked, and the groove filled with a tightly fitted batten of wood to match the planksheer. Another way is to employ a toe rail set at the inner edge of the planksheer as shown in Figure 13-2E. The canvas is tacked along the edge and the toe rail fastened over the canvas with plugged screws. Figure 13-2F shows the most common method of finishing the edge of a canvas covered deck with a half round mahogany or oak molding.

The outermost strake of a strip built deck is edge fastened to the plank-sheer for support, but the outer edge of a tongue and groove deck would be sprung downward if stepped on between beams where unsupported, perhaps

153

to the extent of tearing the canvas and splitting the edge of the decking. To prevent this, and also to support the ends of the deck planks where they run out at the edges, there must be blocks fitted between the deck beams.

Caulked Decks

There are two types of caulked decks. In larger yachts where weight does not make too much difference deck planking one inch thick and upward is laid. In boats of the smaller size where weight is of importance or where the appearance of an old fashioned caulked deck is desired, thinner decking is laid over a sub-deck of marine plywood.

A typical laid and caulked deck is drawn in Figure 13-3 for a sailboat and the construction also applies to powerboats. The planksheer is fitted first as described before, then the narrow strakes are sprung parallel to the edge of the planksheer. The reasons for the narrow strakes are twofold: first, so they may be sprung without too much trouble, and secondly, the narrow material will not shrink and swell much or check. The wood for a laid deck must be clear and should be in long lengths. When butted, the joints are shifted so they are quite far apart in adjacent strakes. The wood must be rift sawn so the grain can be laid on edge because flat grain will eventually lift and splinter, a condition that is both unsightly and hard on bare feet. Suitable woods are good white pine, Douglas fir, Port Orford cedar and Burma teak. The last named is the best and, like most good things, by far the most expensive. It has a natural oil that seems to make the deck everlasting, and it does not have to be varnished or painted. Scrubbing with salt water in the sun will bleach it out to a whitish color so that, together with its long life, there is no deck quite equal to teak.

Teak decks do get dirty and do not look well if neglected, but there are a number of teak cleaners on the market made for just this purpose, and when the decks are clean there is a preparation called Teak-Gard that darkens the teak but slightly and helps keep it in good condition. It is no more difficult to apply than painting with water.

The wood for the strakes of decking should be beveled for caulking as shown in the sections. The bevel may either be cut on both edges of each strake or all on one edge as indicated. The deck is caulked in the conventional manner, but a little more depth is left for seam filler than in the hull planking seams. The best type of old fashioned filler is called seam glue and is heated for application. The seams are generously filled and the excess scraped off after it is hard.

Paying, as seam filling is called, with the old type seam glue is a rough job for the amateur, so it is advised that he use a thiokol base seam filler as made by Minnesota Mining and Manufacturing Co. and several others. It is best to stick masking tape on the decking, leaving only the width of the seam exposed. The caulking is available in cartridges for use in an ordinary cheap caulking gun. The seams should be filled from the bottom up to avoid the entrapment of air, and they should be overfilled. When compound has cured the excess can be cut off easily with a really sharp chisel.

An inch and one-eighth or quarter thick deck will have strakes about and inch and three quarters wide, and this proportion is about right as the thickness of the decking becomes greater in larger boats. Your plans will specify what your architect wants. It is suggested that you use flat head screws as listed in the table, Figure 6-2. The screws will be countersunk and plugged with bungs of the same wood as the decking, and due to the plug size needed for a good screw there will be room for just one fastening at each deck beam. Note in Figure 6-2, that the screw gauge may be reduced for decking, resulting in a smaller bung at times.

It is noted in Figure 13-3 that the strakes may be herringboned at the center line like the strip built deck or nibbed into a king plank as drawn. Either way there must be blocks under the deck at the center line to take fastenings. It is not desirable to let deck seams run under cabin sides, and to avoid this the strake next to the cabin opening is made wider, as drawn in Figure 13-3. Sometimes the decking strakes are run parallel to the cabin sides instead, requiring the ends to be nibbed into the planksheer as well as the king plank. Quite a lot of fitting is needed, as the taper on some of the nib ends will be very long. Still another way of decking is to run the planks straight fore and aft, nibbing both into the planksheer and a margin plank around the cabin (unless the cabin sides are straight too), and there must be blocks under the deck for fastening the plank ends where the lengths run out at the sides. You will find that Figure 13-3 is not only common but pleasing to the eye. When planking is completed the seams are caulked and payed, then the entire surface of the deck is planed and sanded smooth.

Teak strakes laid over a sub-deck should be at least ⅝ inch thick, which is enough for counterboring and plugging the screw heads, and the seams should be machined for caulking with a thiokol type compound only. The plywood sub-deck should be at least ⅜ inch thick for stiffness.

The ultimate is to make the sub-deck watertight by fiber glassing, then if leaks develop in the teak layer it will not run into the boat or rot the plywood. As an alternate the teak can be laid in thiokol compound to act as a seal similar to the function of the fiber glass.

Chapter 14

DECK JOINERWORK

T HE AMOUNT and character of deck joinerwork will vary with the type of the boat. Open boats like day sailers will have simple cockpit coamings while the larger size yachts might have a deckhouse, cabin trunk, hatches, watertight cockpit and bulwark rail. This work should be done carefully and neatly because, regardless of how well you have built your hull, the occasional visitor will make a snap appraisal of your boat based on the appearance of the deck structures. Proper maintenance, too, is necessary, for nothing looks worse than bare and stained woodwork, peeling varnish or scarred and dirty paint. Even though it is said that a book cannot be judged by its cover, our best advice is to take a great deal of care when finishing parts that meet the eye and to keep them looking shipshape.

Finishing with Varnish

Traditionally the finest yachts have varnished deck joinerwork of teak or mahogany, even though today these may be faces of plywood rather than solid lumber. These woods are moderately hard and resistant to scarring, but either of them can be dented by abuse. Their natural appearance, though, has appeal to many, and such a finish takes work to initially produce and to maintain. These woods have open grain that must be filled for a smooth finish. Clear, natural filler is used for teak, while paste filler stains of desired color are applied to the mahoganies. The wood must be sanded to a perfectly smooth finish before filling, then the filler, thinned to brushing consistency, is spread on and allowed to dry to a dull appearance at which time the excess is wiped off across the grain with clean cotton waste or rags. This is easy after a little practice. After a day of drying the first coat of varnish can be applied, then sanded with fine sandpaper when dry. Repeat for about six coats and you will have something to be proud to show your friends. You must keep the work and workshop free of dust while varnishing.

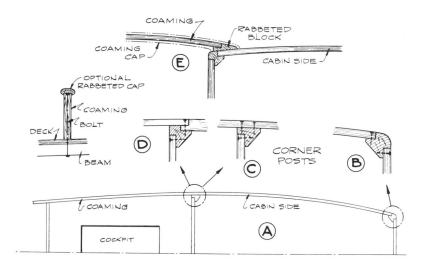

FIGURE 14-1.

Finishing with Paint

There is a word about painting in Chaper 16. We want to point out here that you may be painting wood deck joinerwork, such as Philippine mahogany, either solid or plywood, fir or Duraply plywood, or fiber glass covered wood. For the finest appearance, and indeed an all paint finish can be very attractive as well as less trouble to maintain, the wood must be just as smooth as though it were to be varnished. With a paint finish the heads of screw fastenings need not be plugged because countersinking below the surface and covering with a polyester putty will do as well. This is an advantage when working with material that is thin. Use only a good grade of marine paint. Start with an undercoater, apply glazing compound to smooth out irregularities, sand smooth, apply second undercoater, glaze again if necessary, and sand lightly and carefully before painting with first finish coat. Sand lightly again to kill the gloss, then apply second coat of finish.

Cabin Trunk and Cockpit Coaming

The plans of your boat will show you the kind of cabin and coamings, together with heights and half-breadths, type of toe or bulwark rail, size and location of hatches and other related information, so the best we can do is discuss joinerwork details in general. The largest structure you will tackle is the cabin trunk, or deckhouse depending upon the design. If the curve of the cockpit coaming on deck is a continuation of the cabin side it will be best and easiest to make them both out of one long piece as in Figure 14-1A. Long, wide mahogany boards are usually available but, if not, the width can be made up by edge joining the board with glued splines. If the cabin side is plywood longer than standard panels, these can be made up in the same way.

The shape of the bottom edge of the cabin side, whether it is to rest on the deck or overlap it, is best obtained with a template of thin wood carefully held in place at the deck opening and scribed to the shape. The top edge is taken from the mold loft floor where it was laid down from the plans, and remember to leave a little extra on the top edge so it can be planed to the camber of the trunk top.

The old timers dovetailed the corners of the trunk, almost unbelievably exacting and time consuming work that truly was a sight to behold, while general practice nowadays is to fit the ends into corner posts suitably rabbeted as shown in Figures 14-1B and C and to fasten with glue and plugged screws. When making corner posts do not finish the rabbet to net dimensions before assembly. Rather make the rabbet deeper by 1/16 inch or so than the thickness of the cabin sides and after assembly work off the radius corner to a perfect fit.

The sides of the cabin, rather than being vertical, should be sloped inboard toward the center line slightly to keep them from appearing to lean outboard. Sometimes for esthetic reasons the cabin sides are sloped inboard considerably. This can be a chore for the amateur builder but the results are often more than pleasing. It is easy to fit the cabin sides inside the deck beam headers as shown in Figure 14-2B but difficult to keep the joint watertight unless the deck is fiber glassed and the fabric turned up against the cabin side for a couple of inches. If the cabin sides are finished bright, making turned up fabric impractical, great care must be taken to fit and bed the cabin sides against the deck edge to insure watertightness. Better construction is to set the cabin sides as shown when the deck is canvas covered or fiber glassed, but with a laid and caulked deck the best way is to make a rabbeted sill piece as sketched in Figure 14-2C. This job is a real challenge, to say the least.

When trunk sides of solid lumber are specified to be as thick as 1¼ inches thick they should be fastened with bolts through the deck and beam header, with the bolts countersunk into the top edge. Drilling must be very carefully done so as not to ruin the lumber. When the cockpit coaming is thinner than the cabin side make it a separate piece and let it into the trunk at the after end as shown in Figure 14-2D. When the cabin and the coaming are not in a continuous curve the coaming is usually fastened to the cabin sides through a rabbeted block, Figure 14-2E.

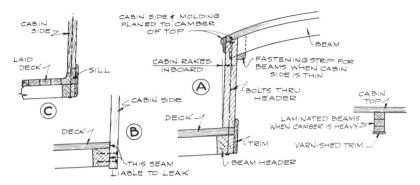

FIGURE 14-2.

Strangely enough, the writer has seen only one rather shapely cabin trunk for a sailboat that had strip built sides, nailed and glued same as planking of this type, because with the mast stepped through the trunk top the cabin has to be strong and this is one way to do it easily, discounting amateur labor. Female forms were set up against which to clamp the strips athwartship, the work went quickly and the trunk was very strong.

Sometimes the intersection of the cabin roof and sides is designed with considerable curve at the edges like Figure 14-3A or even more so. Depending upon whether the roof is single or double planked it might be impossible to give a quick bend to the plywood edges, especially in view of the curve in plan view. In this case a solution is to strip plank the edge as shown in the figure.

Toe Rail

Small sailboats are fitted with toe rails on deck (Figure 14-4) which are used as a foot hold when the boat is heeled, and from long use they have come to be looked on as decorative as well as practical. The rails are either set slightly inboard of the deck edge or at the inboard edge of the covering board, as mentioned in Chapter 13, and are fastened with plugged screws. Where joints are necessary the butting pieces are scarphed and the under edge of the rails has scuppers cut at and near the low point of the sheer, so that rainwater and spray will drain overboard. The rails may be of the same thickness throughout, but more often they are tapered on the inside face. Small toe rails may be of constant height from end to end, but frequently they taper, the heights being shown on the lines plan.

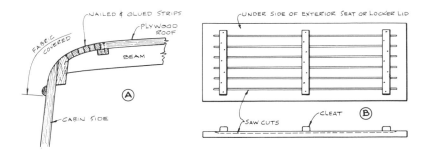

FIGURE 14-3.

Bulwark Rail

Larger boats have what is called a bulwark rail, always tapering in height and usually tapering in thickness. Details are shown in Figure 14-4B. They are secured by drift bolting about every 18 inches through the deck into the sheer strake, and are topped with a neatly shaped cap, screw fastened and plugged. The cap is sometimes omitted for economy. Joints in both rail and cap are always scarphed, and the bottom of the rail is scuppered to free water that otherwise would be trapped on deck. If no deck scuppers (pipes inside the hull to drain water from deck overboard through the hull near the waterline) are fitted, then the bottom of the rail scuppers must be at the deck to drain rainwater, but when there are deck scuppers the bottom of the cuts in the rail are placed about a half inch above the deck so that ordinary rainwater will not run through them to streak the topsides with dirt. The forward end of the rail is fitted into the stem rabbet, and the cap is shaped as shown at the stem and across the transom.

Installation of the bulwark rail will call for some ingenuity on the part of the builder. Templates should be made of thin wood, sprung in place, shaped on the bottom edge to fit to the edge of the deck, then the rail heights at the stations are laid out and a batten run to fair the top of rail. It will be a problem to hold the template in place and will vary with the type of boat. Bear in mind that the outside face of the rail conforms to the hull sections, that is, it is not installed vertically on a normal boat, and thus the bottom edge bevel constantly changes. Jigs from the cabin sides and coamings and across the fore and after decks must be devised to hold the template in place, and then the rail while fastening. It is very likely that the forward section of the rail, at least, will need steaming to get it in place, and much care must be taken to fair the rail sections into each other at the joints, so they will be smooth.

160

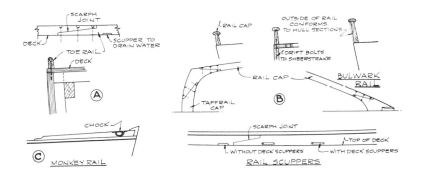

FIGURE 14-4.

Bulwarks for the larger boats can indeed try the patience of the inexperienced builder. In certain cases laminating can eliminate some of the heavy work and of course this is especially true when more than one boat is to be built, but laminating requires a jig that takes some planning and time to construct. See Figure 4-4D.

Monkey Rail

Powerboats are dressed up with a short monkey rail forward, Figure 14-4C. This is handy as a foothold when handling an anchor in a heavy sea and can be fitted with chocks for anchor and dock lines.

Sliding Hatch

A sliding hatch is necessary to give headroom over companion ladders and elsewhere. The hatch must be rugged enough to take the weight of a man sitting or standing on it. The cover that slides may be flat across, but is much better in appearance when cambered like the deck. It can be of plywood, either one or two layers, but is usually made as shown in Figure 14-5. The sliding cover may be flat across, but is better in appearance when cambered the same as the deck. Make the cover on a pair of beams sawn to the camber, using material ⅞ inch thick and about 3 inches wide, with the butting edges grooved for soft white pine splines which stiffen it as well as prevent leaks. Waterproof glue the joints and fasten the top pieces to the beams with plugged screws. The logs may be of a variety of styles as shown in Figure 14-5, some of which are easier to make than others. A common slide is shown in sketch A with brass tongues on the beam ends to slide in grooves in the logs. The edge of the cover is protected with a piece of split brass tubing, while the top of the logs are sheathed with strip and the two interlock to keep spray out of

161

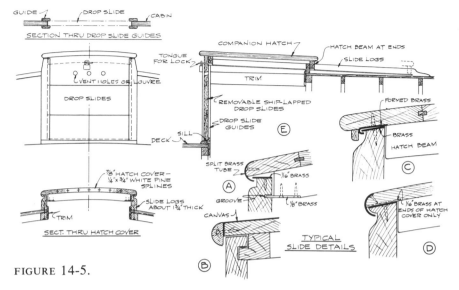

FIGURE 14-5.

the hatch opening. The arrangement in sketch B is similar in operation, having a rabbeted beam header to slide in the log groove. The top of the log may be sheathed if desired, and the molding on the edge of the cover makes it adaptable to canvas covering. The covers shown in sketches C and D do not have grooves in the logs, but ride directly on the logs instead, making it necessary to sheathe them to prevent wear of the surface. In C the sliding friction is minimized by having an angle between the brass strips, so contact is at one edge only. In D there is a piece of brass let into the cover at the ends only, and it should project slightly, so the wooden cover will not touch the log. The arrangements shown in the sketches are typical and others can be devised. The metal parts can be stainless steel, but brass is quite easy to work.

An elevation at the center line of a sliding hatch is illustrated by sketch E, Figure 14-5. The length of the logs is determined by the distance from the aftermast hatch cover beam to the apron on the cabin top at the forward end of the hatch opening. Beyond the required length the logs are finished with an ogee curve. Fasten the logs to the deck beams and headers with plugged screws. The bottom edge of the logs just forward of the apron must have scuppers cut in them to drain water trapped between the logs.

Companionway Closure

The simplest way of closing the opening in the aft end of the trunk is to fit drop boards which slide between guides as shown in Figure 14-5. A slot can

162

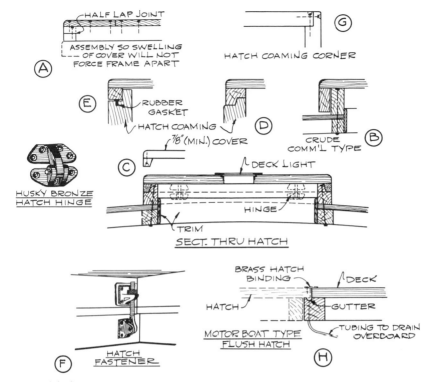

FIGURE 14-6.

be cut in the top slide to take a brass locking tongue screwed to the bottom of the hatch cover beam, or a cabinet lock may be fitted. The top slide should also have ventilation holes or louvers to circulate air through the boat when it is locked up. A shaped sill is fitted on the deck to keep water from running off the slides or main deck into the cabin. Double doors are sometimes substituted for the drop panels.

Hatches

Openings in the deck are covered with hatches made to be watertight or reasonably so. At sea, particularly, hatches that leak are an unspeakable nuisance, making for discomfort during the watch below, so every effort should be exerted to construct them so they fit well and function satisfactorily. The pieces forming the cover are preferably splined as described for the sliding companion hatch. The frame around the cover is half lapped at the corners (here, again, the old professionals used dovetails which we consider

163

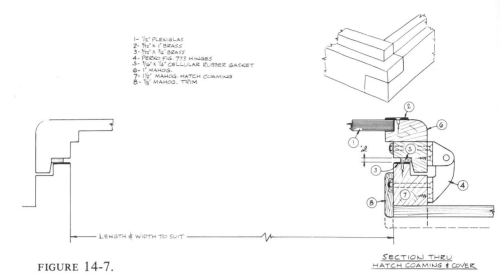

1- ½" PLEXIGLAS
2- ³/₃₂" x 1" BRASS
3- ³/₃₂" x ¼" BRASS
4- PERKO FIG. 773 HINGES
5- ⁹/₁₆" x ¼" CELLULAR RUBBER GASKET
6- 1" MAHOG.
7- 1½" MAHOG. HATCH COAMING
8- ⅛" MAHOG. TRIM

LENGTH & WIDTH TO SUIT

FIGURE 14-7.

SECTION THRU
HATCH COAMING & COVER

too difficult for the amateur), and it is very important that the detail in sketch A of Figure 14-6 be followed. If the half lap is reversed from that shown so the end screws in the top pieces are in the side frame that is parallel to the top pieces, the swelling of the top in width will force the corner joint apart. In other words, all screws across the width of the top must be in the same piece of frame. The hatch coamings vary in detail according to preference or practice, but all are either through bolted or fastened from the bottom with long husky screws. The corners of the hatch coamings are dovetailed together or rabbeted and screw fastened as shown in sketch G, Figure 14-6, and set in marine bedding compound on the deck. In fact bedding compound is used to keep out water under everything fitted on deck. Use either the time tested products of Kuhls, Dolphin, etc., or thiokol base compound. Sketch B illustrates a crude workboat type hatch not very suitable for a yacht, and although frames like C are to be seen they are too light to be any good and should be modified into something like D, which will stay together and is fairly watertight when dogged down. The type shown in sketch E has the coaming grooved for a rubber gasket, but a refinement of this is the hatch construction shown in Figure 14-7, which is the best of the lot and not too difficult to build. It is a mistake to make the parts of hatches too light. Flimsy hatches and hatch hardware just do not stand up to the abuse they must take. The hinges shown in the figure are made by a couple of the marine hardware firms and are quite satisfactory. Through bolt the hinges wherever possible. Note that the hatch in Figure 14-7 is shown with a plastic top. This is optional, but it admits a lot of light to spaces like the galley. It is a bit risky to use a hatch with a plastic top on the main deck of a sailboat where a crewman is liable to jump on the hatch with considerable force. If a light is wanted in a main deck hatch it is safer to use a round one with bronze frame shown in the section through hatch in Figure 14-6.

When the deck joinerwork is to be all painted a hatch cover of marine plywood, fiber glassed if fir, is satisfactory. Some like to hinge the hatches at both forward and after sides, which is effected by fitting two sets of hinges and replacing the individual pins with a removable rod to engage both hinges on the desired side. The covers are locked from below with cast brass hooks and eyes, or dogged down tight with a bronze fastener of the type shown in sketch F (available from marine hardware concerns) located at the corners opposite the hinges. Such fasteners are especially good where a gasket must be pulled down.

Flush Hatches

Cockpits usually have flush hatches over engines, tanks and storage spaces and often are constructed as shown in sketch H, Figure 14-6, in an effort to keep rain, spray and washdown water from running into the bilges and dripping on equipment on the way. This usual method is pretty poor because it does not take much water to overflow the shallow gutters or much dirt to clog the drain. A better method is a system of channel shaped sheet metal gutters attached to the hatch opening framing, wide enough to project under the opening, and having a good sized overboard line, say ½ inch at least.

Watertight Self-bailing Cockpit

A watertight cockpit as fitted in sailboats is simply a well sunken into the deck and provided with drains. The floor or sole of the cockpit is subject to much wear, and therefore canvas will need replacement at more frequent intervals than that on the main deck. As a result a caulked sole is often used even though the main deck is canvas covered. The sole is laid on beams which may extend to the hull sides, or it may be supported by beam headers which in turn are suspended from the main deck headers by long rods with threaded ends for nuts. See Figure 14-8A. Two types of water tables around the edges of the sole are shown, either of which may be used with a caulked sole. The cockpit ceiling may be permanently installed or fitted with hinged doors for access to storage spaces not occupied by fuel and water tanks, exhaust piping, etc.

Many prefer cockpit seats lowered below the main deck level (Figure 14-8B) for the feeling of security it gives. If the boat has a raised doghouse

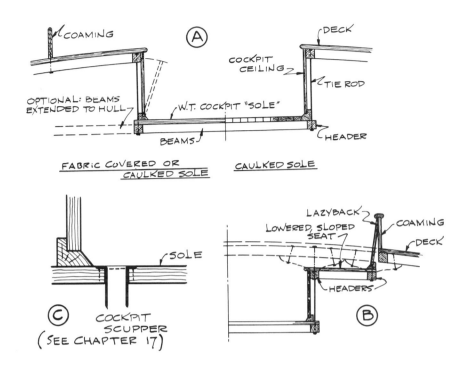

FIGURE 14-8.

the architect must plan the lowered seats with care in order not to restrict visibility of the helmsman. The seats require beams and headers as shown for support, and are most comfortable if sloped and fitted with a slanted lazy-back. Shown dotted in the sketch are blocks under the main deck beams at the ends of the cockpit to which the seat headers are bolted. Sloped seats must be scuppered with copper tubing to drain water, and may be arranged with hinged sections over storage spaces.

Seats and Locker Lids

Hinged seats and locker lids on deck are prone to warp from changes in moisture due to rain and sun. This occurs in both solid lumber and plywood. One way to minimize this is to make a series of cuts parallel to the long direction and on the under side of the piece. This is done on a table saw or with a portable hand circular saw. Cleats are fitted as shown in Figure 14-3B.

166

Sheer Guards

The hull guard at the sheer of the boat, if it is the type that is designed for one, can vary from a simple half round or rectangle for the smaller boats to a fairly heavy built up guard for the larger hulls. In the latter case it can be no small job to make and install considering the shape of the deck in plan and the changing bevel of the sections of the boat from bow to stern. The most difficult part is at the bow of a powerboat with a full deck line forward and a lot of flare, requiring a heavy guard to be laminated to the shape of the deck line and sawn to the bevel of the sections. The fastening of guards is very important, for they are there for the purpose of protecting the hull and not to come loose when called upon to do some work.

Lower guards to protect hulls at the stern where there is tumble home (hull wider below the sheer than at the sheer) take some hard knocks at times and also must be securely fastened. Depending upon the construction of the hull and deck at the sheer, the sheer guard sometimes needs blocking between the frames to take the fastenings, which preferably are through bolts for heavy duty guards.

Chapter 15

INTERIOR JOINERWORK

F ROM THE beginning of this manual it has been assumed that the builder is familiar and reasonably skilled with woodworking tools and that he has made some of the projects generally built for a house or as a hobby. With this experience the cabin joinerwork should prove to be the easiest task in the construction of the boat. The joints and finish can be as plain or as fancy as desired, commensurate with the ability of the builder.

The boat designer's drawings of sections through the interior should show details of joinerwork construction methods but, in case these are lacking or sparse, we will show some typical structural methods. In a small craft there are not too many different details to be planned, although there might seem to be a multitude of them the first time around, and even in a hull large enough to sleep four or more persons there are only a few bulkheads and doors, the rest of the interior joinerwork consisting of berth tops and fronts, lockers, drawers, galley work top and the all-important ice box. Any finished carpentry in the nature of cabinet work is enhanced by neat fitting joints and smooth finish so that time spent in fitting parts and pushing sandpaper really pays off with the satisfaction of a job well done.

Waterproof plywood makes the interior work much easier than in years past because this material saves labor by permitting parts to be made quickly cut from large sheets rather than to be fabricated from narrow boards. Bulkheads and large partitions are a good example as these can be made in a fraction of the time formerly needed to make them either panelled or of tongue and groove material, and plywood is by all means more attractive than the latter.

Assuming that plywood will be used, the finish can be any of several basic types. The first of these is a real wood finish such as plywood faced with mahogany, teak or other kinds available in waterproof panels, stained or natural, finished with multiple coats of varnish, each rubbed down with fine sandpaper between coats. Moldings for trim around locker openings, etc., must be made of solid lumber of the same species as the plywood face selected. Flats such as table tops, exposed shelves and the like are best covered with Formica or similar material to match the natural wood finish, but in the case of covered parts the plywood can be of inexpensive fir. The natural wood decor is for the perfectionist who has the time, skill and patience to make perfect fitting joints throughout.

Another choice is a completely painted finish or a combination of paint with natural wood trim such as mahogany. For a painted finish the use of faced plywood like Duraply is recommended because it will save one or more coats of paint and helps kill the grain of the wood. Even though most of the work is planned to be painted it is practical to cover the galley counter and other flats that receive hard wear with Formica.

A third choice is to cover most of the surfaces that are vertical with one of the tough, washable vinyl wall coverings applied with waterproof adhesive, and paint the parts that are not practical to cover with color to harmonize. Again the horizontal surfaces that take wear and tear should be Formica covered or painted. The trim can be painted to match or contrast, or be natural wood finish.

Still another alternative finish is to use Formica as far as practical on both horizontal and vertical surfaces, either in colors or wood grains. The reader should realize that the word Formica is a trade name for but one of a number of brands of phenolic finishing materials available. It is a little tricky to work until you get used to it but an attractive and unusually durable finish results. The panels are applied to clean plywood with so-called contact cement applied to both surfaces and allowed to set up dry to the touch, which it does rapidly, before joining them. Once the two cement coated surfaces contact each other they are stuck for good, so positioning must be carefully done. One method of preventing premature contact is to use what is known as a slip sheet, made of a piece of brown paper the same size as the Formica part to be cemented. The cement coated surfaces are allowed to set up dry to finger touch, the slip sheet is laid on the wood while the Formica is lined up perfectly, then while holding the parts aligned the slip sheet is pulled out from between the surfaces so the cemented parts will meet.

Plywood helps keep the weight of joinerwork as light as possible, for there is no sense in installing permanent useless weight in the form of furniture that is needlessly over strength. The plans for the boat should specify the thickness of the plywood but, if not, a general guide for bulkheads is ½ inch, ¾ inch in the larger hulls; dresser tops, counters and minor partitions need not be over ½ inch in any boat where weight saving is desired. Shelves in lockers and elsewhere can be ⅜ or ½ inch depending upon the area. Be guided by common sense because with glued and screwed parts high strength can be achieved with plywood.

Sometimes in sailboats the mast is stepped on deck and the thrust has to be carried to the hull. In some cases the bulkheads in the immediate vicinity of the mast are used for this purpose and thus they may be heavier than normal.

When bulkheads or partitions are larger than can be cut from one plywood panel the pieces must be joined. The simplest way is to use a butt strip of plywood, glued and screwed, but this does not look well unless it can be concealed from view. The neatest butt is made with a spline as shown in section A of Figure 15-1, using a glued plywood spline, but you must have the woodworking machinery to cut the rabbets accurately or have a mill do it for you.

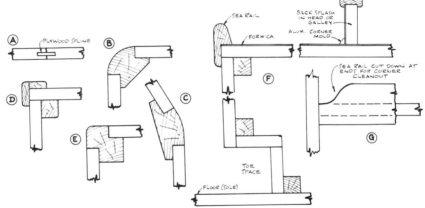

FIGURE 15-1.

Sections B through E in the figure are ways of building corners for bulkheads, while F is a vertical section through a galley or bathroom counter with a toe space at the floor. This is well worth the trouble. Also worth the work is to cut down the height of sea rails near the ends of counters and locker tops so dirt can be cleaned out at the corners as shown in G of Figure 15-1. Sea rails are used to keep things from falling off counters and should be about an inch high, or even higher when you have something in mind like retaining a portable radio.

Where berth platforms, shelves and the edges of bulkheads and partitions are against the hull the edges are curved and must be fitted by a process similar to spiling planking, and require the use of heavy cardboard or light wood for making a template. In the case of a horizontal part the template board must be held level athwartships for the most accurate results, while the template board for a bulkhead must be held normal to the center line of the hull. Similarly, a line through the points of a divider's or carpenter's compass being used for scribing or making points for a horizontal part must be normal to the center line of the boat; level when scribing the shape for a bulkhead. If this is not done the shape will not be right and unnecessary fitting will be required. Bevels so the part will fit the hull can be taken off at intervals and marked on the template board. The template board is cut to the scribed line and used as a pattern. See Figure 15-2.

Bulkheads are often located on one side or another of a frame. Fastening to the frame is simple unless the frame is not plumb vertical, which is often the case when the frames are bent rather than sawn, requiring the frame to be shimmed to true up the bulkhead. It pays to be particularly careful when framing a boat to have the bulkhead frames as true as possible. When a bulkhead is located between frames a strip similar to the frame must be installed to fasten the bulkhead to the hull. In vee bottom hulls and in some round bottom hulls a strip can be bent cold to the inside of the planking, but where the shape is too great for this you must resort to the steam box to make the wood supple, or scribe or saw a frame to shape, or make a strip with a lot of saw cuts as shown in Figure 15-3A. The spacing of cuts is determined by trial and a strip like this is preferable placed where not visible in the cabin if possible.

Drawers are best made of solid lumber, using ¾ inch for the fronts, ½ inch sides and backs rabbeted for a bottom of ¼ inch plywood or hard board such as tempered Masonite. They must have a device to prevent them opening at sea. See Figure 15-3B.

Fastenings in interior woodwork are screws for the most part. Where nails are used never economize falsely with steel nails unless they are hot dipped galvanized. In joinerwork of plywood many of the fastenings can be hidden by the trim. In varnished trim the fastenings are counterbored and plugged for screws or concealed by matching putty if the fastenings are nails set below the surface of the wood. Plugs in varnished work are set in either Weldwood glue or spar varnish.

In Figure 15-3C is shown a typical detail section through a berth.

Do not expect plated steel hardware like hinges, drawer pulls or lock sets to survive for long in a boat. Admittedly expensive, the hardware should be brass or bronze, either plain or chrome plated.

Ventilation

Ventilation of the hull is one of the most important items contributing to the long life of a wooden boat. Passage of air must be provided at all times, all

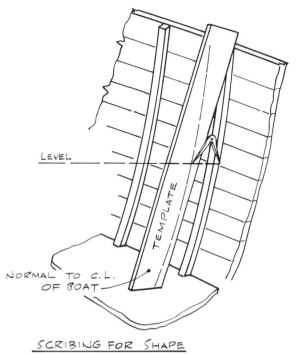

SCRIBING FOR SHAPE
OF BULKHEAD

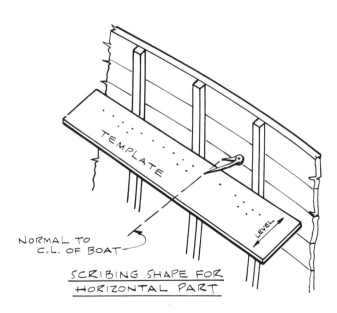

NORMAL TO
C.L. OF BOAT

SCRIBING SHAPE FOR
HORIZONTAL PART

FIGURE 15-2.

172

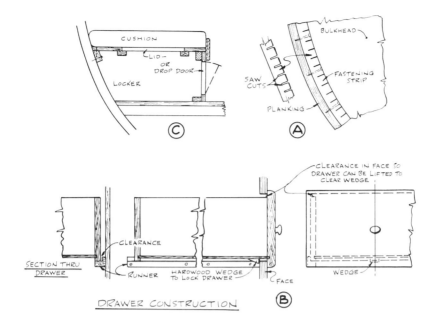

FIGURE 15-3.

the while keeping fresh water from entering the boat and becoming trapped, and it must be remembered that the boat may be kept at a mooring or an uncovered slip, unprotected by a roof for most or all of its life. Aside from getting air from the outside to the inside it must be able to flow through the boat after it gets inside. Other than patented devices made of molded plastic, etc., the most practical ventilator ever developed is the cowl ventilator that Noah may have used, but mounted on a box with a baffle against water as illustrated in Chapter 17. This will provide air from the outside, so for it to circulate there must be openings in hull ceilings (this is a hull lining against the frames, often used for esthetic reasons, rather than an overhead as in a house), and lockers. Where bulkheads are watertight each compartment must be provided with a source of air for ventilation.

Doors to lockers and cupboards should have vents for passage of air at top and bottom, not only for the preservation of the hull but also so clothes and other stowed gear will have a chance to dry out and thus reduce mildew. A few suggestions for locker door ventilation and typical door frame and stop details are shown in Figure 15-4.

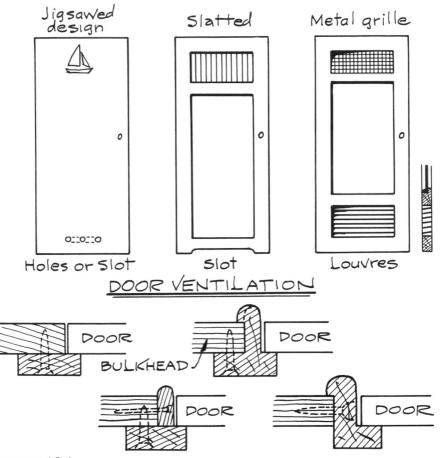

FIGURE 15-4.

Ceiling

Ceiling is a lining on the inside of the hull used either for concealing structure, for protecting stowed gear from sloshing bilge water or for strengthening the hull. In the latter case, in the larger yachts the ceiling is usually 40% of the thickness of the planking, spiled to shape when the hull form requires this, and the strakes wedged tightly together before fastening. For appearance the inner edges of the ceiling are lightly beveled so the seams show a vee on the inside, and before fastening the outside of the strakes is painted or treated with a wood preservative before fastening in place. In the

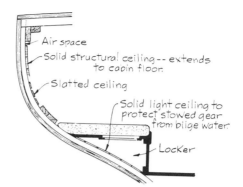

- Air space
- Solid structural ceiling -- extends to cabin floor
- Slatted ceiling
- Solid light ceiling to protect stowed gear from bilge water
- Locker

FIGURE 15-5.

finest yachts the fastenings are counterbored and plugged where visible in the quarters. This type ceiling extends upward at least from the cabin sole, and an inch or two of space is left between the topmost strake and the under side of the sheer clamp for the circulation of air.

In small boats light ceiling ¼ to ⅜ inch thick is sometimes used for the sake of appearance and may be slatted if desired. At the outboard side of a bunk the ceiling prevents discomfort from the frames pressing against your body, but one of the best reasons for ceiling in small boats is to protect stowed gear under berths and in the bottom of lockers from being wetted by sloshing bilge water when the boat is heeled down in a lump of a sea. For this purpose the ceiling seams must be tight, and thin tongue and groove can be used. The weight of small boat ceiling should be kept light, for it adds little strength and excessive thickness is useless. White cedar or pine is suitable and may be fastened with nails or screws. Ceiling is shown in Figure 15-5.

In boats where the shape of the topsides will permit forcing a sheet type ceiling into place it is sometimes made of light plywood or hardboard, the latter either plain or perforated with many small holes such as "pegboard."

Cabin Sole

Cabin sole is the proper name for the flooring or decking inside the hull. It must have hatches for ready access to the bilge, tanks, piping, valves, etc., and in small boats a removable panel on the center line is usually sufficient to serve all purposes, but make sure of this because there is nothing more frustrating than not being able to get at a seacock, for instance, and lack of access can be downright dangerous in an emergency. Plywood is an excellent material for the sole because it saves much labor and can be fitted in large pieces. The plywood can either be painted for the simplest finish or covered

175

with vinyl flooring in one piece or laid in the squares same as at home. There are aluminum and stainless steel hatch bindings for use with the vinyl coverings. Do not make the hatches too tight, for in a boat the plywood will swell just enough to make a hatch bind.

In a sailboat it is practical to have a sole with a non-skid surface by adding a compound to the final coat of paint. It is not pretty, but practical. Also non-skid is a sole of bare teak, very expensive, and it will hold grease stains, but also very practical.

In cabins where a carpet is practical the sole needs but one coat of paint. A carpet is warm on the feet on a chilly morning, but requires cleaning with a vacuum to be properly shipshape, and it should not be used near the weather hatch of a companion without a roof over it. A recent development of indoor-outdoor carpet made of synthetic fibers that will not absorb moisture has become very popular with boatmen. It is light enough to be taken up and cleaned on the dock.

The sole is the first of the interior joinerwork to go in the hull so must be carefully planned ahead for the hatch locations, and it must be adequately supported by beams and headers.

Portlights

Frequently misnamed portholes, portlights are fitted in the sides of the cabin to admit light and air. They are made of cast bronze in round, oval and rectangular shapes (Figure 15-6A) and can be found illustrated in any marine supply catalogue. The rectangular ports are also manufactured in larger sizes and are available in cast aluminum alloy to save weight. All are made watertight by means of a rubber gasket fitted in a groove in the hinged cover which is dogged down against the frame with screws and wing nuts (Figure 15-6B). At the present time the oval or rectangular port is favored over the round in cabin sides for the sake of appearance. Where the height of the cabin side permits use of the rectangular shape the greatest clear opening for overall size is gained, an important consideration in hot climates.

A small amount of rain water or spray will collect at the bottom on the outside of the portlight if the cabin has tumble home and will spill to the inside of the boat when the port is opened. Sometimes a drain can be devised by drilling a sloping hole through the spigot and the cabin side, but this invites rot if the hole through the wood is not properly sealed. To keep the water from draining on to a berth or elsewhere a wooden or sheet metal gutter of sufficient capacity can be installed under the port on the inside and sponged out when necessary.

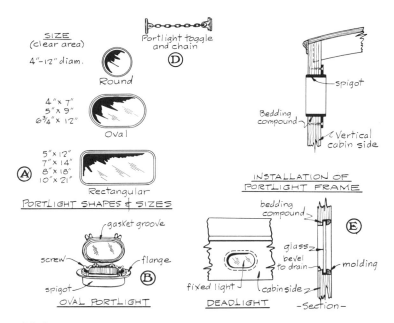

FIGURE 15-6.

It is usual to have the hinge at the top and to provide a little bronze chain and toggle (Figure 15-6D) to hold the port open. If a sloppy hole is cut in the cabin side for the spigot of the frame the workmanship can be concealed on the outside by fitting a finishing ring around the spigot, but these are not considered attractive. It is best to cut the hole to an exact fit, with room only for bedding compound. The portlights are bought with spigots for cabin sides 1½ inch or 2 inches thick, but may be cut to suit. Finishing rings as well as removable insect screens are available from portlight manufacturers.

In small boats, or where the budget is limited, fixed deadlights may be substituted for portlights, although opening ports in the forward end of the cabin are seldom omitted under any circumstances because they let in air while head to wind at anchor. Deadlights are made by cutting a rabbeted hole of the desired shape and size and fitting husky glass, at least ¼ inch thick, set in a generous amount of bedding compound, then finishing off by securing the glass with glazier's points and putty or with a molding. Although outside the scope of the usual amateur's tools, the rabbeting of the cabin sides can be neatly done with one of the high speed portable routers. Wooden molding must be sawn to shape and consequently has cross grain, making it

177

difficult to fasten without splitting. As a substitute the marine hardware people carry quarter round lead molding in various sizes which can be bent to shape and nailed or screwed in place. See Figure 15-6E.

Round brass deadlight frames are made for use in hatch tops. Small and moderate size boats have one light centered in the hatch top, while larger boats sometimes have as many as four lights in their large hatches. The deadlight frames must be set in bedding compound to prevent leaks.

If aluminum portlights are wanted to save weight, by all means try to get them with anodized finish. The additional expense is well worth it.

Thermal Insulation

A considerable number of boats are airconditioned nowadays, and when this is done it pays to insulate the overhead in the living quarters. This can be done with glass fiber insulation that is available with a film on one or both sides. This material can be cut to fit between the deck beams and stapled in place. The only way to make it look decent, though, is to install headlining on the under side of the beams.

Headlining

The covering for the under side of the deck beams, if desired, can be Formica type material, perforated Masonite or vinyl material made specifically for the purpose. The latter is by far the lightest in weight and is not too difficult to install if you look at other boats to see how it is done. Automobile upholstery shops sometimes will make an installation in boats. The Formica or Masonite headliners are a carpentry job, so the builder can tackle it. The biggest problem is installing backing blocks where seams are necessary and at the edges, so you are lucky if the cabin is small enough to avoid joints. Seams and edges are covered with wood, or metal molds made for the purpose.

Icebox

The icebox that looks so simple when used will be found to be a very time-consuming and relatively expensive job, if it is any good, before it is finished. For this reason, if any of the ready made boxes suit your boat you will be much better off buying one. There are several makes on the market of about 4.5 cu. ft. in capacity that hold 50 pounds of ice. They are all plastic except for the necessary metal and have polyurethane insulation, just about the best. They are built for under-counter installation. If space permits and the capacity is needed it would not be ridiculous to use two of them, either side by side or stacked. These boxes are also made as electric refrigerators, but

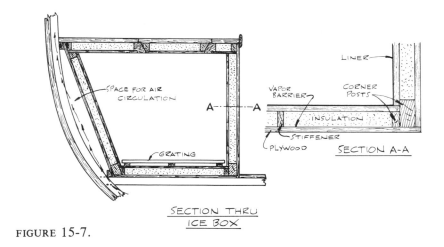

SECTION THRU
ICE BOX

FIGURE 15-7.

we are not going to get into the matter of batteries, chargers, generators and shore lines that are needed for even the smallest refrigerator because the service conditions can vary so widely.

One of the most important points about building an icebox into a wooden boat is to leave space between the hull and the box structure for the circulation of air, and to treat the hull that will be hidden with a wood preservative or paint. Space is always limited in a boat and to make the most of the area allotted to the icebox the outboard side should be shaped somewhat to the hull form. The section in Figure 15-7 is typical of the situation in many boats, and here again plywood simplifies the job. Basically the box consists of an inner and outer shell with insulation in between and a watertight liner inside.

First make the outside box, leaving the top off, and brace it to the hull, making sure not to obstruct passage of air, as noted above. Add posts in the corners and intermediate stiffeners on bottom and sides to support the inner shell and to take its fastenings. Then the inside of the outer box is coated with bitumastic paint and while still wet the box is lined with tar felt paper laid with overlapping joints. This is a vapor barrier. The insulation, and we suggest polyurethane foam available in planks, is then cut to fit between the corner posts and the stiffeners. Next make the inner plywood box. The drain must be considered, either overboard or to a sump tank if the bottom of the box is below the water line because it is an invitation to rot to drain fresh water into the bilges. The sump tank can be removable for dumping overboard or piped with a two way valve to the bilge pump. Of course the

179

drain should be at the low point of the bottom of the box.

Before making the box top the liner must be fitted. This can be galvanized steel, copper, Monel or a stainless steel sheet with soldered, watertight joints. This is not a trivial matter, so you might consider fiber glassing the inside of the box. Due to the corners this will be tedious, but it can be done and makes a good job. Finish up with gel coat for smoothness.

Whenever possible, a top opening is best for the icebox because less cold air is lost when the box is opened. Sometimes a front door is unavoidable, but the cold air will pour out quickly, and so will the contents when rolling at sea.

The finished weight of a built-in box is significant. Limit the outside of the box to ½ inch thickness, the inside to ⅜ inch. In fact, you might look into omitting the inside wooden box and fiber glassing right on the insulation.

Finish the box with light wooden gratings in the bottom, and fit adjustable partitions to separate food from ice.

Chapter 16

MISCELLANEOUS DETAILS

HERE SEEM to be optional ways, some of them good and some bad, of doing everything. Just remember that there is no compromise in the quality required to produce a seaworthy boat. The reader is again urged to take advantage of every opportunity to inspect boats of all types and to study the details of construction. Such observation, coupled with opinions of the experienced, will soon reveal the best way to handle a job.

Patterns for Castings

While all fittings for a power boat may be purchased from the stocks of marine hardware manufacturers, there are always a few items for a sailboat that are special. Here the amateur can save money, enjoy making patterns, and have a bronze foundry pour the rough castings. To name a few of the fittings that are usually special for the sailboat, there is the jibstay fitting, permanent backstay fitting, propeller aperture casting, rudder gudgeons and pintles, and sometimes light cast bronze hanging knees and floors when tanks are located under the cabin floor. The standard fittings may be homemade too, but this does not pay unless you have time to burn.

The pattern making and casting processes will be but briefly outlined, as many with wood and metal working experience will know all about them already. Any kind of wood may be used for patterns provided it is given a smooth finish, but soft pine is preferred because it is easy to work. The fitting is drawn full size on the wood, using fine lines for accuracy (pattern makers use a knife rather than a pencil), but because the molten metal will shrink during cooling the pattern is made oversize by the amount of shrinkage. The shrinkage of bronze is 3/16 inch per foot, which must be allowed, and if any amount of work is to be done a two foot shrinkage rule should be purchased to make the layout work easier. Such rules can be obtained at good hardware stores, and are made in shrinkages of ⅛ inch, 3/16 inch, etc., per foot of length. A two foot rule made for 3/16 inch shrinkage will actually measure 24⅜ inches.

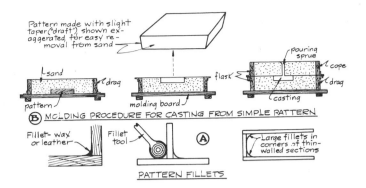

Pattern made with slight taper ("draft") shown exaggerated, for easy removal from sand

sand

drag

pattern

molding board

flask

pouring sprue

cope

drag

casting

(B) MOLDING PROCEDURE FOR CASTING FROM SIMPLE PATTERN

Fillet-wax or leather

Fillet tool

(A)

Large fillets in corners of thin-walled sections

PATTERN FILLETS

FIGURE 16-1.

Inside corners on patterns have fillets for strength in the casting and ease of molding, and large thin sections at an angle to each other have proportionately larger fillets, A in Figure 16-1. Fillets may be purchased from a pattern maker's supply house in strips made of wax which are stuck in place with a heated fillet tool as shown in the figure or made of leather and fastened in place with glue. For a small job you can get along with parrafin wax as used to seal homemade jelly. Knead the soft wax and work it into the corners, making it uniform and smooth with a fillet tool, which is simply a steel ball on a handle and made in various diameters, or with a dowel or metal rod. Give the finished pattern several rubbed coats of shellac or varnish to smooth it so it will not stick in the molding sand. Also, when the pattern is made you must consider how it will be withdrawn from the mold and give the sides of the pattern a slight taper, called draft, so it may be easily removed by the molder. This is better understood by referring to B of Figure 16-1.

For small work such as your boat fittings a small platform called a molding board will be used, and on it will be placed a box without ends to retain the sand used for the mold. The finished mold consists of two boxes one upon the other, called the cope and the drag, and together the assembly is called a flask. Dowel pins on the cope fit into sockets on the drag and keep the two in alignment. The pattern is placed in the drag, covered with sand of such a nature that when packed hard it will stick together, then the drag is turned over. With the pattern still in the mold the surface of the sand is coated with a powder so that when more sand is added the two surfaces will part, then the cope is added, filled with sand and rammed solid. The cope is lifted off and turned over and the sprue, a passage for pouring the molten metal, as well as small vent holes to carry off gases, are cut with

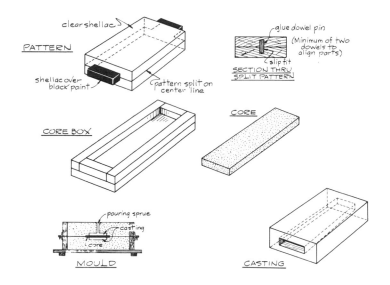

FIGURE 16-2. *Pattern, core and mold for simple hollow casting*

molder's tools. The pattern is removed from the drag, leaving a space to be filled with metal.

A flat pattern as shown in the figure is easy to remove, but a deeper one or one with a complicated shape is more difficult to take out without breaking the sand unless the pattern sides have proper draft. The casting is ready to be poured when the cope is replaced on the drag. The sprue is cut off the finished casting by the foundry.

The molding procedure for the simple block pattern in B of Figure 16-1 is easy, but a study of the mold in Figure 16-2 will show that to produce a casting shaped like the pattern in the figure will require a pattern split along the center line. Further, if the casting is to have a hollow portion, it must be kept free of molten metal and this is done with a core of sand shaped like the hollow. A simple core as shown is molded in a box with an open top, rammed full of core sand and baked to make it hard and strong to withstand pouring. Cores of irregular shape are molded in a split box with dowel pins. In the pattern the core is extended beyond the length of the casting so the imprint of the core extension in the mold will support the core, and this is shown in the figure. The core print, as it is called, is painted black so the molder will understand the core. When the casting has cooled and taken from the mold the core is easily broken out.

183

Castings

The metal for your fittings should be as specified by the designer. For fittings that are loaded like a jibstay fitting or rudder straps, the metal should be manganese bronze with a tensile strength of not less than 60,000 pounds per square inch. An alloy of somewhat less strength is suitable for parts like cleats and chocks.

Ballast Keel

The ballast keel casting for sailboats will be of either cast iron or lead, bolted through the keel or through both the keel and floors as preferred by the architect. Bolts will be as shown on the plans and are the largest diameter fastenings used in the construction of the boat. They are made from rod threaded on both ends for nuts, and on the inside of the boat are set up on heavy washers under which are grommets consisting of a few turns of cotton wicking soaked in red lead. Tobin bronze or Everdur bolts are used to hold lead keels, while good galvanized wrought iron or Monel are used when the keel is cast iron.

Because of the weight of the metals, 450 pounds per cubic foot for cast iron and 710 for lead, the size and location of the ballast must be carefully figured by the designer and just as carefully reproduced by the builder. Templates for the keel are made from the mold loft lines and, as noted under *Patterns for Castings,* the keel pattern is made with a shrinkage rule. Shrinkage of lead and iron castings is ⅛ inch per foot.

Cast Iron Keel

When the keel is iron the pattern is made of soft pine, and for a rectangular keel (Figure 16-3A) the job is quite simple. For a more shapely keel the pattern entails more work, and in either case the sections should be constantly checked for accuracy as the pattern nears the finished shape. The pattern for a shaped keel is made of layers of pine anywhere from 1 to 2 inches in thickness, screw fastened and glued together. Those familiar with model building can see that the "bread and butter" method of construction may be applied by drawing waterlines through the keel, spaced the same as the thickness of wood used, then sawing each layer roughly to shape before fastening together.

The holes for bolts through an iron keel are cored, and care must be taken to locate the cores in relation to the bolt spacing, always taking shrinkage into account. The core in the bottom of the keel is enlarged in diameter to take the nut, allowing length for cementing over the nut to close the hole in the casting. A core box is made only for the longest core needed, as the molder can break them off to proper length for the shorter ones. When required, a centerboard slot is also cored. The iron casting should be given a coat or two of red lead before it starts to rust if possible. Later on it can be finished by applying coats of trowel cement and sanding smooth.

Lead Keel

More and more frequently of late builders make a male pattern for a lead keel the same as for iron, and have a sand casting made by a foundry. This is an easy way out for the builder if a casting can be made at a low enough cost over the price of the metal, because a pattern is relatively easy compared to the mold needed into which to pour the lead when the job is done at the boat shop. A rectangular lead keel mold is quite simple (Figure 16-3B), as it may be made with planks as shown and either wood or plaster fillets when necessary to shape the corners. It must be remembered that the keel will be heavy, necessitating husky braces and shores to support the weight and a strong mold that will not break apart when pouring. The inside of the mold is given a thin coat of plaster to prevent burning easily. The plaster and the mold must be perfectly dry before starting, as the lead will spatter if poured into a wet mold and workmen may be burned. For amateur builders this really spoils the fun.

The mold for a shaped lead keel (Figure 16-3C) is quite a task and is a good reason to have the keel sand cast in a foundry. As shown in the section, forms are made to the outside of the keel, plus the thickness of mold, at stations and half stations, then they are set up rigidly (Figure 16-3D), and the mold is strip-built inside of the forms. As the strips are fitted they are edge nailed to each other and to the forms. The inside is finished to a set of templates representing the finished keel plus shrinkage and gouges, and round bottom planes used for this work. The casting will reflect the degree of smoothness of your mold.

Lead, fortunately, has a low melting point, but the least you will need in the way of equipment is a large iron melting pot, supported by bricks so a roaring wood or charcoal fire can be built under it, and several iron ladles. Better still is a melting pot with a pouring spigot or pipe leading over the mold and a metal trough to distribute the molten metal over the length of the keel. The top of the open mold must be level. A centerboard slot can be taken care of by a plank of proper thickness to act as a core. More than enough lead must be on hand to allow for discrepancies, and some of the pigs may be placed in the mold before pouring. Several hands will be needed because the pouring must be carried on to completion before the top of the

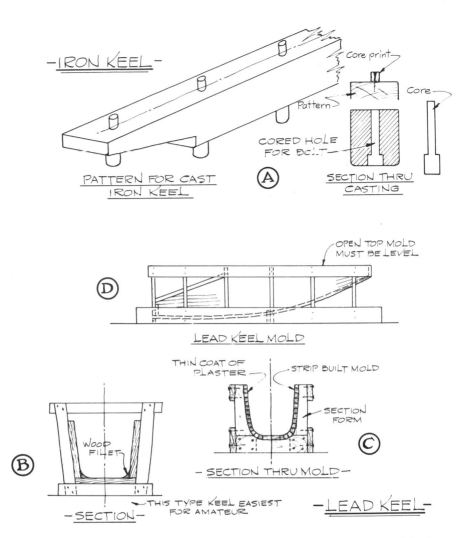

FIGURE 16-3. *An iron keel is sand cast in a foundry, while a lead keel is either sand cast from a pattern or cast in a mold at building site*

lead already in the mold starts to solidify.

Start to pour when the lead in the pot is hot, distribute it in the mold, skim the slag from the top, and puddle the molten lead to prevent the formation of air pockets. Add pigs to the pot as you pour, and they will quickly melt in the hot lead if the fire is kept blazing. Allow at least a day for the casting to cool before removing the mold. The top surface of the lead casting can be smoothed with a woodworking hand plane. The holes for the keel bolts are drilled with a barefoot wood auger or with a twist drill lengthened

186

by welding a rod to the end and preferably used in an electric drill of ample capacity. Either drill must be frequently withdrawn to clear the lead shavings and kerosense is used as a lubricant. Where necessary the outside of the keel is smoothed with coats of trowel cement, and the cement sanded. Liberally coat the keel casting with thick white or red lead where it fits against keel and deadwood.

Chainplates

Chainplates perform the function of transmitting mast loads to the hull, and must be designed equal to the task. The construction plan should show these important fittings in detail with sizes and number of fastenings. It is a simple matter to calculate the strength of the metal parts, but their fastening to the hull can be insufficient. The area of the wood in the hull against which the bolts bear must be equal to the strength of the shroud. Sometimes the chainplates are bolted through the planking and a frame, and are located either on the outside of the planking or between the planking and the frame, but it is advantageous to use a backing block between frames cut to bear against the clamp and bolt it through the block and the planking. See Figure 16-4A. A block of this type eliminates cutting frames with fastenings, somewhat weakening the hull at the point of shroud attachment.

Inside chainplates are to be preferred, as on the outside they will show unless neatly let flush into the planking, and the metal may bleed and discolor the topside paint. It is best to use nonferrous metals such as bronze or Monel for both plates and bolts, as there have been many cases of chainplates torn out under stress due to corroded parts. This may result in a broken mast at least. There are several types of small boat chainplates peculiar to the various classes, and these are shown in detail on the plans for the boats. Referring to chainplates in general, the end of the lug extending above deck should have only slightly rounded edges so as not to reduce strength unnecessarily. The hole through the deck should be filled with compound or fitted with a brass collar set in compound to stop leaks.

Sailing yachts of the more expensive type with a waterline length upward of twenty-eight feet are fitted with a rectangular bronze plate between the frames and the planking to which lugs for the shroud turnbuckles are bolted or riveted. Diagonal metal straps extending to the keel are riveted to the plate and screwed to each frame crossed and the keel. This arrangement, Figure 16-4B, distributes the rigging loads over a large area and prevents distortion of the hull, called hogging, often noticed in the sheer line of old boats. The planking rather than the frames is carefully notched for the straps as each strake is fitted.

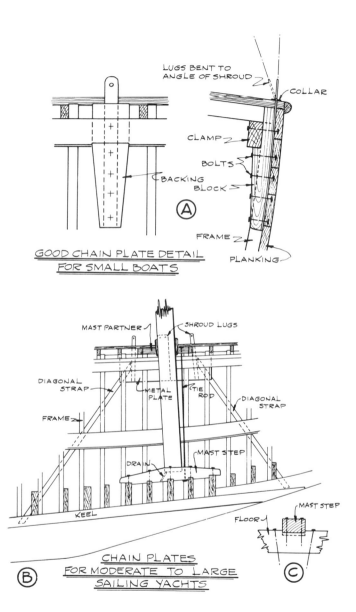

LUGS BENT TO
ANGLE OF SHROUD

COLLAR

CLAMP

BOLTS

BACKING
BLOCK

BACKING
BLOCK

FRAME

PLANKING

GOOD CHAIN PLATE DETAIL
FOR SMALL BOATS

(A)

MAST PARTNER

SHROUD LUGS

DIAGONAL
STRAP

METAL
PLATE

TIE
ROD

DIAGONAL
STRAP

FRAME

MAST STEP

DRAIN

KEEL

MAST STEP

FLOOR

CHAIN PLATES
FOR MODERATE TO LARGE
SAILING YACHTS

(B)

(C)

FIGURE 16-4.

188

Spars

Rarely does a modern sailboat have spars that are not hollow and there has been a definite trend toward aluminum alloy extrusions made for this purpose. There are several manufacturers of aluminum spars that make them up ready for installation in the boat. On the other hand wood is still extensively used for hollow spars. The simplest mast is a hollow rectangular box, relatively easy to make. Wooden spars are preferably made of mast grade clear Sitka spruce because it is a light strong wood, with clear fir and pine running rather far behind as second choice. Inasmuch as a mast is a column, the maximum sectional area is required at midlength of the longest unsupported panel, so to further save weight aloft the mast is tapered from the point of greatest cross-sectional area to the head and sometimes to the heel as well. The edges on which sails are set, the top of the boom and the aft side of the mast, are made straight so the sails will set as they should.

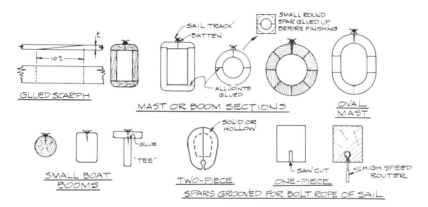

FIGURE 16-5.

When using modern waterproof glue, fastenings in spars are not required or even desirable, as they add weight up high where it is detrimental to the stability of the boat. As a matter of fact, hollow glued spars were in use years before truly waterproof glue was known, water resistant casein glue being relied upon together with coats of varnish to protect the joints from moisture. Sitka spruce, fortunately, is available in lengths to forty feet, and the majority of amateur built boats will have spars that fall below this limit. When joining is required, the individual pieces are scarphed on the flat, the length of the joint being made about ten times the thickness of the piece, and considerable patience as well as sharp tools are needed to make a per-

189

fectly fitting featheredged joint of this type. Theoretically a glued joint is as strong or stronger than the wood, so that splices could be adjacent to each other, but inasmuch as a glued joint will be locally stiffer than the adjoining unjointed pieces it is best to stagger the scarphs as much as possible. Figure 16-5 shows a scarph and typical hollow spar sections in use today.

The section next in simplicity to the rectangular box section is the round spar made of hollowed out halves. The tee boom is used on the smaller sailboats, which also sometimes have solid rectangular booms. Some of the sailboat classes use a solid mast routed out for the boltrope on the luff of the mainsail. These are either made by hand gouging or machine routing the halves separately and gluing together, or are made in one piece by first making a circular saw cut and then routing the groove with a very high speed cutter having a shank slightly narrower than the saw cut. The box mast with the fore and aft pieces rabbeted is preferred by some builders because it is easier to control skidding of the glued surfaces when clamping. The larger spars, both the oval section and the round section made of staves, are the most difficult to make and would be quite a job for the amateur. Of the two the oval is the easier in the smaller sizes, as it consists of two round halves and two tapered side pieces. The wall thickness of oval and round spars is always tapered in the interest of weight saving.

Hollow Rectangular Spars

Probably the easiest way for an amateur to make a box spar, unless he has extensive machine tools, is to order the spar material dressed four sides to the dimensions at the maximum section of the spar. It is desirable to add a slight thickness, say one-thirty-second of an inch, for dressing up and finishing after the spar has been glued. With such material at hand there is nothing to do but taper the pieces in accordance with the architect's detail plans. This is done by laying off the width at the spacing shown on the plan for the spar, fairing with a long batten, then sawing and planing the edges to the lines. The width layout for the forward and aft pieces is done from a center line because both edges are shaped. Duplicate sides may be temporarily nailed together and made at the same time. Be sure to keep the edges square or else a perfect glued joint with 100 per cent surface contact cannot be made. When only one or two spars are to be made, a makeshift spar bench may be devised by nailing a series of short boards horizontally to a wall or fence, with legs down to the ground to support the outer ends. See Figure 16-6A. All should be level and at the same height, or the top edges shimmed to be so, as upon them will be placed the side of the spar that is to be straight, that is, the aft side of the mast or the top side of the boom.

190

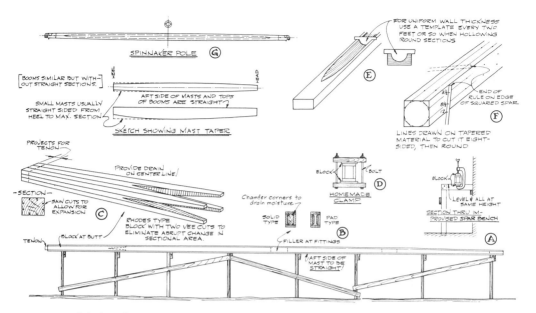

FIGURE 16-6. *Spar making details*

Shellac the inside of spars, care being taken not to coat the surfaces that will be glued. Use a marking gauge to scribe the width of the side pieces on the forward and aft pieces and shellac between the lines. The filler pieces at the ends of the spar and elsewhere as called for by the plans are fitted and shellac is omitted also in way of these. Because solid filler blocks have been known to swell and either split the spar or cause poorly glued joints to open up, some prefer the pad type fillers glued to the inside before assembly as shown in sketch B, Figure 16-6. A long solid filler as fitted at the heel of the mast is bound to locally stiffen the mast due to the sudden increase in sectional area. Naval architect Philip Rhodes prefers a block cut as shown in Figure 16-6C to avoid this situation and also advises running saw cuts longitudinally on the block to allow for expansion. Provide drain holes in all solid fillers in masts except the one at the head so moisture will not collect and start rot.

When everything is ready, mix the glue strictly in accordance with instructions, paying particular attention to those regarding temperature and working life after mixing. Once mixed, spread the glue quickly and thoroughly. Before gluing make sure there are enough clamps at hand, and it is surprising how many are needed as there should be one every few inches or so to apply the pressure required for the glue. Although the boom clamped up in Figure 16-7 is larger than the average amateur would attempt, it is a good illustration of the number of clamps used by the builder to insure a perfect job. All kinds of clamps may be utilized if the opening is sufficient to clamp the spar plus pieces of scrap used under the clamp pads to distribute pressure and prevent scars. If your number of clamps is short of the amount needed you can make satisfactory spar clamps of two husky pieces of oak or ash with bolts in the ends at least one-half inch in diameter. See sketch, Figure 17-6D.

The clamps should not be removed for at least twenty-four hours to allow the glue to develop full strength. Finish the spar by scraping the excess glue from the seams, round the corners, and then sand all sides smooth, gradually working down to fine abrasive paper. If a varnish finish is wanted, and Sitka spruce has a beautiful appearance when finished clear, do not apply less than four or five coats, carefully sanding off the gloss between coats.

FIGURE 16-7. *A 20 foot long round hollow boom glued and clamped, show-ing large number and close spacing of clamps*

Round Hollow Spars

Even though the boat has a rectangular mast and boom the spinnaker pole (Figure 16-6G) will be round, made in halves and symmetrical around the center line. First get out two pieces of stock that will be square when clamped together and equal to the diameter of the pole in the middle. Mark center lines on the mating surfaces of the material, then lay out the inside of the pole, that is, the part to be hollowed. Make hollowing templates, Figure 16-6E, for points every two feet or so apart and constantly use them to check as the wood is cut away. The templates control the wall thickness of the finished spar and guard against walls that are too thin or not uniform in thickness. The hollow portion is ended in a quick taper as shown on the sketch so that pole end fittings will be attached to solid wood.

When the halves have been glued together the spar again must be laid out on the outside and then the square assembly is tapered. It then will measure equal to the outside diameter of the pole at any point. The next step is to cut the corners off the square and make it eight-sided. This is done by drawing guide lines, Figure 16-6F. At any point along the length of the tapered square the end of a rule is placed even with one corner of the wood, then pivoted until the 12 inch mark coincides with the opposite corner. Points are made on the wood at the 3½ and 8½ inch marks on the rule. These figures are used as an example and are varied to suit the diameter of the spar. For ease of layout the rule should be almost square across the spar and the layout is accomplished by reducing the ratio of 12-8½-3½ by a common divisor to suit the spar. In most cases the spar will be small, say 5 inch diameter, in which case 2 is used as a divisor. Therefore the end of the rule is held on one corner of the spar, the 6 inch mark on the other corner, and points made at the 1¾ and 4¼ inch marks. Repeat this about every foot, and run a batten through points to draw a line. With guide lines on all four sides it is a simple matter to make the spar eight-sided with drawknife and plane, then round it off to be finished by sanding.

A round mast for a marconi sail will be straight on the aft side but the method of making it is the same.

Rigging Attachments

Not too many years ago almost all masts were round and the upper ends of the standing rigging were spliced in a loop, dropped down over the mast head to the location wanted and held in position by shoulder cleats on the mast. With the introduction of the marconi rig and the systems of stays for supporting it came masts elongated in section, and then the manufacturers of wire rope started to make what is called strand, a rope consisting of a single wire core with eighteen wires twisted around it. This is known as 1 to 19 construction, has more strength than any other rope of the same diameter, and is the logical rigging to use to reduce windage. It is very stiff and difficult to splice and therefore is not suitable for looping around a mast, particularly one with an elongated oval or rectangular section. Consequently spliced rigging has practically disappeared and the ends of the wire rope are fitted with swaged terminals or hot sockets, either of which is attached to the mast with tangs. Most tangs are made of strong sheet metal like Everdur or Monel and are held to the mast by one bolt and a number of wood screws calculated to take the outward and downward stress components of the stay. It is the job of the naval architect to design tangs that are both light and strong, and each tang is usually carefully detailed for the job to be done.

The tangs can be made by a machine shop, one of the rigging specialists, or the enterprising amateur can tackle the sheet metal work by fitting his bandsaw with a metal cutting blade. Besides making the tangs exactly accord-

FIGURE 16-8. *Strong, simple tangs for double lower shrouds. Note hollow bolts to save weight and clips for spreaders*

ing to plan, the builder must drill the mast with care for all the tang fastenings. Loose holes will permit the tangs to slip, possibly overloading a few of the fastenings instead of letting them all do their share of the job. Fore and aft bolts for tangs have nuts on the aft side of the mast, necessitating a batten under the sail track in order to have it straight. Without a batten the track would have to curve out over the nut and back to the mast again and would affect the set of the sail. The batten is glued to the mast and cut away for the nuts. Battens are not always necessary on booms but are desirable to prevent sail slides from binding due to contact with the boom at their edges. The screws for sail track go through the batten into the wall of the spar. At certain points of extra strain, such as the extreme ends of a track and at the reefed positions of the mainsail headboard, through fastenings rather than screws should be used. Figure 16-8 shows tangs for double lower shrouds on the main and mizzen masts of a ketch. These particular tangs are strong, simple and well made with tube bolts to save weight. A few inches above the tang bolts are straps encircling the mast with clips for the heels of spreaders.

Mast Step

The compressive load from the mast is taken by the mast step, which is of some hardwood like oak. The step is given a length of several frame spaces to distribute the load over the hull, and in boats of any size is placed in notches in the floors after first having been notched itself. When carefully done the resulting joint at each floor will prevent movement of the step in any direction, and in addition it is drift bolted to the floors, Figure 16-4C. The mortise in the step to take the mast tenon should have a drain hole drilled at the low point so that water will not collect and rot the step. A typical step is shown in Figure 16-4B, but like many other boat details there are other types of steps, particularly in small craft, and details will be found on the plans.

Vertical Tie Rod

The forces from the thrust of the mast and the upward pull of the rigging tend to collapse the hull, so that in moderate sized boats it is well to fit a tie rod between the mast step and mast partner as shown in Figure 16-4B. The rod is threaded on both ends for nuts which are set up over washers. Just take up the nuts snugly when installing, as there is no need to try to pull the deck and step together.

Marking the Boot Top

Nothing looks worse to yachtsmen than a ragged division between the topside and bottom paints. Assuming that the builder has had the foresight to mark the designed waterline at the stem and stern for reference during construction, just about the easiest way to mark the boot top is to first plot the straight waterline at frequent intervals along the hull and then lay off heights to the boot top as scaled from the plan of the outboard profile. Level straight edges are set up at the ends of the boat as shown in Figure 16-9, then a length of thin strong cord is stretched tightly between the edges and moved inboard until it barely touches the hull and the point marked. By moving the cord in and out on the straight edges alternately at opposite ends, points on the waterline may be marked as often as desired. Be sure to keep the cord tight, for if it is allowed to sag the waterline will not come out straight. If the boat is level fore and aft and there is room to work, a builder's level or transit may be used to run in the line. The boot top or stripe is usually curved (sheered) for appearance, and offsets above the waterline can be taken from the plans and plotted as shown in the figure. A batten is nailed on the hull to fair the points and mark the line by scribing with the broken end of a hacksaw blade or similar device, or with a so called race knife made for scribing wood.

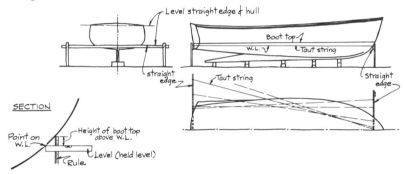

FIGURE 16-9.

Types of Rudders

A rudder consists of a wood or metal blade and a stock through which force is transmitted to the blade and around which it pivots. Except for common types of power boat rudders it is attached to the hull by hangers called gudgeons and pintles. The location of the rudder is either inboard, meaning forward of the after end of the waterline, or it is hung outboard on the transom. Further, the rudder is either unbalanced, with all the blade area abaft the stock or pivot point, or it is partly balanced, with a percentage of the area forward of the stock. In the case of the latter the force required to turn the rudder is reduced.

Motorboat Rudders

Modern power boat rudders are now almost invariably made of metal although formerly they were often of wood. They are sometimes of galvanized sheet steel with a split stock through which the blade is riveted. The most common and more durable than steel has a blade of cast manganese bronze bossed for a rolled bronze or Monel stock which is inserted in the head of the rudder. Figure 16-10A shows this type rudder supported at the top by the rudder port, a stuffing box to prevent a leak where the stock enters the hull, and at the bottom by a pintle riding in a hole in a metal skeg. A spade type rudder is sketched in Figure 16-10B and is made the same, but

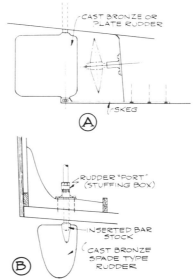

FIGURE 16-10.
Powerboat rudders

is not supported at the bottom and is more liable to catch lobster pot buoys and the like. It is a clean design and results from an effort to reduce underwater resistance by cutting away the deadwood, so there is no way of supporting the bottom of the rudder. On twin screw boats a spade type rudder is used behind each of the propellers and gives excellent steering qualities. The two types of rudders sketched may be purchased in a number of sizes.

There are many ways of linking power boat rudder to the steering gear and the plans should show how the designer wants it done. Needless to say, the steering system must be laid out with care, but by the time you have come this far with boat building the work will not be found difficult. Where wire rope is used the sheaves over which it runs must be accurately aligned with the wire and strongly fastened so they will never pull out.

Small Sailboat Rudders

Small centerboard sailboats have an outboard rudder as shown in Figure 16-11A. The blade may be of one or more pieces depending upon available material, but in any case it should be doweled with galvanized iron or brass rod to prevent warping and the grain of the wood should be alternated from piece to piece for the same reason. The blade area below the surface of the water is streamlined in shape, as indicated on the sections in the sketch, with the maximum thickness being held about twenty-five per cent of the blade width from the leading edge of the rudder. Using the common variety of gudgeons and pintles as seen in any marine hardware catalogue, the rudder will probably float up and become disengaged from the boat, leaving the skipper with a tiller in hand but no control over the boat. To prevent this the rudder may be weighted with an insert of lead heavy enough to offset the buoyancy of the blade, or the upper pintle can be drilled for a cotter pin just below the gudgeon. The tiller is fixed, or preferably made to hinge so it can be raised when tacking.

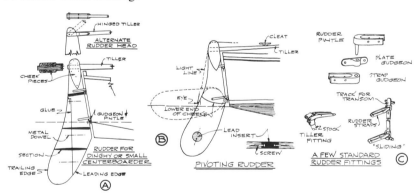

FIGURE 16-11. *Small boat rudders and fittings*

In shoal water localities the small boat outboard rudder is often made with the blade pivoted so that it may be raised to clear an obstruction (Figure 16-11B). This is done by pivoting the blade between long cheek pieces riveted securely to a filler of the same thickness as the blade. A lead insert is needed to prevent it from rising due to buoyancy or the forward motion of the boat. A light line is used to raise the rudder while sailing over shoal areas.

Some of the standard fittings available from marine stores are sketched in Figure 16-11C. Besides these, Merriman Brothers and Wilcox, Crittenden and Company each make a set of fittings for small outboard rudders that prevent the rudder from coming off, yet the rudder is readily removable from the transom. Rudder fittings should be bolted rather than screwed to the transom.

Large Sailboat Rudders

Figure 16-12A shows the rudder for a keel sailboat in which the stock is run down far enough to take a few bolts through the piece of blade next to the stock. A strap is fitted as shown at the end of the stock to prevent bending from the pressure of water against the blade when the rudder is turned. At the bottom of the rudder a pintle and gudgeon are fitted for support. Unfortunately, like most rudder fittings, the variety of rudder shapes and thick-

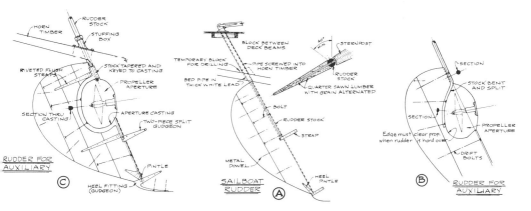

FIGURE 16-12.

nesses is so great that stock fittings are not available and patterns must be made for castings. These fittings are usually detailed by the architect with enough dimensions so that, together with templates made on the hull and rudder, the necessary patterns can be turned out for the use of the foundry. It is inadvisable to use anything but nonferrous metals for rudder fittings because the constant operation will soon wear off any surface plating. One of the best materials for rudder stocks is tough strong Tobin bronze or Everdur shafting, while the cast parts are of a good grade manganese bronze with tensile strength of not less than 60,000 pounds a square inch. Do not skimp on the quality of fittings because the rudder is important.

Larger rudders must be made of pieces doweled or drift bolted together as indicated. The size of dowels and bolts should be shown by the designer and may be decreased in diameter near the trailing edge where the blade is thinner so the wood will not be weakened by the fastenings. Dowel holes must be parallel or the pieces cannot be joined together, and all fastenings must be kept in the middle of the blade to prevent their coming through when tapering the blade. Drift bolts used in heavier rudders do not have to be parallel to each other, and when driven at varying angles lock the pieces together. Drifts driven from the trailing edge have a slot cut far enough in from the edge so the head will be hidden, then a piece of wood is inserted to fill the slot. The enlarged section in Figure 16-12A shows how the blade is tapered. It may be seen that the amount of work to make a rudder should not be underestimated.

If the builder is fortunate enough to have a thickness planer some hand labor can be saved by planing each piece to its thickness at the forward edge. Otherwise all tapering is done with plane and spoke shave. The sketch also shows how the grain is alternated in adjacent pieces to prevent or minimize warping, and how the after edge of the sternpost is hollowed out so water will flow past the deadwood onto the rudder with a minimum of disturbance. As mentioned in Chapter 8, the edge of the sternpost is sheathed with copper about 1/32 inch thick for protection from worms and to eliminate painting, which is practically impossible anyway without unshipping the rudder. The sheathing is carried around the sides an inch or so and secured with copper tacks. The forward edge of the rudder blade begins aft of the center of the stock so the rudder can be turned hard over without fouling the sternpost. With the rudder arranged as shown in Figure 16-12A, water is kept out of the hull by screwing a threaded brass or bronze pipe into a hole drilled in the horn timber. The hole must be just the right amount smaller than the pipe so the threads will take hold, and must be drilled at the correct angle. The best way to start the auger is to cut a block as shown dotted in the figure with the face at right angles to the center of the stock. This can be laid out from your mold loft drawings and a drilling guide devised.

Rudders for Auxiliaries

When a sailboat is fitted with an engine and the shaft is on the center line there must be a hole or aperture cut in the deadwood and rudder in which the propeller can turn (Figure 16-12B). The aperture should not be larger than necessary, but the size must be such that the propeller blades when

200

revolving will not strike the rudder. The edge of the aperture can be checked on the mold loft floor by setting up on the propeller center line a semicircular disc of the same diameter as the propeller, then a piece of thin plywood or heavy cardboard is hinged on the center line of the rudder and an aperture cut away by trial until the rudder can be swung forty degrees off center and still clear the propeller blades. See sketch 16-13.

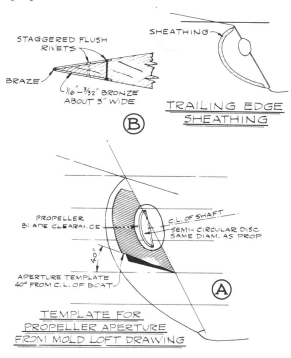

FIGURE 16-13.

It is not sufficient to end the rudder stock at the top of the aperture. Therefore it must be carried either partly around the opening as shown in Figure 16-12B, or completely encircle the aperture as shown in Figure 16-12C. Sometimes the method in the latter figure is carried out by casting the complete stock in one piece from upper end to the pintle below the aperture, but a long pattern is needed, the casting is not the easiest to make, and quite a lot of machining is required to finish the job. A shorter casting around the aperture as shown is hard to beat for strength, and except for filing rough spots from the casting, the only machining needed is to taper

201

bore and keyway the upper end for the stock, drill holes in the lugs for the blade straps, and turn a pintle or bore for an inserted pintle on the lower end. The blade straps shown are cut from flat bronze and secured with countersunk rivets. The stock, of course, is made from bronze shafting, tapered and keyed to match the aperture casting and secured with a pinned nut on the lower end. A rudder made like this may be removed from the hull without digging a deep hole by taking off the two-piece split gudgeon and the stock and lifting the rudder enough to disengage the bottom pintle from the heel gudgeon. A stuffing box is shown on the horn timber. This will very likely be a special job, as seldom can standard fittings be adapted due to angle between stock and horn timber. The upper end of the stock of any rudder has a keyway for a standard tiller fitting, or in larger boats for a wheel steerer. There are several varieties of each of these items made by the marine hardware manufacturers.

An expensive and by no means necessary refinement to a rudder is to bronze sheath the trailing edge as illustrated in Figure 16-13B. This is made by templating the shape of the trailing edge and bandsawing the sheathing from a sheet of bronze about 1/16 to 3/32 inch thick, and there is much waste. The edges of the curved strips are filed smooth and laid on the rudder to mark the rabbet to be cut so the sheathing will be flush with the surface of the blade. Fastening is by means of countersunk head rivets as shown, and the trailing edges are brazed together, then ground reasonably sharp. Sometimes the rudder on a new boat will vibrate so that it chatters considerably, a condition remedied by sharpening the trailing edge somewhat, but the sheathed rudder is perfect from the start and is usually fitted on cruisers and racers of the finest quality.

Steering Controls

There are various means of transmitting power to the rudder, starting with the simple tiller for an outboard rudder shown in Figure 16-11A. When the rudder is inboard under the hull more complicated methods must be used. Some sailboats have an Edson type steerer with wheel and gearing attached to the upper end of the rudder stock. These gears must be carefully aligned and securely fastened to the structure. Other sailboats have the wheel further away from the rudder and use a wheel with pedestal steerer connected to a quadrant on the rudder stock with a length of sprocket and chain and wire rope running over sheaves.

There are several types of steerers for powerboats. One method uses a reduction gear steerer at the wheel and chain and wire rope similar to the sailboat pedestal steerer. Others use a gearbox at the wheel or elsewhere in the system and connect to the rudder arm with shafts, solid or pipe. A more modern type of steerer suitable for small to medium sizes of boats uses a rack and pinion at the wheel and a heavy push-pull cable from the rack to an arm at the rudder. This is by far the simplest type of steerer and is seen in many boats because it is the least expensive to install.

The fortunate builder has good detail of the steering system on his plans, otherwise he has been left on his own to work it out. The steering should be installed before too much of the interior joinerwork has been built. It is most important that all steering gear parts be fastened securely to prevent movement of units such as the steerer and wire rope sheaves, and the latter should be through bolted as well as carefully aligned to reduce friction and eliminate wear on the wire rope. All parts should also be nonferrous.

Water Trap Vent

There should be a circulation of fresh air through a boat even when it is closed up otherwise. The vent shown in Figure 16-14 was developed for sailboats at sea some years ago and remains popular and practical for any type boat because it permits ventilation while excluding rain and flying spray. The cowl can be turned as desired for best results. The removable screen should not be used unless there are insects because screens reduce the effective opening by about 25%. The cowl can be one of the pliable rubbery plastic kind that bends when a rope crosses it. The tube into the boat can be plastic, aluminum, or copper. The box can be installed either fore and aft or athwartship.

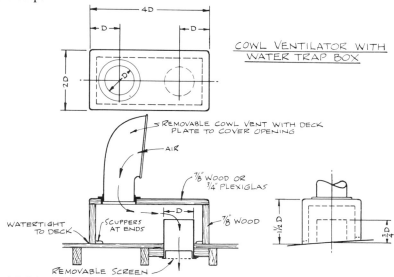

FIGURE 16-14

203

Painting

If you are inexperienced in boat painting the best advice we can give is to listen to the experts—the marine paint manufacturers. The majority of these are old line companies, some over a hundred years old, and the competition is such that many of them have prepared booklets of instructions for painting every part of the boat. Ads offering these can be found in the boating magazines.

Fuel Tanks

Due to the danger of explosion and fire the construction and installation of fuel tanks should not be taken lightly, and both are well covered by standards of the American Boat and Yacht Council and the National Fire Protection Association written by people with long experience. The standards are only as good as compliance with them, so heed them well (see Recommended Reading).

Probably the utmost in quality for both metal gasoline and diesel fuel tanks is welded Monel. Although approved for gasoline tanks, steel is the least desirable of the metals because it will corrode outside from the atmosphere and inside from water derived from condensation. In many cases, though, financial considerations limit the choice to steel. So-called black iron is acceptable for diesel fuel tanks, but never galvanized, and these tanks must have a built-in corrosion factor by making them thicker than usual, consequently heavy in weight.

At this writing fuel tanks of aluminum alloy are not approved by the standard making bodies, but this will probably come along in time, nor is fiber glass, although it is used for tanks on diesel trucks and will likely be approved for marine use in time. Both aluminum and fiber glass tanks are actually in use in many boats, and apparently with success, but the mills often grind slowly for one reason or another.

Of equal importance to the construction and installation of the fuel tanks is the fill, vent and supply piping, and these too are well described by the published standards. When these are installed of good materials and carefully made up joints then you can rest easy. One of the critical items is the fuel valves. These must be of the packless type, otherwise the fuel can deteriorate the packing around the stems and leak.

Tank Capacity

Figure 16-15 shows tank shapes commonly used in boats and how to calculate capacity by figuring the volume in cubic inches and dividing by 231

TANK CAPACITY IN U.S. GALLONS
(DIMENSIONS IN INCHES)

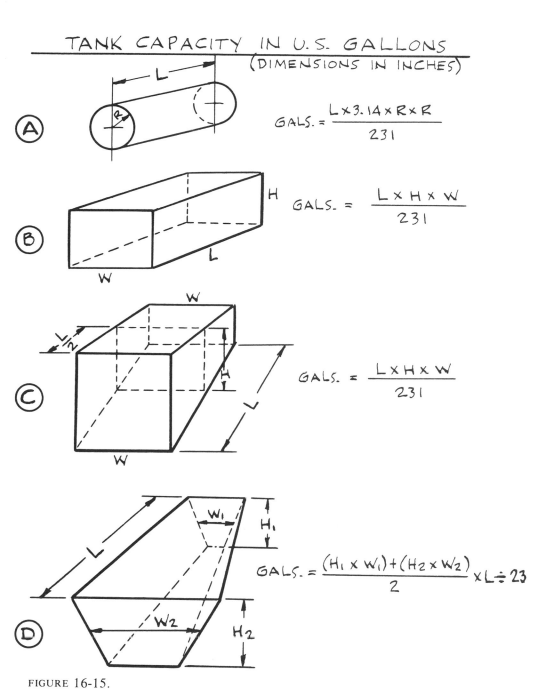

(A)
$$GALS. = \frac{L \times 3.14 \times R \times R}{231}$$

(B)
$$GALS. = \frac{L \times H \times W}{231}$$

(C)
$$GALS. = \frac{L \times H \times W}{231}$$

(D)
$$GALS. = \frac{(H_1 \times W_1) + (H_2 \times W_2)}{2} \times L \div 23$$

FIGURE 16-15.

to find contents in U.S. gallons. Boatbuilders seem to always work the capacities from inch dimensions. If dimensions are taken in feet the cubic capacity is multiplied by 7.48 for the answer in gallons.

The cylindrical and rectangular tanks A and B are straightforward to figure. Shape C is typical of a tank installed under the cockpit of a sailboat. The sides are parallel but the top and bottom are not due to hull shape. The cross sectional area W times H is the average of the area of the ends, or the same as the area at midlength of the tank. Shape D is often used for tanks located under the floor of a cabin, and again the volume is the length times the average of the area of the ends. The W measurements are taken at mid-height of the ends.

Plumbing

The plumbing in most boats is relatively simple, and instructions are easy to come by from the manufacturers of such equipment as toilets and water pressure systems. Copper tubing is the good old standby for hot water piping; for cold water lines a good grade of hose will do. Of importance is the piercing of the hull anywhere below a line about a foot above the normal water line of the boat. All such pipes should have standard through-hull fittings and seacock type valves. Needless to say the valves must be kept in operating condition and also must be where you can get at them to shut off in an emergency in case something happens to the piping inside the boat. In fact when a boat is to be left untended for any length of time it is not a bad idea to close the seacocks and eliminate worry.

One word of advice about toilets. Install the intake seacock forward of the outlet seacock.

Engine Connections

Water and fuel lines to an engine should never be rigidly piped because vibration will cause a rupture in time. Water connections to the engine should have a section of hose, while the fuel line should connect to the engine by means of a length of flexible hose made for the purpose. Water connections can be made with hose slipped over the pipe or tube and held in place with stainless steel hose clamps, but use threaded ends, not clamps, on the fuel hose to the engine.

Propeller Shafts and Bearings

Shafts are made of either Tobin bronze, Monel Alloy 400, Monel Alloy K-500 or one of the stainless steels such as Armco 17-4 PH or Allegheny

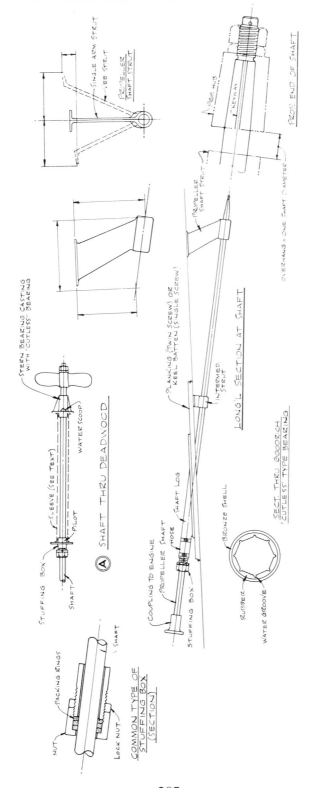

SINGLE ARM STRUT
VEE STRUT

PROPELLER
SHAFT STRUT

PROP HUB

KEYWAY

PROP END OF SHAFT

PROPELLER
SHAFT STRUT

OVERHANG = ONE SHAFT DIAMETER

STERN BEARING CASTING
WITH "CUTLESS" BEARING

STUFFING BOX

SLEEVE (SEE TEXT)

WATER SCOOP

PILOT

SHAFT

(A) SHAFT THRU DEADWOOD

PLANKING (TWIN SCREW) OR
KEEL BATTEN (SINGLE SCREW)

INTERMED
STRUT

LONG'L SECTION AT SHAFT

COUPLING TO ENGINE

PROPELLER SHAFT

HOSE

SHAFT LOG

STUFFING BOX

BRONZE SHELL

RUBBER

WATER GROOVE

**SECT THRU GOODRICH
"CUTLESS" TYPE BEARING**

NUT

PACKING RINGS

SHAFT

LOCK NUT

**COMMON TYPE OF
STUFFING BOX
(SECTION)**

207

FIGURE 16-15A

Ludlum Almar 362, the strengths being in the order listed. Tobin bronze is an old standby and is used for economy rather than maximum strength, but for unprotected shafts especially such as in typical twin screw motor boats a stiffer, stronger shaft is more practical and the cost is not proportional because the stronger materials can be smaller in diameter.

If your boat plans do not specify the shaft diameter, American Boat and Yacht Council Standard No. P-6 has charts for selecting the sizes of shafts for the materials mentioned above and also for bearing spacing.

Typical shafts have a keyway machined on one end for the propeller shaft coupling to the engine, while the outboard end has a taper with keyway to match the propeller hub bore, and then threads for the propeller locking nuts. The shaft tapering must be carefully done so the propeller will fit properly and is best left to a shaft supplier who is set up for this work. Dimensions for machining the shaft end and propeller hub have long been standardized, at least in the U.S., and the SAE data for this is usually tabulated and illustrated in the catalogs of the propeller makers. When setting up the length of your shaft, allow one diameter of the shaft to overhang the stern bearing or strut.

Figure 16-15A shows a longitudinal section at the shaft center line of a twin screw motor boat. The same section applies to a common type of single screw motor boat, with keel batten and cutaway skeg. It shows the usual modern arrangement of rubber necked shaft log with a stuffing box inboard to prevent water from leaking into the boat around the shaft, and a strut to support the shaft at the propeller. Intermediate struts are used when the shaft is sufficiently long to require additional support.

The stuffing box and the shaft log are both of bronze and are connected by a short length of rubber hose secured by clamps. The hose helps to reduce vibration. Shaft logs are manufactured in several angles that have proven the most useful for the majority of boats but may have to be shimmed with a wedge of wood in your boat to get correct alignment. The base flange of the shaft log must be made watertight either by the use of several thicknesses of canvas gasket all liberally soaked in "marine aviation glue" or, simpler, with a thiokol base compound. Wherever possible the base should be through fastened with silicon bronze bolts, otherwise wood screws of the same metal.

The shaft hole through the wood should be treated with polyester or epoxy resin because the hole is difficult to clean and paint later with the shaft in place and therefore susceptible to worm damage. This precaution is very important indeed.

Some shaft logs are designed with a tube integral with the base. The tube is a lining for the shaft hole and is cut off flush with the outside of the hull. This type of shaft log is rather special and not used as frequently as the kind that terminates at the base.

Another type of special shaft log that should be mentioned is sometimes used in moderate to large sized boats where the shaft is quite long in proportion to the diameter so that it is desirable to have a bearing between the first intermediate shaft strut and the engine. In this case shaft logs are made that have a short length of bearing. The bearing is housed so the forward end is not exposed to a flow of water, so water lubrication is provided by engine cooling water tapped into the log forward of the bearing. The water used is part of that usually piped into the exhaust line for cooling, but the diversion is not detrimental because only a small amount is sent to the shaft log bearing. This type shaft log is made up special, not found in marine supply catalogs.

A part of the propulsion set-up that almost always is a special item is the propeller shaft strut. These are single arm or the vee type as specified by the plans, and due to the angle of the shaft and the shape of the hull it is nearly impossible to find a stock strut that will fit the job. There are, however, some small adjustable struts on the market that might just do. Otherwise enough dimensions on a sketch as shown in Figure 16-15A or a mock-up must be sent to a strut manufacturer so he can make up one or a pair to fit the boat. We are not advertising anybody in particular, but over the years the Columbian Bronze Corp., Freeport, New York, has actually made thousands of special struts, so they have many patterns that may be adapted with small alterations. Most struts are made of cast manganese bronze.

Struts are fastened through the planking and blocking inside with silicon bronze or manganese bronze bolts with countersunk oval heads, have a screwdriver slot to hold the bolt from turning while tightening. These bolts are best ordered from the strut manufacturer, specifying the length needed.

You may as well have the strut maker install the bearing in the strut. It is hard to beat the Goodrich "Cutless" type bearing, made of rubber bonded to an outer bronze shell and with grooves for water that not only provides lubrication but minimizes wear on the shaft by washing out silt and particles of sand. The bronze shell of the bearing is lightly pressed into the strut and secured with one or two set screws. The bearings are four times the shaft diameter in length when used as the aftermost bearing, and often reduced to half length in intermediate struts so that one standard bearing can be cut to make two.

Figure 16-15A also shows a typical arrangement when the shaft of a single engine boat goes through deadwood. The stuffing box is inside the hull, the stern bearing outside. The latter has a Cutless type bearing and a water scoop on each side of the casting for bearing lubrication. The stuffing box can be had "rubber necked," with a piece of hose between the stuffing box and the casting. Both stuffing box assembly and the stern bearing are stock items of marine hardware and readily available.

Water will fill the hole for the shaft and must be prevented from leaking into the hull through joints in the deadwood structure. This is done by fitting a tube between the stuffing box and stern bearing castings, either a lead sleeve as shown in A of the figure (the lead is easily flanged by hammering or on special order from a supplier like Columbian Bronze). The pilots of the castings can be tapped for the ends of a threaded pipe. The castings should be fastened to the wood with hanger bolts.

The stuffing box packing is square, either waxed braided flax or Teflon impregnated asbestos braid, installed as individual rings with the joints staggered so they are not all in line and possibly leak.

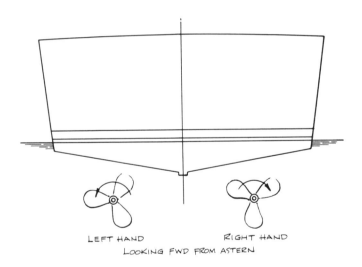

LEFT HAND   RIGHT HAND
LOOKING FWD FROM ASTERN

FIGURE 16-17

Hand of Propellers

Screw propellers are made either right hand or left hand. Looking forward from astern, a shaft that turns clockwise requires a right hand propeller and a shaft that turns counterclockwise takes a left hand propeller. It is customary for the propellers in twin screw boats to be of opposite rotation and to turn outboard as shown in Figure 16-17 but there are exceptions to this.

Pulley Drives

The boat builder is often faced with figuring out a vee belt pulley ratio when it is planned to drive a bilge pump or extra generator from a power take-off pulley on an engine. The formulae below are handy for finding pulley diameter or speed in RPM.

Driven pulley:

$$RPM = \frac{\text{diameter x RPM of driver}}{\text{diameter of driven}}$$

$$Diameter = \frac{\text{diameter x RPM of driver}}{\text{RPM of driven}}$$

Driving pulley:

$$Diameter = \frac{\text{diameter x RPM of driven}}{\text{RPM of driver}}$$

$$RPM = \frac{\text{diameter x RPM of driven}}{\text{diameter of driver}}$$

Aligning Couplings

If there is misalignment between the engine and propeller shaft couplings there will not only be unneccessary vibration when the engine is running but also possible damage to the rear bearing and seal of the reverse gear. The shaft should be installed first and the engine mated to it. If there are only

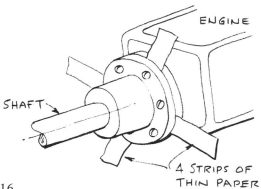

FIGURE 16-16.

two support bearings for the shaft, the stern bearing or strut bearing and a rubber necked shaft log, block up under the shaft inboard of the shaft log to prevent the shaft from sagging at the rubber neck. Lacking a feeler guage, test for alignment between the coupling halves by inserting four strips of paper as shown in Figure 16-16. You can tell by gently pulling on the strips whether the pressure, and thus the gap, is the same for all pieces. Hardwood and thin brass shims are used under the engine mounts until the alignment is as perfect as possible. The final test is to tighten down the engine and still have good alignment of the couplings.

Many engines are equipped with adjustable mounts that need but a wrench to lift or lower them a few thousands of an inch, and some of the larger engines have jacking screws built into the mounts for the same purpose.

If aligning of the engine is done with the boat out of water it must be tested again when water-borne because some hulls change shape and this will throw out the alignment that was done while hauled out.

Engine Controls

The engine is almost always located some distance away from the steering station of the boat so that remote controls must be installed for operating the throttle, reverse gear, and sometimes an emergency shutdown in the case of two-cycle diesel engines. This used to be done with complicated linkages of rods, pipes and bell cranks, and was a job of major proportions. One of the greatest boons was the advent of the hydraulic reverse gear, requiring but finger tip effort on a small lever on the gear instead of many foot-pounds of effort needed to operate the old manual clutch. This led to the push-pull cable controls now seen in most boats, a method that drastically reduced the time and cost of installation. The engine control system consists of an attractive set of levers at the steering station and two push-pull cables running from the levers to the engine, one each for gear and throttle. Simply by naming the engine, the control maker usually has kits for connecting the engine end of the cables to the gear and throttle. These save hours of making brackets for each job.

The length of cables between control levers and the engine is almost unlimited, but they should be installed with a minimum number of bends, and the bends must be easy. A little time planning the cable runs will show which way has the least number of bends, thus is the preferable one. The control manufacturers furnish really good instructions for making the installation.

A variation of a control head with two levers per engine is the single lever control favored by many operators. Two cables per engine are still required, so the installation is planned same as when there are two levers.

Electrical

Now here is a part of boatbuilding that can get the builder into a lot of trouble, especially if the design calls for equipment of more than one voltage, an auxiliary generator, and both A.C. and D.C. When this is the situation the best bet is to call in a good marine electrician, and they are not numerous. In large yachting centers there are usually firms that specialize in this work, otherwise the first place to try is a boat yard sizable enough to have an electrician.

A small or moderate size boat can really be quite simple electrically if the craft is not loaded with electrical gadgets, but even though the ABYC and NFPA standards specify type of wires to be used, wire sizes, etc., someone still has to design and plan the system, so because of possible dangers the best road is still to have the job done by an expert.

Safety

A sound hull does not necessarily make a safe boat and, due to an increase in mishaps with the vast growth of pleasure boating, there has been a great deal of effort expended to establish standards for the safe installation of equipment and fittings that might otherwise endanger boats and the persons aboard. This is all to the good because in their enthusiasm to get going the newcomers are likely to do foolish things due to lack of knowledge. Faced with governmental regulation if something were not done to correct hazards to safety, the boating industry moved to set standards for the guidance of all concerned with the building of boats, professional or amateur.

A simple illustration of a hazard is an underwater connecton for a pipe through the hull such as an inlet for toilet flushing water or engine cooling water. If a hose is slipped over the through hull fitting the hose can rot out in time or it can be cut in one way or another and the boat will flood and probably sink. Therefore there should be a valve, or seacock, attached to the through hull fitting and the hose connected to the valve. This arrangement permits the seacocks to be closed when the boat is unattended and eliminates a hazard at each opening underwater.

Another example is a copper gasoline line installed as taut as possible between the tank and the engine, without a loop in the tubing or a flexible hose connection to the engine. Vibration will eventually fracture the tubing and the contents of the tank will empty to the bilge and probably explode. There are many other hazards to safety that can be built into a boat and until relatively recently written information about them has been scarce, but now the situation is different.

One organization, the American Boat and Yacht Council with head-quarters at Room 1603, 15 East 26th Street, New York, N.Y. 10010, is composed of naval architects, engineers, representatives of manufacturers, marine surveyors and insurers, and the standards that have been set by these volunteer workers represents thinking of immeasurable value to the safety of property and human life. It is practically impossible for a designer, although he gives enough information to build a good boat, to completely detail every item and system that go to make up the finished boat ready in all respects to go to sea. But at least now he can refer to standards available to guide the builder to the safe installation of such things as fuel tanks and piping, exhaust piping, low voltage direct current wiring and circuit protection, hatches and door, cockpits and scuppers, fire extinguishing equipment and engine compartment ventilation, just to skim the list. The ABYC standards, which continue to be increased in number, are published in a manual *Safety Standards for Small Craft.*

The insurance underwriters are naturally interested in the safety of yachts and have had regulations for the guidance of their surveyors for many years. Although not as broad in scope as the ABYC standards, rather limited to fire prevention from fuel and electrical sources, the National Fire Protection Association standards are called *Motor Craft (Pleasure and Commercial),* NFPA No. 302 and, due to close cooperation with the ABYC, this is conveniently included in *Safety Standards for Small Craft.* The builder is urged to acquire the ABYC manual and study it carefully because there is much of value to be learned and there will be more as time goes on. In fact, to the new boatbuilder the information should be priceless.

A step for safety beyond mere words has also been taken. Manufacturers can now have their products tested for compliance with ABYC standards and so labeled when the product meets the requirements. This is reassuring to the uninitiated when purchasing such items as ready-made fuel tanks, a good sized investment with much safety at stake. The agency that does the testing is the Yacht Safety Bureau, which has the blessings of the National Association of Engine and Boat Manufacturers, and products that have been approved are marked with the bureau insignia.

Drilling and Tapping

Drilling metal and tapping threads for machine screws or bolts is almost unavoidable when building anything but the simplest boat. To help you get away from hit or miss methods when guides are not handy Figure 16-18 has been included to show tap drill sizes for the commonly used sizes of screw threads.

TAP DRILLS FOR U.S. STANDARD THREADS		
SIZE	NO. OF THDS. PER INCH	TAP DRILL
No. 8	32	No. 29
No. 10	24	No. 25
No. 12	24	No. 16
1/4"	20	13/64"
5/16"	18	1/4"
3/8"	16	5/16"
1/2"	13	27/64"

FIGURE 16-18

Equivalents

1 fathom	6 feet
1 inch	25.4 millimeters
1 knot	1 nautical mile per hour
1 nautical mile	1.152 statute miles
1 British gallon	1.2 U. S. gallons
1 U. S. gallon	231 cubic inches
1 ton (long)	2240 pounds
1 ton (long) fresh water	36 cubic feet fresh water
1ton (long) sea water	35 cubic feet sea water
1728 cubic inches	1 cubic feet
1 cubic foot	62.5 pounds fresh water
1 cubic foot	64 pounds sea water
1 meter	39.37 inches
1 foot	.3048 meters
1 foot high column of water	.434 lbs. per square inch
1000 watts	1 kilowatt
1 killowatt	1.34 horsepower
1 horsepower	746 watts

RECOMMENDED READING

Wood Handbook (Handbook No. 72), Forest Products Laboratory, U.S. Department of Agriculture. Superintendent of Documents, U.S. Government Printing Office, Washington, D.C. 20402. Contains much basic information on wood of interest to the boatbuilder at one time or another.

Wood: A Manual for Its Use as a Shipbuilding Material, Volumes I, II and III, Department of the Navy, Bureau of Ships. Available from Superintendent of Documents as above. Good information on the specifications and storage of wood for boatbuilding use, moisture content, structural design of parts, storage of boats, etc.

Understanding Boat Design, Edward S. Brewer and Jim Betts, International Marine Publishing Company, Camden, Maine 04843. A basic introduction to the subject for the boat buyer, amateur builder, and beginning yacht designer.

Safety Standards for Small Craft, American Boat and Yacht Council, Room 1603, 15 East 26th Street, New York, N.Y. 10010. Industry standards for Construction and the installation of equipment of value to the boat builder, especially the parts on electrical wiring and installation.

Motor Craft (Pleasure and Commercial), NFPA No. 302, National Fire Protection Association, 60 Batterymarch Street, Boston, Mass. 02110. Standards for fuel tanks, engine exhaust systems, electrical installation, etc., much used for guidance by marine insurance surveyors when inspecting boats. Available from NFPA as a booklet, but usually is included as part of the ABYC **Safety Standards for Small Craft.**

Marine Design Manual for Fiberglass Reinforced Plastics, Gibbs & Cox, McGraw-Hill Book Co., New York. As indicated by the name, this book is a guide to the design of fiberglass and resin structures for hulls and boat parts and is the only such publication of this nature at this time.

Ship and Aircraft Fairing and Development, S.S. Rabl, Cornell Maritime Press, Cambridge, Md. Worthwhile, clearly illustrated information on lofting details.

Aluminum Boats, Kaiser Aluminum & Chemical Sales, Inc., Oakland, Calif. Historical background of aluminum alloys for boat construction, examples aluminum craft and construction details.

Recommended Aluminum Applications for Boats and Yachts, Special Information Report S-1 of the American Boat and Yacht Council, address as above. A valuable guide to avoid the misapplication of aluminum alloys in boat construction.

National Fisherman, 21 Elm Street, Camden, Maine 04843. A monthly newspaper that always carries fishing boat and yacht designs, articles and pictures of all kinds of boatbuilding.

Fiberglas Boats, Construction and Maintenance, Boughton Cobb, Jr., (Yachting Publishing Co., 50 West 44th Street, New York, N.Y. 11036): This covers basics in Fiberglas construction.

Boat Owners Buyers Guide (annual), 50 West 44th Street, New York, N.Y. 10036. An extremely detailed and up to date listing of sources for materials, parts, equipment, engines, kit boats, plans for boats and naval architects.

INDEX

A

Abbreviations, lines plan, 51
Adhesives, 45
African mahogany, 17
Alaska cedar, 18
Aluminum boats, 27
American Boat and Yacht Council, 204, 214
Anchorfast nails, 36, 40–44, 136
Ash, white, 18

B

Backbone, 70, 87
Ballast keel, 184
Battens, lofting, 54; body plan, 60
Batten seam planking, 129
Bevels, 79, 102
Bevel board, 79, 81
Bilge stringer, 109
Boat cedar, 16
Body plan, 59
Bolts, 34, 35, 39
Boot top, 195
Brass, 31
Broad strakes, 120
Bronze, manganese, 184; silicon, 31
Bulkheads, 170
Bulwark rail, 160
Buttock(s), 49, 62; ending, 62

C

Cabin sole, 175; trunk, 157
Camber, deck beam, 143
Carriage bolts, 35
Carvel planking, 114
Castings, 184
Cast iron keel, 184
Caulking, 123, 126; cotton, 124; decks, 154
Cedar, white, 16; Port Orford, 16;
    Western red, 16; Alaska, 18
Ceiling, 174
Chainplates, 187
Chine, 52
Clamp, 107, 139
Clinker planking, 127
Cockpit, 165
Companionway, 162
Controls, engine, 212; steering, 202
Copper, 32; nails, 39

Copper napthanate, 23
Countersinks, counterbores, 37–39
Couplings, aligning, 211
Cypress, 16

D

Deadwood, 83
Decay prevention, 23
Deck, 147; tie rods, 144
    tongue and groove, 147; strip built, 148;
    plywood, 149; canvas covered, 150;
    Fiberglassed, 152; planksheer, 153;
    caulked, 154; laid, 154; paying, 154;
    joinerwork, 156
Deck beams, 141; camber, 143; strong, 143;
    half, 143
Deck framing, 139
Deck line, 48
Decking, 147
Diagonals, 49; fairing, 61; ending, 62
Diagonal planking, 133
Diagonal straps, 187
Double planking, 130; diagonal, 133
Douglas fir, 15
Drawers, 171
Drift bolts, 34
Drilling and tapping metal, 215
Dynel, 25

E

Electrical, 213
Electrolysis, 32
Engine stringer, 110; beds, 112
    mounts, 211; alignment, 211;
    controls, 212
Epoxy resin, 25, 46, 152
Equivalents, table of, 216

F

Fastening metal fittings, 45
Fastenings, 30
Ferro-cement hulls, 29
Fiberglass, 20, 25, 26, 152
Fin keel, 86
Fir, Douglas, 15
Floor timbers, 106
Frames, steaming, 101; bending, 102
Framing, 99; round bottom, 100; vee bottom, 78, 99; sawn, 99; bent, 100
Fuel tanks, 204

G

Galvanic corrosion, 32; series, 33
Galvanized iron, 30
Garboard plank, 119, 131
Glue, 45
Gripe, 87
Guards, sheer, 167

H

Hackmatack, 18
Hanging knees, 144, 146
Hanger bolts, 39
Hatch, sliding, 161; deck, 163; flush, 165
Headers, 143
Headlining, 178
Honduras mahogany, 17
Horn timber, 87

I

Ice box, 178
Insulation, 178
Interior joinerwork, 168

J

Joinerwork, deck, 156; interior, 168
Juniper, 16

K

Keel, 83; powerboat, 84; sailboat, 86; ballast, 184; cast iron, 184; lead, 185
Knees, quarter, 141; lodging, 144; hanging, 144, 146

L

Lag screws, 39
Laminating wood, 22
Lapstrake planking, 127
Larch, 18
Lauan, 17
Laying down, 47
Lines, 47; drawing, 47; plan abbreviations, 51
Load waterline, 49
Lodging knees, 144
Lofting, 47; tools, 53
Lumber, 12

M

Mahogany, 17; Mexican, 17; Philippine, 17; African, 17; Honduras, 17
Mast partners, 144; step, 195
Metals, galvanized iron, 30; brass, 31; silicon bronze, 31; Monel, 31; copper, 32; stainless steel, 32; manganese bronze, 184; casting, 184; Tobin bronze, 184
Mexican mahogany, 17
Miscellaneous fasteners, 43
Mold, 26; molds, 70
Molded plywood planking, 133
Molding, 24
Mold loft, 53
Monel, 31, 204
Monkey rail, 161

N

Nails, copper, 39; clout, 40; galvanized, 40; boat, 40; threaded, 40; Anchorfast, 36, 40–44, 136; Stronghold, 36, 40–44, 136
National Fire Protection Association, 204, 214
Northern white spruce, 17

O

Oak, white, 15
Offsets, 51; table of, 55

P

Painting, 126, 157, 204
Patterns for castings, 181
Pentachloraphenol, 23
Philippine mahogany, 17
Pine, yellow, 15; white, 16
Piping, 204, 206, 213
Planking, 114; carvel, 114; spiling, 117; broad strakes, 120; width scale, 120; stealer planks, 122; caulking, 123; smoothing, 125; lapstrake, clinker, 127; batten seam, 129; double, 130; plywood, 132; molded plywood, 133; diagonal, 133; strip, 134; fastenings, 123
Planksheer, 153
Plans, 6
Plumbing, 206
Plyfoam, 27
Plywood, 19, 169; planking, 132; sizes, 20; exterior, 21; deck, 149